Midnight in the Garden of Evel Knievel

Giles Smith is the author of *Lost in Music*. He is a former Sports Columnist of the Year. He writes about sport for the *Daily Telegraph*.

Also by Giles Smith

Lost in Music

GILES SMITH

Midnight in the Garden of Evel Knievel

Sport on Television

PICADOR

First published 2000 by Picador

This edition published 2001 by Picador
an imprint of Macmillan Publishers Ltd
25 Eccleston Place, London SW1W 9NF
Basingstoke and Oxford
Associated companies throughout the world
www.macmillan.com

ISBN 0 330 48189 4

1 3 5 7 9 8 6 4 2

A CIP catalogue record for this book is available from
the British Library.

Typeset by Intype London Ltd
Printed and bound in Great Britain by
Mackays of Chatham plc, Chatham, Kent

Contents

1997

Contents

2000

Introduction

Manchester United clinching the Treble; Tyson biting Holyfield's ear; Schumacher barging Hill off the track in Australia; Sampras sweeping Wimbledon clean; Christie going for gold; Argentina beating England on penalties; Germany beating England on penalties; everybody else beating England on penalties. You name the massive, era-defining sporting incidents of the last decade – I wasn't there. I was at home, watching on the television, like pretty much everyone else. And then I wrote about it.

I wrote about it in a weekly newspaper review which considered only television programmes about or containing sport. No soaps or Jane Austen adaptations; no histories of the Cold War or documentaries about joyriding in Bradford; no Inspector Morses, no game shows and no chat shows (unless sports people happened to be on them); just sport. Going in, in 1994, it looked like a narrow field (though that turned out not to be the case), and it was certainly an open one. Televised sport would occasionally crop up in general television reviews once the real business of talking about Jane Austen and the Cold War was done with, during, perhaps, Wimbledon fortnight, or an Olympics or a World Cup – those times when sport bulked so large in the schedules that you could hardly walk around it. Otherwise TV sport was pretty much left alone.

But it made sense to dwell a little longer on sport as it was refracted through the television screen because this was, after all, the way most people came into contact with it. Forty thousand people might attend the big Saturday football match, but six million would watch it later that night on

Match of the Day, so it would almost certainly be worth thinking about the way television framed the spectacle for them. It was also the case that, by 1994, sport was beginning to occupy more and more space on television. The occasions on which you could hardly walk around it were growing in frequency.

I had a couple of ideas about what such a narrowly defined newspaper column should and should not do. Obviously, merely collating – in the manner of *Private Eye*'s 'Colemanballs' – examples of the mistakes made by commentators and analysts under the formidable pressures of live broadcasting (pressures which, by rights, call for our sympathy and admiration rather than for our smooth mockery), would be a heartless and far too easy way to generate laughter. So, naturally, I set out to do as much of that as I could.

But it grew clear that these articles could, if they wished, do more than just make jokes at the expense of John Motson. They could attempt to cut to the vital heart of the sporting issues thrown in their path – whether by Cantona's kung-fu kick or the religious beliefs of Glenn Hoddle or the retirement, in a big strop, of Linford Christie. And *then* they could make jokes at the expense of John Motson.

There was live sport to write about, of course – more and more of it as time went by. Entire channels devoted to it. But I kept an eye out, too, for sports people cropping up outside their natural habitat – for sport's little invasions of the mainstream. For these, too, seemed to be on the increase, as if sport were taking over the world. Lennox Lewis on *Sportsnight* was clearly one thing; but Lennox Lewis on *Des O'Connor Tonight* – that was another. I came to prize an appearance by members of the England rugby squad on *Jim Davidson's The Generation Game* almost as much as I prized

Vinnie Jones's spectacularly incautious performance on *Ready, Steady, Cook*. But not as much as I prized an ill-advised showing by Ruud Gullit on a themed late-night Channel 4 programme which required him to wear a white towelling dressing gown. And what was harder to swallow: Ian Wright's noisy transition from footballer to chat-show host? Or Jimmy Hill's appearance on *This Is Your Life*, which caused a drastic and mind-boggling demolition of the received wisdom about him? (It made him seem like a nice man.)

But most of all there was the sport. Hours of it. Days and weeks of it. Eons in the company of Murray Walker and Alan Hansen, Sid Waddell and Peter O'Sullevan, David Coleman and Barry Davies. Grand Nationals and Grands Prix. Test Matches and Tours de France. Boat Races and boxing bouts. World Championship Darts tournaments and Winter Olympics. Plus the unique challenge to the viewer's conditioning and staying power which is the month-long football World Cup.

Looking back, I see how these reviews amount, inadvertently, to a kind of sports diary. Many of the big moments are there – albeit as they landed in someone's living room. (And frequently those landings were spectacular; sometimes there is no substitute for not actually being there.) The reviews also map the manoeuvres in what is our era's biggest broadcasting battle: the one being fought on the fields of sport. They report on the brazen aggression of Rupert Murdoch's BSkyB, the collapse of the BBC as the nation's official keeper of sport, the bold comeback by ITV, the rearguard action of Channel 4, and the weird arrival on the field of Channel 5.

But the other story the pieces tell is about the relationship between television and sport, their accelerated intimacy in our time, their complicated marriage. Ours is the age of the cable and digital exclusive; of pay-per-view and the footballer as satellite-dish-salesman. For ages – since way before Henry Cooper even considered splashing it all over – people have assumed that sport could be used to sell almost anything: crisps, credit cards, car parts, deodorant. Now those with most to hope and fear from sport's supposed commercial magic are the people using it to sell television. And by television, one does not just mean the hardware – though sport is felt to be very good at flogging that. (In the advertisements placed in newspapers by electrical retailers, the pictured televisions tend not to be showing Colin Firth in *Pride and Prejudice* or Jimmy Stewart in a cosy film or Michael Buerk reading the news; they tend to be showing Dwight Yorke of Manchester United. Except in the weeks before Wimbledon, when they tend to be showing Tim Henman. Rightly or wrongly, a fairly straightforward assumption is made about what people are principally looking for in a television.) Now sport is employed to sell television as hard as it is employed to sell televisions.

It is our pleasure and privilege to live in the somewhat eerie and uncertain light after the dawn of deregulated broadcasting, when television channels are no longer our gift (give or take a licence fee) from a benignly smiling government with a keen interest in keeping us off the streets, but are available to us at a range of additional prices, if we are prepared (and can afford) to take our risks at the stalls of a clamorous and sweaty bazaar. The people manning those stalls cling to at least one certainty: that sport is the must-have commodity, the big display item, in among the cheap carpets and cast-offs.

The single biggest broadcasting ground-shaker in recent history was the launch of the satellite broadcaster BSkyB.

When BSkyB went up – proletarian and proud of it, and causing the terrestrial channels to splutter indignantly in their smoke – it was not with the promise of bold and uncompromising wildlife programming and a new vehicle for Noel Edmonds, it was with football. Football was bread and circus in one, viewer-friendly package. Nothing, it was felt, would move those dishes like the prospect of live Premiership matches. Weekly. Twice weekly. Thrice weekly, if necessary. With matches from the lower leagues and from Scotland and from Spain to fill the gaps on the nights where there was no Premiership football.

Similarly, when OnDigital pitched themselves into the market for the provision of digital decoders, it was not with the offer of an unprecedented commitment to historical documentaries and a saucy, blindside raid on the BBC's *Songs of Praise* franchise; they signed a heavyweight boxing bout and access in its entirety to the Champions League football (itself a competition broadly expanded with the specific needs of Europe's television stations in mind). On the grounds that you can never have too much football, OnDigital then did a deal to broadcast in Britain the German Bundesliga, which would have been unthinkable as little as two years previously.

The same bug bites the basic terrestrial channels: sport moves money. The first thing the fledgling Channel 5 did, to convince advertisers that they were serious about securing audiences, was buy the rights to an England football international. All in all, television's new-found synergism with sport has had the most unlikely consequences. For us, the trade in sports rights has ceased to be a dry specialism and become instead a plausible general topic of conversation. (What? No Cup Final on the BBC?) So provocative was Channel 4's purchase of Test cricket deemed to be, that it earned more headlines and caused more debate than anything the channel have done since they broadcast those explicit films with the red warning triangle in the corner of the screen. People caught up in the business (mere television types) have found their status weirdly transformed. When ITV outbid the BBC for the rights to Formula One motor racing, the commentator Murray Walker moved overnight from distinguished commentary-box motormouth to big-time player in a multimillion-pound takeover bid. In August 1999, 400 people were killed in a train crash in India, but the *Guardian* didn't have room for that on its front page because Desmond Lynam had defected from the BBC to ITV and – tell you what – that was a story.

How sport itself bends and buckles under television's avid attentions is a narrative to follow carefully if you are interested in sport. Once it had been observed that sport could drive the sales of set-top boxes and magnetize the monthly subscription fees, television began to own and drive sport and sports began to thrive or shrivel according to the quantity and quality of their television coverage. Right now, sports can swiftly be divided into two groups: those enriched by television and those desperate to be so. (There is no sport so small that it isn't quietly dressing itself for a future televisual bonanza – pool, bowls, snowboarding, you name it.)

Yet sport might end up preferring a little more distance. Ironically, television's keen-eyed, technical-driven inquisitiveness has begun to threaten sports with dissolution. Television creates a state of almost perpetual controversy, in which no sport could run for long except as farce. What hope for the referee or umpire against television's heat-seeking close-ups and infrared night-sights? What can the referee Dermot Gallagher tell us about a football match that fifteen different cameras on super-slow-mo cannot? (Quite a lot, almost certainly, but it's a difficult argument to mount, in the face of all that technical armoury.) Cricket now routinely defers in its judgements to the superior wisdom of the camera; football, presumably, will be obliged to find a way.

Right now, the remote control for my set-top box clicks up to channel number 72. It offers more viewer-choice than I could ever have imagined, and at the same time less than I could ever have feared, because nearly all of it is junk. But the exceptions include the sports channels. They're really good, and this is probably not said often enough. Even Eurosport's coverage of tractor-pulling from Hanover sets standards of care and competence which daytime ITV can only dream of. But then things ought to be smoother because the relationship between broadcaster and sport is now tightly knit. They're in it together. Once there were sports events, and cameras turned up and covered them; now a man in headphones beside the pitch waves to let the referee know that television is ready for him and the game can start. Increasingly, sport takes place when television tells it to and because television wants it to. Consider the career of Naseem Hamed which, as a subscriber to Sky Sports, I have been able to measure in hype and entrance music. He is not simply made for television; he is very largely made by television and he is not alone. Our sports arenas tend ever more towards the condition of television studios; and our sports tend ever more towards the condition of television packages.

Join us after the break, then, for some pieces about sport and television – and, necessarily, an increasingly strenuous attempt to keep tabs on where one stops and the other begins.

1994

WORLD CUP OPENS; DIANA ROSS MISSES PENALTY

19 JUNE 1994

First of all, that controversial penalty incident. Diana Ross appeared to be clear through, played well on-side by Oprah Winfrey, with Daryl Hall way behind her and several hundred school kids with pompoms flailing hopelessly in her wake. And suddenly, out of nowhere – a minute remaining, scores level – the referee pointed to the spot. And of course, she blew it – scooted it pathetically past the left-hand post. One small kick for Ross, one giant hoot of derision for everyone else.

Easy to say now that she never really got her head over the ball, but of course, on the world stage, in the pressure-cooker atmosphere of global football, this most basic of skills can desert you. Just ask Chris Waddle, who skied one in Italy in 1990 – and he didn't have to cope additionally with singing a medley of his greatest hits while concentrating on keeping important parts of his anatomy inside a small silk shift. The argument that the death-or-glory endgame format reduces the game to little more than a lottery certainly gained momentum on Friday night: there may never be a more appropriate moment to call for Fifa officials to ban the penalty shoot-out as a means of deciding opening ceremonies.*

* It may be that the sport dearest to Diana Ross's heart is not football at all, but actually rugby league. See page 91.

It was left to William Jefferson Clinton, who plays up front for the USA, to restore some order. 'The World Cup has captured the imagination of our country,' he said, his words just audible above the low rumble of a nation snoring. And finally there was football.

The traditionally gruesome opening game won't have done much to wake America – not the most obvious country in which to stage a football tournament, but very rich, which might have something to do with it. Awesome but boring Germany took on plucky but careless Bolivia, famous for their stunning home record – though, as Barry Davies pointed out, home in their case happens to be at one of the highest altitudes in the world and it was felt the oxygen packs may well have impeded the opposition. The new FIFA initiatives designed to stamp out lawlessness mean if you're seen breathing with your mouth open, you get sent off. This happened to Marco Etcheverry of Bolivia. Nearly everyone else got booked (offences included failure to produce a hanky and yawning without covering the mouth). The first goal of the tournament went in midway through the second half and Davies made his first reference to 'German efficiency' approximately ten minutes later.

The ITV team were out in Dallas on what looks like a disused game-show set, and gloating madly, converting their betting metaphors into dollars and referring frequently to the boundless warmth of the American welcome. Late on Friday, they were rewarded with an interesting 2–2 draw between South Korea and Spain, along with another sending off (Spain's Miguel Nadal, for forgetting his mother's birthday) and a pack of yellow cards (sniffing, mostly). The sun was out and the wince factor was high. 'The first thing that comes to mind is the lack of height from this Korean side,' said Trevor Francis, though he later confessed to a lurking admiration for 'the lad Shin'. 'You'll find a lot of the Korean players sounding very similar, as well as looking very similar,' said Alan Parry. Thank you for that, Alan.

The BBC declared there were five billion people in the world and two billion of them would watch the World Cup final. This seemed striking but plausible. Over on ITV though, outside the central television building in Dallas, Matthew Lorenzo, who must have been taking several as yet undiscovered planets into consideration, confidently informed us the tournament would be seen by '30 billion'. Still, who's counting?*

PROFESSOR SAYS DRUGS ARE JUST FINE

6 NOVEMBER 1994

On *Open Space* this week (BBC2), Ellis Cashmore, a Professor of Sociology at Staffordshire University and the author of a book called *Making Sense of Sport*, got up and said: 'Let's do drugs.' Or words to that effect. 'I'm not convinced that drug-taking in sport is cheating,' said the Professor, who was calling for a ban on the ban.

Actually, the logic here is not that difficult. There are

* Declared television audiences for big sporting events now almost routinely exceed the earth's population. This is because television companies – who like to impress advertisers with big numbers – count not the number of individual viewers, but the number of times each individual viewer turns on over the course of the event. If you switch over for a few minutes and then turn back, or even if you pop out to the kitchen for five minutes to make a cheese sandwich, you become, as far as television is concerned, two viewers. People in television get rich for having these kinds of idea.

rules which prohibit drug-taking. While those rules are in place, to break them deliberately is to cheat. But anyway, it seems clear that the complexities of the prohibited drugs list are a bit of a joke and, for athletes, a complete headache – for which they're not allowed to take Nurofen. I've done a lot of Lemsip in my time without noticing myself subject to startling bursts of pace, but this is a drug on the prohibited list.

Still, just because the restrictions are in a tangle, it doesn't necessarily follow that you drop them all together – unless you're Professor Cashmore, who argued that sport now dangled before athletes all manner of cash incentives and, with drug prohibition, the athletes were 'being denied the opportunities to capitalize on them'. This was possibly one of the most morally vacuous statements heard on television since *The Borgias*, a weirdly capitalist version of the 'society's to blame' argument.

Unconsidered here were the clean athletes who worry about the after-effects of performance-enhancing compounds. One has to overcome one's feelings about Carl Lewis, the American sprinter and purist and the self-appointed representative of this constituency, and remember that there are many athletes who don't take tissue-enhancing drugs, not because they are pious and high-minded, but because they don't want to find themselves, in their retirement, growing an additional head between their knees. What becomes of them if the authorities give drugs the nod? And if drugs are going to play a legal part in competitive sport, at what point do we start injecting children? At twelve? At nine?

Then again, maybe the Professor's got a point. Maybe we should just think: 'To hell with it; break out the laughing powder.' It would certainly be good news for Britain: overnight, Glasgow would become one of the top three cities of sporting excellence, right up there with New York and Marrakesh.

It would also give television commentators something new to talk about: 'Interestingly, Debbie has opted to ditch the Night-Nurse-and-crushed-Polos combination which stood her so well in Stockholm and this afternoon favours a handful of magic mushrooms left to marinade overnight in a can of Tizer.' And there would be whole new areas of pontification for the studio expert panels: 'The home-grown leaf versions of these drugs are, of course, less potent than the manufactured resins. Jimmy?'

We'd need, of course, to modify the way in which sporting records are kept. Currently in athletics, if a record has been broken in particularly favourable weather conditions, the record books will say so. This could easily be adapted, so you would end up with: Fred Bloggs, 400m World Record Holder (heroin-assisted). Or: Frida Bloggovitch, European and Commonwealth Shot-Put Champion (but, like, really out of it at the time).

Unambitious of the Professor, surely, to stop at drugs: let's have a sports-wide amnesty on rule-breaking. Let's make ball-tampering in cricket legal, so that Michael Atherton can fiddle around in his trousers with impunity. Let's avail 800m runners of the field in the middle of the track; after all, the glory of the winning line is there as an incentive and to make them go all the way round is surely to deny them their opportunity to capitalize on it. And let's make handball perfectly routine practice in football: it was only the pressures of the money and fame at stake that made Maradona pat that one into the net against England in the 'Hand of God' incident in 1986. How could he have been expected to behave otherwise?

Professor Cashmore made this programme himself and got to have a high old time. He showed himself thumping away at a punch bag. He loomed on to the screen in fetching close-up. He even flashed up a credit at the beginning which read 'A Film by Professor Ellis Cashmore' though, lacking a plot, movie stars, car chases and a cinema release, this looked suspiciously like a television programme to me.

Unfortunately, there was no means of subjecting the Professor to a post-broadcast dope test, so we cannot be sure if he himself was on drugs; but he was certainly on television, which may in the end be the most dangerous drug of them all, leading in many cases to a willingness to put views chiefly to draw attention to oneself and, perhaps ultimately, to a complete collapse of the synapses.

FOREMAN RETURNS TO THE FACTORY

13 NOVEMBER 1994

After big George Foreman knocked down quite large Michael Moorer in Las Vegas last weekend, people were quick to hold up the new heavyweight boxing champion as a beacon of hope for the ageing, a victor over the tyranny of youth. It's probably fair to say, though, that most of us would hope to reach forty-six in slightly better shape than Foreman – a bit less heavyweight. As they say in boxing, the punch is the last thing to go, but the waistline is the first.

The fight was brought to us live by the cable station Wire TV, who had bought wholesale America's HBO coverage, and as George entered, one of the American commentators (either Rick or Arnie, it was hard to tell, not least because both of them spoke at the same time almost continuously) said, aghast: 'Looks like he's put on ten or fifteen pounds since the weigh-in.' Indeed, Foreman seemed to be getting larger all the time, inflating in front of our eyes. You could imagine uncomprehending small children in the audience, tugging on their parents' sleeves mid-bout and saying: 'Daddy? Can I have a go on the bouncy Foreman?' If the fight had gone the whole way, the chances are they would have had to pop him in order to get him back inside the dressing room.

In these circumstances, the fight was never going to be a dignified thing. Foreman's main tactic seemed to involve impersonating a multi-storey car park, while stopping Moorer's punches with his left hand and occasionally bopping him with the right. Foreman's left eye was starting to close during round two. So were both of mine.

In a vigorous effort to keep us awake, sensitive microphones, poised in the corners, picked up the goings-on between rounds. Whether or not you rate this recent innovation an advantage will very much depend on how you feel about hearing, in bright, clean Nicam digital stereo, Michael Moorer emptying his sinuses into a bucket. It should be said, much of the trainers' babble is tough to follow for the outsider; a lot of stuff about stepping in, stepping out, coming round the right side, coming round the left side, and wearing pink pyjamas when he comes. But it was hugely satisfying to hear Foreman's man, at the end of the ninth, tell his wheezing charge: 'You gotta put this guy down – you're behind, baby.' And out went George and he put the man down.

There was pandemonium in the ring and also at the commentary desk, where Rick and Arnie took to screaming simultaneously as if Michael Jackson had just come on. Interviewed in the ring afterwards, wearing a large pair of shades,

Foreman said: 'When you wish upon a star, doesn't matter who you are, anything your heart desire, can come to you.' There's a song in there somewhere.

'He didn't look at all out of place in there,' Lennox Lewis said to Desmond Lynam after *Sportsnight*'s midweek showing of the fight. Pray that Lewis never becomes a town-planner in your district. Lynam was concerned to focus on the thought of a forty-six-year-old man taking that amount of punishment about the head. 'Seems ridiculous to me,' he said. Sometimes it can seem that only Desmond Lynam stands between televised sport and complete madness.

CHEATING BASTARD ROBS DAMON HILL

20 NOVEMBER 1994

A scene from the Adelaide Formula One Grand Prix drama which you may not see replayed on BBC's *Sports Review of the Year* when it comes round: Michael Schumacher, having written his car off against the surrounding wall, has just managed to eliminate Damon Hill from the race by the unusual and not entirely AA-recommended method of driving directly across Hill's bonnet. Hill manages to get back to the pits where the Williams team stare mournfully at the irreparably bent wheel strut. The title race is over, Schumacher is now champion and the Benetton team celebrates – much bouncing around and hugging of flame-retardant boiler suits.

At the centre of the throng, the camera picks out a particularly beefy mechanic with a joyous leer on his face. And, as he bounces, we see him send down the pit lane, in the direction of the Williams team, a fat-fingered V-sign. How sweet to retain, in your moment of victory, the grace and self-possession to offer your defeated rivals a token of your esteem – a big, fruity, Formula One fuck-you.

If you hadn't taken any of the many opportunities offered this season by Schumacher and Benetton to develop intensely inimical feelings towards them, it was hard to resist this one. It seemed to confirm your worst suspicions about the piece of driving you had just witnessed. Under pressure from Hill, Schumacher had come to grief. If Hill had been able to squeeze through at this point, he was home clear. So did Schumacher try to mend his error by fixing Hill?

As Jonathan Palmer in the BBC commentary booth put it, the 'charitable view' was that, despite the breakages sustained in his collision with the wall, Schumacher genuinely believed he was still in the race, that he could go on for another fifty laps. In other words, though we could see that Schumacher's car lacked half a chassis and had no left wheels, in the heat of the moment Schumacher thought it was nothing more than a cracked wing-mirror and some damage to the paintwork.

That's the 'charitable view'. But why be charitable? The bastard cheated. Most of us have been in enough supermarkets to recognize the old Sainsbury's trolley manoeuvre when we see it; the one where you wedge the trolley diagonally to hold a place between two checkout queues and then leave it there while you go off to pick up those final few items by hand. Metaphorically speaking, Schumacher had wilfully diverted Hill down the Household Goods aisle, leaving himself free to saunter over to Wines and Spirits.

Needless to say, the tabloids cut up rough and ugly about the outcome on Monday morning. 'Kraut KOs Damon In Title Storm,' said the *Daily Star*. 'What a schunt,' it added. 'Hun-acceptable Face Of Motor Racing,' declared the *Sun*.

Trust the tabloids to hit the fast lane and follow the signs all the way to the Second World War. It's digraceful to confuse the fact that Schumacher is a cheat with the fact that he is a German. The former he need not be; the latter he cannot help.

1995

CANTONA HITS THE FAN; ENTIRE NATION TREMBLES

29 JANUARY 1995

Gary Lineker, back from playing football in Japan, started his new job as soccer chat-meister – a spot of co-presentation on Football Focus, some punditry on *Match of the Day* and *Sportsnight*, a place in the studios of Radio 5 in midweek and also a column in one of the less reputable Sunday papers*.

And what happened? Virtually the entire Football League programme was wiped out by the weather; those games which weren't might as well have taken place on one of the more complicated rides at Waterworld; and Manchester United's finest player flung himself horizontally into the chest of a Crystal Palace supporter. Welcome back to English football, Gary.

Lineker looked about seventeen when he left for Japan and since he's been back he looks about twelve. *Football Focus* packed him off to the Tottenham training ground to examine the new spirit under manager Gerry Francis. 'Something had to happen – and it has done,' said the striker Teddy Sheringham in a statement which gets more puzzling

* In 1999, Lineker went all the way and succeeded Desmond Lynam as the host of *Match of the Day* – some vindication for the BBC's youth policy.

the longer you look at it. 'Jurgen Klinsmann's taken to it like a duck out of water,' said Gerry Francis. In verbal whirlpools like these, you can see why broadcasters go for Lineker's calming influence.

So it was good to have him around on *Sportsnight* for the Cantona incident – someone who could quietly point out that abuse is the native language up there in the stands. How serious was Cantona's kung fu moment? Well, Desmond Lynam had a pair of glasses on – that's how serious it was. 'One of the most amazing things I've ever seen at a football match,' said Lineker from somewhere inside a courageous mix of checks and stripes. 'Extraordinary to go in feet first,' said Des, analytically. 'He's lost les marbles,' said Gary.

It has to be said, the actual Cantona incident was a good deal less tawdry than the torrent of pieties written in its wake. There has been much sad head-shaking and accusing Cantona of 'bringing the game into disrepute'. No one has attempted to back up the implicit allegation that the game was in some sort of 'repute' before this happened. Some have referred to 'a stain upon football', as if a new stain would even show up on soccer's bib at this point, what with all the ketchup, the brown sauce, the mud and the dribble.

Should we extend any sympathy towards Matthew Simmons, the man whom Cantona clattered? There he was, innocently going about his business as a football supporter – royally relishing the misfortune of an opponent – and suddenly he's one-on-one with the wayward French genius. This would be a bit like a computer game crashing out of the screen at you. It's understood that the aggression directed by fans at the pitch is a kind of fantasy aggression, that the abuse is a kind of virtual abuse. If real consequences followed from the vigorous accusations of incompetence one makes inside football grounds, Chelsea's Paul Furlong and I would be out in the car park on a weekly basis. Frankly, I wouldn't fancy myself. Would I berate him in similar tone and terms and at the same volume if I met him outside the ground? No, I would not. I would be reduced to a state of speechless fawning and sycophancy. The football stadium is an enclosed world in which normal rules do not apply. It may be no bad thing for us to be reminded by Cantona of the frailty of that construct.

Then again, there are accusations of incompetence and there are other kinds of abuse. Until all the evidence is gathered and marshalled, we can't be entirely sure what Simmons said to inspire Cantona to hop over the barrier and have a word with him. Given Cantona's famously intellectual mien, perhaps the surest way to wind him up would be to challenge him on a philosophical basis. It may well turn out, in the fullness of the police inquiry, that what Simmons actually shouted was: 'Eric! Your conception of individuality is diluted! You're acquiescent and you know you are! Come and have a go if you think you're Sartrian enough!'

But, as I understand it, they don't have lot of time for existentialism down at Selhurst Park. So one is more inclined to believe the statements from Wednesday night's eye witnesses who maintained that what Cantona faced as he left the pitch was a torrent of abuse relating principally to his origins in France and the desirability of his returning there as soon as possible. In which case, I beg to differ with Gary Lineker's verdict that what Cantona did was 'inexcusable'. There is an important initiative in place at football grounds across the country to stamp out racism. It appears Cantona may only have been interpreting this campaign in a baldly literal manner. It was not the kind of protest which Martin Luther King instructed us in. Best to show racism a clean pair of heels. But failing that, how about a dirty set of studs?

ICE SKATING NEARS THE EDGE

6 FEBRUARY 1995

An exciting week at the European Figure Skating Championships in Dortmund. The BBC was offering condensed evening reports, with Sue Barker repeatedly promising us sightings of 'the ever popular Finns'. If you really wanted to go ice crazy, you could catch every single minute live on the satellite channel Eurosport. When I tuned in the presenter was getting worked up about 'a very promising couple from Poland – twenty-third in the world and a lot of people are making very positive noises about them'. At which point, I decided to catch it later on the BBC. There's only so much fun you can have.

The BBC had Alan Weeks and Barry Davies elucidating the moves rinkside – the doubles, the triples, the double triples, all of which make the sport sound like a particularly reckless happy hour in a City cocktail bar. Weeks sat in on the routines as they happened, pointing out the good bits ('Yet another one!') and Barry Davies glided in at the end of each to talk us reflectively through the replays and smooth us through the judging. We looked again at Ilia Kulik, the precociously gifted seventeen-year-old with the precociously voluminous batwing sleeves. 'Took an extra turn after the landing,' Davies pointed out. If you did that in our house, you'd end up in the spare bedroom. Here, the cost was greater – lost points on the technical side – though Kulik triumphed even so, becoming, as Weeks put it, 'a name we're going to be very close to in years to come'.

Sue Barker had also promised us 'the entertaining' Phillipe Candelaro and along he came, a man, it turned out, so entertaining he had dyed his hair. 'One of the great characters of the sport,' said Weeks. 'He didn't have grey hair this morning. He, as I said, is one of the great characters of the sport.'

We've seen this hair-colour-as-index-of-fun-factor gambit before, when Andy Townshend, the Republic of Ireland midfielder, went carrot-topped midway through the 1994 World Cup Finals, and, let's face it, it didn't exactly turn him into Groucho Marx. Candelaro had taken out an additional humour insurance policy, though, by adopting a pair of stripy trousers. 'Inviting the audience to clap along with him,' noticed Weeks. This was clearly a tragic figure we were dealing with here. 'Heh heh!' said Weeks. 'Quite something very special,' he added. Sadly, Candelaro took a tumble on the way round and by the end even Weeks was forced to conclude this was 'not quite the character we've seen in the past'.

Let no one say that ice skating is a sport without claws. The misbehaviour, the sullenness and the downright ungraciousness which brightens so much of our sporting calendar has its place in the rink, too. The fixity of those skaters' smiles is our firmest guarantee of this. The lavishly talented French star and all-round tantrum chucker Surya Bonaly, forced to take a lousy second place this week, stood on the podium at the concluding ceremony and removed her medal in protest during the national anthem of the Japanese victor. Hard to imagine a future for her in diplomacy. But easy to imagine a future for her in sport – especially if Nike decide to break into skatewear and need an attitude-primed billboard star.

But to some degree, this is a sport in crisis. It is no longer enough to come out and fling yourself about athletically to a few minutes of Mantovani. Now the pressure is on to garb yourself in a themed outfit, hit the ice running and enact the entire plot of *Miss Saigon*, complete with helicopter sequence. When Candelaro got marked down, Barry Davies was forced to wonder whether, for a few of the judges at least, 'this is sport, not a show'. And when the Russian Olympic Champion, Alexander Urmanov, appeared in a reassuringly old-fashioned pair of tight disco trousers and did a routine which involved no acting, no gesturing for the crowd's participation and positively no hair-dye, it was like a throwback to another age. 'He just came out and skated to the music,' said Weeks in a tone of something like amazement.

One fears that these distractions might have arisen out of boredom. Perhaps as an athletic challenge, the sport has become too easy for those who excel at it. There's only so many triples you can do in sequence before you run out of rink. It may be time, then, for the sport's governing body to intervene, to complicate the ice dance again in the interests of competition. For example, by the simple expedient of introducing on to the ice a few fences, as at the Horse of the Year show, the concentration of the athletes would be re-focused. There would be less time for them to think about costume and drama if they were working out how to avoid barking their shins on a stripy pole or a section of polystyrene brickwork. Or perhaps a portion of the competition could take place underwater. This would call for the development of completely different muscle-groupings but it would at least provide all competitors with an opportunity to deploy the ever popular fins.

ENGLAND FANS RIOT IN DUBLIN; MATCH ABANDONED

19 FEBRUARY 1995

For several minutes we had been watching whole segments of seating drop out of the upper tier. Martin Tyler in the commentary box talked to Nick Collins on the touchline. 'Has it been a case of throwing seats?' he asked. Nick implied that, yes, that did seem to be why there was now a large abandoned area in the stand, a throng of people on the pitch and lots of uniformed men running around with truncheons. Tyler pressed him again: 'And Nick can you confirm that it is England fans totally causing the trouble?' Nick said it was difficult to see.

When it went off at Lansdowne Road on Wednesday night, the worst place to be was in that lower tier, helpless beneath a shower of wood and glass. But it wasn't so great at home either, watching it on Sky Sports, ducking in your seat from a barrage of muddled remarks. For the most part, we would prefer to ignore the fact that the sport we watch has connections – be it with far right activists or with anything outside the stadium's walls. We're happier when the evening's action can be contained within *Sportsnight* and doesn't have to spill over on to *Newsnight*. Sky's live coverage made excruciating viewing for two reasons: partly because some of the things which were said were plain excruciating, but also because the situation was so unfair on those saying them. There were hints of Heysel in 1985 here – a live sports event unfolding and growing beyond the bounds of sport, and the commentators finding their job description has changed beyond recognition.

Imagine, for example, being Nick Collins on Wednesday. You've gone along intending to spend most of the game eavesdropping beside the England bench and hoping to squeeze a couple of breathless words out of David Platt at half-time, and suddenly you're a battle correspondent, jostling for a position near the front line.

Similarly, the programme's producers don't employ the former England international Alan Ball to comment as a sociologist. They employ Alan Ball to . . . well, actually, I don't know what they employ Alan Ball to do, but it certainly isn't to deconstruct some of the patterns behind errant social behaviour. On the one hand, he said these were 'mindless thugs' and on the other they were a highly organized and disciplined paramilitary force who 'knew exactly what they were doing'. And just to confuse matters further, as the image of a baffled boy wearing an Ireland scarf appeared on the screen, Ball suddenly came over all misty-eyed and uncle-like. 'Says it all,' said Ball. 'He's gone with his dad to see probably his heroes from England – he's probably only read about them in magazines and his dad has said, "Come on, I'll take you along to watch them play and see them in the flesh, live football." And they're subjected to mindless people . . .'*

Back in the studio, Richard Keys announced to the camera: 'They shouldn't let them out. They should nick the lot, because somebody in there knows who was doing this.' It was hard to know what was more alarming: the images of the crowd members in England shirts converting

* Never short of an arresting perspective on things, Alan Ball once maintained that England's World Cup victory in 1966, in which he played a part, was 'the greatest team achievement of the twentieth century'. Something to mull over there for participants in, say, the Apollo space programme.

their benches into missiles, or the sight of Keys, tight-lipped and advocating indiscriminate imprisonment, a thought ripped from Block W in his mind and tossed recklessly into our living rooms.

In the struggle to find an appropriate tone, the further up the rhetorical scale everyone climbed, the more out of touch they sounded. When the game was cancelled, Tyler said, 'The ultimate price has been paid here for the folly of a few', as if he was reading the lesson at a service of remembrance. He went on: 'There's just a terrible feeling of dismal sadness, sorrow, say what you like – shame is the word that constantly comes to mind.' 'Ban them for life,' said Gerry Francis. 'And that means literally banning them for life,' he added.

On *Sportsnight*, Desmond Lynam had his glasses on again, which is always a mournful signal that all is not well. Jimmy Hill talked, rather movingly, I thought, about the particular awfulness, for his generation, of seeing England fans use the Nazi salute. When they screened some rugby league, it was possible to experience an intense relief. At last, you thought: some sport. About five minutes in, there was a fist-fight and a couple of sendings-off.

Newsnight's piece involved a qualified sociologist, the Irish sports minister and the MP Kate Hoey. Hoey's baloney ranged from absurd piety ('it's something that brings disgrace on all of us') through to noisy tub-thumping. 'It's very important that someone takes the initiative,' she said before calling for 'an immediate inquiry' – the politician's standard means of looking active and on the case while merely saying 'would somebody somewhere please do something about this?'*

* Kate Hoey succeeded Tony Banks as Labour's Minister of Sport in 1999. Early on in her reign she led a vigorous, but alas unsuccessful, campaign against footballers spitting.

Beside her, Phillip Cornwall from the magazine *When Saturday Comes* quietly pointed out that when we talk about the long period of time since England fans were in trouble at an away match, all we mean is that England haven't played away for a long time – since 1993, in Rotterdam, when there was trouble. It was suggested that some of the 'known' thugs should never have made it to Ireland: Cornwall indicated that you can't detain or restrict people who have no criminal records. These were by no means happy things to think about, but it was heartening, at the close of a cheerless evening, that just about the only person talking calmly and sensibly was a football fan.

SHOWJUMPING: SEX ON FOUR LEGS

26 FEBRUARY 1995

As the saying goes, there's no business like showjumping. And there's no programme like Channel 4's *Cutting Edge* for getting down to business. 'Women in jodphurs with boots and spurs and a little whip in their hand,' said one of the hapless contributors to Monday night's documentary. 'Er . . . you know, shows the outline of their bum and their legs . . . I think it's quite sexy.'

Put a little less feverishly by the woman doing the voice-over, the premise of *Jumpers* – in which the cameras nosed into horseboxes and stables, in search of a hidden world – was that showjumping has 'always enjoyed a glamorous image'. Well, perhaps by comparison with, say, carpet bowls. But for many of us, showjumping has tended to enjoy, not a glamorous, but a faintly absurd image – the stuff of late-night sports programming in which horses named after television sets and car spares attempt to clear polystyrene walls and giant flower arrangements while Raymond Brooks-Ward shouts 'Come on, Virginia' and 'Oh no!'

Jumpers included a clip of an event in which riders zip round the course as usual, but then abruptly abandon their horses, jump into a bright red jeep and burn off across the sawdust to complete a test of driving proficiency (no jumping required in this segment, fortunately). First Prize: £15,000-worth of Japanese car. In this the sport approached closely the condition of a high-risk It's A Knockout, but you could argue that showjumping always has the potential to appear that way, even at its more straightforward.

The programme mentioned only one item in support of the glamour claim; the Jilly Cooper novel *Riders*. But Cooper is not exactly renowned for her gritty, close-to-the-facts documentary style, so this was like claiming that beagles are renownedly thoughtful animals and producing as evidence a set of Snoopy cartoons. In the event, what was revealed here was that showjumping is a lot less glamorous than you think (assuming you think it's glamorous at all) and quite a bit more absurd.

Much was made of the graft in the background. The Horse of the Year Show might look like a fancy dress party, but behind the scenes evidently there's muck and mud and endless training and a lot of driving to Leicester in mid-winter in a lorry with a bust heater. Tim Stockdale, Britain's No 15, reckoned he had broken nearly every bone in his body in his quest to rise into the Top 10. He once jumped a seven-foot fence at Wembley with his collar-bone strapped up and can no longer straighten one of his fingers as a result of stitching a wound himself, in order to be able to make a competition. You'd say he was a frantic glory-seeker, except that there didn't seem to be much glory around. Not only was there no press at one of the events Stockdale regularly attended, there was also no audience.

The programme also introduced us to Ronnie Massarella, who, with a name like that, should really have been leading a Big Band in the Sixties but who settled instead for becoming the manager of the British showjumping team. Ronnie, we were forewarned by the voice-over, is 'plain-speaking', a term which always sets alarm-bells ringing, being frequently a synonym for 'plain stupid'. As it turned out, Ronnie laughed a lot, while unleashing on us a set of sexual politics which might have raised an eyebrow in the court of King Arthur. It was put to him that women seemed to play a strangely minor role in the British set-up. 'I do like girls,' explained Ronnie, who was filmed, rather touchingly, through a enormous tumbler of white wine at one point. 'I'm very fond of them actually. But you can't get to them like you can men. You can give men a good bollocking and tell them what you think.'

Enter Oliver Skeete, former bus-driver, sheetmetal worker and bouncer who, at thirty-eight, has been riding horses for just three years (as he pointed out, you didn't tend to see a lot of horses in Acton when he was growing up) and is intent on becoming Britain's first successful black showjumper. Skeete has decided that the sport needs 'a personality, someone with a bit of character, a bit of panache, somebody who's going to promote the sport.' We followed Skeete to some no-hoper pony trial or other in a deserted barn. First Prize: £10. The camera looked on in disbelief as our personality – riding Tascam Mini-System or Mazda Clutchbox Boy or some such – turned in a performance which was, literally, devastating. It left no pole untouched. You wouldn't want to query Skeete's control, but the horse did appear to destroy a couple of those fences with its chest. 'Going over a fence for me is better than having sex,' said Oliver. And probably a much rarer experience.

The encouraging (and very modern) thing about Oliver was that, although he displayed almost zero competence in the arena, at least he could handle the autograph hunters. 'I know how to keep them at bay,' he said. And without professional distinction of any kind as yet, he has already found a publisher for his autobiography, *Jumping the Odds*. A hero for our times, really.*

L'AFFAIRE ERIC; ENTER RIMBAUD

5 MARCH 1995

Near the start of *The Cantona Affair* (BBC2), a journalist declared that 'it's easy to put top spin on a Cantona story'. But as we've seen in some of the coverage generated by the kung fu assault on Matthew Simmons, it's easy also to swing wildly, catch the thing at some laughable angle on the top edge of your racket and balloon it on to the next-door court. So how would *The Cantona Affair* fare?

Essentially, this was a previously shown interview spruced up and rejigged to incorporate the recent misdemeanour. There was no new comment from Cantona, sadly. But at least we got to look again at some of Eric's finest seconds: that peachy goal against Wimbledon, that extraordinary shot which hit the bar against Chelsea, and that blissful moment in France when he returned the ball to the referee with a touch more vigour than was strictly essential. Against the

* For Oliver Skeete's heroic appearance on the Saturday morning children's programme *Live and Kicking*, see page 63.

rules, a bad example to youngsters, not to be encouraged, etc., but it was an athletic achievement of its own kind to be able to hit the referee that hard from that distance.

Connections were explored between Eric and the poet he holds dear, Rimbaud. Simon O'Brien, narrating, boldy insisted on pronouncing it 'Rimbo', presumably in order to steer clear of the traditional 'Rambo' confusion. Fearlessly getting one over on literature, O'Brien pointed out that Cantona had had 'more words written about him than Rimbo managed in a lifetime', a statistic which, for several reasons, seemed a little unfair on the plucky young symbolist from France who did, after all, live in a time before competitive, mass-circulation tabloids and so couldn't always rely on hitting the headlines ('Top Verse Man In Prose Poem Stunner' etc.).

The programme also reflected on the Cantona Nike commercial (in which Eric lists his moments of weakness in a manner at some remove, you could argue, from remorse) in order to initiate some thoughts about the perpetuation of an image. This was a little cheeky because the programme itself was guilty, in its interview sequences, of playing up to received images of Cantona. Not for Eric the standard dodgy two minutes of close-up, outside the bootroom after a game with his hair still wet from the showers. *Standing Room Only* filmed him seated in a blackened studio, strikingly lit from the side, a treatment ordinarily reserved for the various dissident Balkan playwrights and Norwegian underground movie makers who used to pitch up on the *Late Show*.

He was wearing his Nike-endorsed baseball hat – a condition, one would wager, of the interview being granted in the first place – and looked more like a racing driver than a soccer player. And just occasionally, with his jaw tilted up rather imperiously, he would thoughtfully rub the underside of his chin with his thumb and forefinger in the manner made famous by intellectuals worldwide. I am convinced that I have never before seen a footballer doing this.

It is here, I think, that the inevitable comparison with George Best breaks down. It's an easy one to begin to make, given Best's and Cantona's talent-levels and given that both players possessed, or possess, gifts which are inexplicable and therefore difficult for them to talk about or work on. Also, both of them would know something about a kind of suicidal or kamikaze impulse. But, other than that, they may only have in common the red shirt of Manchester United. (Or, in Cantona's case, the red shirt, the green shirt, the black shirt, the blue and white one and, probably before the end of this season, the lilac and cream shirt with apricot shoulder areas and a fetching neckline in jade. A snip from the Megastore at £49.99.)

Best, as clips reminded us here, was always willing to be portrayed as a fun lover, just the man for a champagne fountain or a boutique-opening, and never once tried, even in his darkest moments, to lead us to believe that, behind closed doors at his luxury home in the suburbs, he was in fact writing a thesis about Chaucer. Cantona's temperament is altogether different and the sense of imminent implosion which hangs about him (and is one of the reasons for his attractiveness) has nothing to do with loving the spotlight and threatening to go to seed. If Cantona finally blows it, it won't be in a pub with a bottle of wine in one hand and another bottle of wine in the other. It will be on the pitch, or in the stand on his way off the pitch in some enormous storm of intense, personal seriousness.

Accordingly, the single moment which rang false in the interview was the one in which Cantona alleged, on the topic of Manchester United's secret of success, 'We have lots of fun and score lots of goals.' Lots of goals, yes, and lots of astonishing football. But fun? This is a team whose brilliance often seems directly proportional to the players' ability to get on each other's backs, a team whose emotional condition is perhaps best encapsulated in the perpetually aggrieved face of Paul Ince.* Or in Cantona's furrowed brow.

As predictable as the dawn, Best appeared on the programme and, in a lordly kind of way, suggested that Cantona was indeed a player he would be prepared to pay money to see, but that he could maybe learn to handle the press better. Actually, given Cantona's recent punch-up with a news crew on a beach, there's probably nothing that any of us can tell him, strictly speaking, about handling the press.

JIMMY HILL – THE AWFUL TRUTH

2 APRIL 1995

This week, a judge turned over a two-week sentence on Eric Cantona and an entire nation turned over the judgement of a lifetime on Jimmy Hill, thanks to *This Is Your Life* (BBC1). It's just typical: you think you've found someone you can reliably dislike without any feelings of remorse, and then Michael Aspel turns up with his bloody red book and tells you how they're a quiet saint on the charity circuit and will even shave off their beard, as long as there's thousands of pounds in it for the disadvantaged.

What a turn-around this was. It wouldn't even be fair to say that Jimmy Hill slotted into that possibly mythical cate-

* Or Roy Keane. Or David Beckham. Or Ryan Giggs. Or Paul Scholes. Or Nicky Butt . . .

gory – the people you love to hate. More often than not, hating Jimmy Hill has involved having a really bad time. But from now on, at every point at which one is tempted to turn rancorously against him, one will be haunted by a sequence from Wednesday night's show in which Hill, handed a cornet by one of a cheerful bunch of his old marching-band pals, promptly delivered a quick burst of the 'Eton Boating Song', pausing with perfect comic timing before nailing the high note at the end. At home, blinking away the tears, one was forced to confront the utterly unthinkable: Jimmy Hill In 'Really Nice Man' Shock.

There they all were, on the *This is Your Life* bleachers – Des, Alan, Trevor, Brian Moore, Reg Gutteridge, even 'little' Dickie Davies. At one point an enormous, suited figure rounded the scenery, looking slightly lost. I was still in a state of some considerable personal difficulty following the cornet sequence. It dawned on me that I possibly wasn't going to be able to make it through if we were now, as it appeared, to be shown a heart-wrenching parade of the fellow beings whom, through tireless care and patience, Hill has slowly but successfully restored to a place within the community. But as it turned out, it was the former Wolves and Ireland football international, Derek Dougan.

It had been Dougan's dubious privilege to sit round a table with Hill on an old ITV football discussion programme chaired by Brian Moore. It was his dubious privilege now to cue in a clip. Just as, in the words of Eric Cantona, seagulls follow the trawler in hope of being thrown a sardine, so many of us gather hungrily wherever 1970s television clips are being shown, in the hope of glimpsing a kipper tie. And we were not let down here. In fact, you could have run a trawler aground on the kipper tie Malcolm Allison was wearing.

Allison, whose nearly closed eyes suggested he may well have helped himself liberally to the contents of the sideboard in the hospitality room before filming started, was seen putting forward a forthright – and, you might even say, prototypically Euro-sceptic – view: namely, that all foreigners are 'peasants'. And Jimmy Hill was seen to be intervening on behalf of foreigners and, by implication, on behalf of the future of civilized conversation. It's not a glamorous job – indeed, as Hill has discovered, you run the risk of coming across like a schoolmaster, putting down the unruly pupils while trying, unsuccessfully, not to appear ruffled by them. But someone's got to do it, so it might as well be Hill.

Tributes came from far and wide. Jimmy Tarbuck appeared in a film clip, on a golf course in San Lorenzo. Odd that the *This is Your Life* team didn't grab Tarby less than a week earlier, when he was in a London studio, filming an edition of *Fantasy Football League*: it left you wondering whether, as well as flying surprise guests in from around the world, the programme also flies surprise guests out, just to make things more exotic.

We learned, from Lawrie McMenemy, closer to home, the secret of Hill's unruffled on-screen grooming: even in the most wind-blown aluminium broadcasting shed, on the most God-forsaken Beazer League playing field, Hill stays smooth and smart by taking along, in his briefcase, his own personal make-up compact, complete with mirror, brush and mascara.

Gary Lineker said that Hill 'always fought for the good things in football'. It was Hill who, as chairman of the Players Union, got the maximum wage lifted. But was that such a good idea? Without Jimmy Hill, players would still be earning £20 per week, less tax, and you can see how, in some very straightforward ways, this would be to the benefit of the game. Dennis Wise of Chelsea, for instance, might not have got into trouble for fighting a taxi driver; he would have been in no position to afford a taxi and would have gone home on the last bus, several hours earlier. And Paul Merson, a self-confessed addict for a while to expensive substances, would have had to have made do with sniffing the tip of a felt pen, holding his breath and jumping up and down for two minutes.

Still, such quibbles meant nothing on the night. Desmond Lynam once remarked that if it was possible to unite the Middle East, then maybe even Jimmy Hill and Terry Venables would one day come to an understanding. Wednesday was that historic occasion. 'The word "warmth" comes to me, Jim,' said Tel, as Bill Clinton, Henry Kissinger and Jimmy Carter looked on, smiling proudly.

With Cantona, the judge decreed that his offence, though it clearly brought football into disrepute, should not be punished with a custodial sentence. The producers of *This is Your Life* must surely now face the strictest penalty the Football Association can muster, for bringing Jimmy Hill into repute. In a season hardly short of blows to the game, this is an especially tough one to bear.

SKY SPORTS BUYS RUGBY LEAGUE; PRESENTERS DELIGHTED

25 APRIL 1995

All sorts of confusion has followed the decision by Rupert Murdoch's chequebook to attempt to form a rugby league Super League with exclusive coverage on Sky Sports, not least over the matter of possible mergers between some of the smaller teams. It was reported that Salford and Oldham were considering a merger but couldn't agree where to meet in order to have the discussion. That's how confusing it has got.

No merger difficulties for Sky Sports' rugby league presentation team, however. Eddie Hemmings and Mike 'Stevo' Stephenson are, on the evidence of Friday night's edition of *The Big League*, effortlessly as one on all the radical proposals heard so far. Revisions and redesigns? Bring 'em on. 'We can clean-slate,' said Stevo, inventing on the spot a new, highly American-sounding verb ('Call the VP and tell him I'm gonna have to clean-slate today's lunch-meeting'). 'We can start all over again,' he added.

Of course, it's just possible that our presenters' unerring optimism and joyfulness about these changes to the constitution of rugby league might have something to do with their sense of an impending explosion in the vicinity of their own wage packets. During Friday night's live coverage of St Helen's v. Warrington, Hemmings in particular seemed able to spot harbingers of joy and omens of prosperity almost wherever the camera alighted.

At one point our screens filled with a shot of a small child in the crowd ramming a fistful of Quavers into his mouth, as if trying to push them directly into his stomach rather than go through the altogether boring business of chewing and swallowing.* 'There's the new face of the Big League,' said Eddie, warmly, 'enjoying the match, enjoying his crisps.' If that was the new face of the Big League, then pass the flannel.

Actually, we'd already had half an hour of pure flannel before the game. Eddie and Stevo staged an entirely card-

* The child's mother phoned me in the office the day after publication to complain about this description. But I stand by it.

board debate about the Super League with Eddie lobbing up rhetorical questions of a softness not witnessed since Barry Norman interviewed Michelle Pfeiffer. 'It's got to be right, hasn't it?' asked Eddie. 'It's all about making a great spectacle, so thumbs up,' said Stevo.

At one daring moment, Eddie conceded that some people weren't too happy about the introduction of in-goal referees. 'You'll always get someone who'll knock it,' said Stevo. 'Let's get positive.' 'It's all great to have a chat about,' concluded Eddie.

You got the impression that if a decision was taken to stage the game in swimwear on an enormous bouncy castle and to sanction the use of rubber baseball bats and copious quantities of coloured shaving foam, then this would be greeted back in the studio with a straight face and an upraised thumb, and short shrift for the nay-sayers. Eddie would say, 'Now some people are arguing that replacing the scrum-down with the Grab A Grand sequence from *Noel Edmonds' House Party* is a bit out of whack with the spirit of the game. That's just plain wrong, isn't it, Stevo?' And Stevo would say, 'There are a lot of negative people in this world, Eddie.'

Still, at the moment, it's what happens out on the pitch that counts. Super League initiatives may change a lot about the coverage in the future. Coloured gumshields are obviously a bit of a rage right now, enabling the players to offer the cameras some frankly alarming grins in sky blue and postbox red. But it can only be a matter of time before these spaces are occupied as prime advertising sites – perhaps for Colgate or Listerine.

St Helen's had a player dismissed for a neck-high tackle on Alan Bateman which, if timed correctly, probably would have destroyed a small building. At half-time, big Scott

Gibbs, St Helen's Welsh international, felt obliged to remark that he was 'only grateful that Alan Bateman is still alive'.

Of course, this kind of action is meat and potatoes for Stevo. Or rather, wine. Stevo has been known to greet bloodshed with the words 'the claret is flowing'. The person I watched the game with (a lifelong League fan whose claret runs pure St Helens) opined that Stevo was 'one of the better operators of the chalkboard' (that gimmick whereby analysts get to scribble illuminatingly, or otherwise, on the screen). There was no refuting this. Nor his range of expression: from the outspoken ('Talk about losing your marbles!'), to the obscurely idiomatic ('He's going to earn his corn tonight!'), to the plain unfortunate ('Put that down to an eighteen-year-old piece of brilliance!').

'I'll tell you what, Stevo,' Eddie said. 'Every time we come to Knowsley Road, we get entertainment par excellence.' Another piece of assertion masquerading as conversation. But it didn't conceal anything which anyone would want to debate.

PRINCE EDWARD GETS REAL; CHRISTIE GETS GOING

18 JUNE 1995

Amid much squeaking of rubber sole on wooden floor, Channel 4 took us to a real tennis match. That's 'real' tennis, as opposed to the 'pale imitation' tennis you get at Wimbledon. Imagine a squash match set in an abattoir with rules drawn up by Anthony Burgess. Entertaining viewing? 'Trust me,' said our host, Edward Windsor – Prince Edward to you.

This may look from the outside like novelty casting, but in fact His Royal Highness was the obvious choice for presenter. For one thing, he's a player himself and so can be relied upon to know his 'grille' from his 'tambour' (though we've yet to see him don the shorts and do his stuff). For another, when it comes to explaining obscure institutions, you'd be hard pressed to match a member of the royal family. Also, about as many people play real tennis as have a chance of ascending to the throne.

The programme decided, probably wisely, to skip lengthy explanations in the abstract and elected instead to let us watch some games and pick it up as we went along. Our commentator courtside at Holyport was the Australian player Lachlan Deuchar, who himself sounds like one of the game's targets. ('He's gone for the tambour there, but he's just missed it and clipped the lachlan deuchar') and first up was a mixed doubles – Jonathan Howell and Sue Haswell of England versus Frank Filippelli and Barbara 'Barby' Baker from Australia. I was impressed to learn that Howell currently stands at number nine in the world rankings – until it dawned on me that if I was to sign up myself tomorrow I would probably go direct into the lower twenties by default.

The game was fast and furious and all kinds of other things it was hard to put your finger on. 'He's slipped it into the galleries behind Barby,' said Deuchar. 'No going soft on the girls there!' There was no answer to that. 'The play now unrecognizable from the play earlier on,' Deuchar said later. True, though, to be frank, I hadn't recognized the play earlier on either.

Anyway, true to form, England got whumped, but there's a chance for them, and us, to catch up in the next episode. Normally a bell rings when the ball hits the gallery. And a puff of white smoke rises above the roof of the court whenever anyone inside who is new to the game finally understands what's going on. It's early in the series, I know, but I'm going to stick my neck out here and suggest that it will never replace Wimbledon in the hearts of the nation.

Something, however, is going to have to replace Linford Christie. 'I'm at the stage where I could walk out of the sport any day,' he said during *Sport in Question* (ITV). Any day? What about right after the commercial break? We only popped out for a few adverts and by the time we got back, Linford had decided he wouldn't be going to the next Olympics. 'I'm finished,' he said. 'I can't take any more.'

And suddenly all hell was let loose. The discussion which followed was confused and confusing, to say the least. The rules of real tennis began to look as straightforward as the opening instructions on a milk carton by contrast. Christie said he despised the way 'the media think they make you or they break you', when clearly it was Linford Christie, he said, who made Linford Christie. But then he announced he was giving up because the papers didn't back him sufficiently: in other words, he was granting the papers, in his own case, the absolute power of destruction. He said he ran for the British public, who had always supported him; 'There's no better public out there,' he said. Yet here he was denying that public the chance to see him. He was saying the press meant nothing to him; but it appeared the press meant everything.

In any case, the whole argument seemed to be wrapped up in an impenetrable coat of irony. This was the adored Saint Linford talking – he of the media-friendly track-side stunts with the Union Jack. Linford Christie moaning about his coverage in the British papers is a little like Sarah Ferguson claiming treacherous treatment at the hands of *Hello!*

Asked to be more specific about what had upset him, Christie could only come up with the lunch-box controversy (a gag about the tightness of his shorts which is doubtless politically suspect and probably at once embarrassing and tedious from Christie's point of view, but hardly malicious in intent) and with the generalized complaint that writers had been speculating about his retirement. He didn't add that many of these writers had done so in a tone of anxiousness and concern; nor that with this new revelation, he had promptly made them all dead right.

So, sporting martyr or touchy tantrum expert? This being *Sport in Question*, Jimmy Greaves was on hand to shine the bright torch of his wit into these obscure corners. The contributions of Greaves to these programmes should really be heralded by a passenger announcement: 'We apologize for the delay to your argument. This is owing to a derailment at Greaves Junction.' Greaves thought this might be a good moment to suggest to Christie that he change his shorts. 'Why don't you wear something more suitable?' he asked. Expect widespread media speculation to follow about the contents of Jimmy Greaves's out-to-lunch box.

Linford Christie, incidentally, is right now in the middle of complex financial negotiations with the British Athletics Federation and has an autobiography due out in a month's time. Altogether an inconvenient time to be achieving huge coverage in the papers, then.

ENGLAND LOSE AT RUGBY; PRIME MINISTER RESIGNS

25 FEBRUARY 1995

How bad was England's performance against France in the Rugby World Cup third place play-off? Very bad. Deeply bad. So bad, in fact, that some of us couldn't take it at all. Like those French fans in the crowd whom we briefly glimpsed, ignoring the game and amusing themselves with a live cockerel. Or like the players on the England bench, rendered open-jawed and catatonic with boredom. And about fifteen minutes into the second half, with France up 14–9 and another shoddy Rob Andrew punt descending glumly into no-man's land around the halfway line, the Prime Minister finally said 'sod it' and resigned.

Here was the proof that there is no keeping politics out of sport. A blue strip appeared across the bottom of the screen, courtesy of ITN. I should confess, it was quite a while before I got round to reading it. The slightest experience of watching bad youth programmes teaches us that, when graphics appear at the foot of the screen, it's normally safe to ignore them because the chances are they will only be saying 'get a life' or announcing the release of the new Take That video.

In any case, all through ITV's World Cup coverage, that space along the bottom has only ever housed unrewarding statistical and biographical information about the players – about how fly-half X from team B has kicked thirty-three points in forty-nine internationals and enjoys Italian food and relaxing at home with his wife Maria and daughters Maxine and Jade. These boxes have not at any point in the tournament been the vehicle for warnings of a significant shift in the governmental power base. It was hard to be ready.

Still, there's always a first time. The sign said, 'PM offers resignation as leader of the Conservative Party.' Even here the combination of phrasing and context was slightly confusing. Were we meant to phone in and take him up on the offer? A little later, a second sign appeared saying, 'Major remains PM pending Conservative leadership contest', which clarified matters a little, though without entirely dispelling the suspicion that this was all simply a preliminary to another of ITV's magnificently challenging, multiple-choice quiz questions, which have taxed us all so thoroughly throughout the coverage of this World Cup ('Is the Prime Minister's first name A: John or B: Queen Elizabeth?').

And not long after that, another sign came up saying 'Temporary Fault'. This may just have been a crisp endorsement of the way John Major sees the current break in his service. Or it may have been an apology for the soundtrack which had suddenly deteriorated to the quality of a taxi-driver's CB. Clearly 'Temporary Fault' wasn't referring to the England side who, if their game is to reach the levels displayed elsewhere in the world, face long-term construction work akin to the building of a hydroelectric dam in a remote part of a developing nation.

Eventually, the reverberations of the Major story reached the commentary box. 'Momentous news from England,' said John Taylor, looking anxiously for the implications on the pitch but not immediately seeing any. 'Jack Rowle certainly not aware of that and neither are the players.' Difficult to know how Rowle could have responded tactically – except, perhaps, by implementing immediately, in sympathy with Major, a policy of 'foot up or shut up'.

Some political commentators have argued that Major's response was hasty and overreactive. After all, Tony Underwood was being rested; and Andrew was having what was clearly a rare off-day and will doubtless return rapidly to something more recognizably his regular form on the international stage. Most of us, they argue, would have settled for turning over to another channel or going out into the kitchen to put on the kettle, rather than opening up a leadership challenge and sending the party into turmoil at grass roots level.

But this, I think, is to underestimate the provocation offered in the heat of the moment. The game was about as entertaining as an exhibition of goat-herding. Someone somewhere at the very highest level had to make a stand and stand down.

PRINCE EDWARD 2: TOO MUCH REALITY

2 JULY 1995

After three intensive weeks in a warehouse with Prince Edward, I think I'm finally getting a grip on some of the arcane rules of Real Tennis, which has about as much in common with the game we see at Wimbledon as Formula One motor racing has with dressage. Using imaginative 3D-style computer images and the Prince's own careful voice-overs, the programmes have, it seems to me, finally shone a bright torch on this tricky and, some would say, inaccessible sport.

Basically, as I understand it, the important thing to realize is that the server retains the cutlass as long as the ball makes contact with the armoire and when spades are trumps.

Galleys are out of bounds during any tryst. Bishops can swing either way, but in the event of a cathedral, go directly to jail, do not pass Go and do not collect £200. Professor Plum may only enter the library if in possession of the lead piping. There's a 50-point bonus if you manage to use all your letters. And the last one back is a sissy.

For me, a vagueness still attaches to the scoring system, but ten more programmes and I should be right up to speed. Unfortunately, the series has ended.

TENNIS ENTERS A ZONE; CRICKET FOLLOWS

9 JULY 1995

Interesting developments in Wimbledon's second week. Agassi's shorts appeared to be getting longer as the tournament went on. If he'd made it through to the final, they would have been down around his ankles, so to speak. And Pete Sampras's tongue reappeared, under pressure.

A couple of years ago, Pete's tongue flopped around on his chin as a matter of course, like a thirsty St Bernard's. Then he tamed it – folded it in half, or something – and kept it in, which was generally agreed to advance his game, at least aesthetically speaking. But against Goran Ivanisevic in the semi-final, Pete's tongue was back, just briefly. I thought he might choke. But he swallowed hard and made it.

Later, Pete used the tongue to commend his defeated opponent, 'He was unconscious there for a second,' Pete said, 'unconscious' being, as far as one can make out, a term of approbation in tennis, akin to 'in a zone', and 'thoroughly focused'. 'There are times when he's just not there,' Sampras went on, 'and that's what makes him dangerous.'

As psychoanalysis goes, this was pretty unconscious. But Pete had been out-psyched earlier by Brad Gilbert, Agassi's coach and the author of the handsome coaching manual *Winning Ugly*. Brad is one focused talker. We're looking at a zoned wordsmith here. In fact, the Wimbledon meter clocked Brad's delivery at 139 m.p.h., making him the fastest server of tennis-babble in the tournament's history. 'Tennis,' he said, helpfully, 'is about dealing with the situations, using what you've got on the day.' Agassi's preparation before facing Becker was going to involve deciding 'what he wants to happen under pressure'. Either you were in a zone or you were on a plane – the next one home.

It wasn't just the rapidity of Brad's style that made some of this hard to apply to the game we then saw. When Agassi crouched to receive serve in that final tie-break, was he working out what he wanted to happen under pressure, or was he just trying to concentrate on getting the ball back? This is what is ironic about all the psycho-chat that comes with Wimbledon, both from the interview booth and the commentary box with its perpetual variants on the question 'What will be going through her mind now, Anne?' At this level, when these players really get going, they have no time to think. They have time only to react.

Clearly, given the BBC's coverage, actually going to Wimbledon is no substitute for sitting at home and watching it on the telly, but, for anyone contemplating sending off for tickets for next year, it's become clear that the seats to have are those directly behind the umpire's chair. These may in fact afford a limited view of the court, but they do set you up as the potential recipient of a whole range of tennis and sporting goods, thoughtfully surrendered by the departing players. Of course, your delight in this will depend on how you feel about having to struggle home on the train with a top seed's laundry. But after his semi-final victory, Becker took the time to express-deliver, to someone in the fourth row, a set of sweatbands and a shirt. This was but two days after Pete Sampras had given away a racket. Rumours that the doubles partnership of Knowles and Nestor would be offering free shoes, a selection of wines and spirits and a heavily discounted line of men's fragrances and toiletries turned out to be unfounded, disappointing many who had stayed late into the evening.

Could it be that some of tennis's attitude-speak has rubbed off on the BBC's Test Match cricket team? In this quieter realm, 'Just Do It' normally applies to putting on the kettle. But Geoffrey Boycott, considering Edgbaston's interestingly cropped playing surface, has been referring to 'a result pitch', a piece of hypey verbal mangling with which Brad Gilbert would have been delighted. Boycott in a zone: it's a terrifying thought.

Somehow this doesn't look like the kind of road Richie Benaud will go down. Benaud can achieve a serenity which is positively Bond-like at times. As England's captain stared sorrowfully behind him at the wicket destroyed by Courtney Walsh, Benaud remarked calmly: 'He's made a horrible mess of the ash behind Michael Atherton.'

To be able to preserve this tuxedo'd calm in any live commentary situation is remarkable; to do so while England are batting shows special steel. It's a miracle Benaud isn't in tears most of the time – either of pain or hilarity. On Friday, Graham Thorpe swung with his eyes closed like an apprentice lumberjack. Benaud, for once, began apparently uncontrollably: 'That is one of the . . .' Worst shots ever seen? Dumbest ideas a man could have? Reasons for switching over to *Emmerdale* on the other side? In a flash, our man had somehow chilled himself: '. . . things that will stay in Graham Thorpe's mind for a very long time.'

The umpire had cause to call twice in quick succession for the verdict of the umpire up in the box with the video replay facility. This was over two run-out decisions which our man on the ground wasn't prepared to trust his naked eye on. Convention dictates that the umpire signals his desire for a further witness by holding up his finger and drawing a large television screen in the air. The gesture has, it seems to me, a rather unfortunate relation to charades (as if expecting the crowd to chant in unison: 'It's a book . . . and a TV programme . . . six syllables . . . ') and would perhaps be better – and more honestly – replaced by an exaggerated shrug, indicating, 'Search me. I was unconscious.'

A TIME TO DANCE, A TIME TO FIGHT

6 AUGUST 1995

The opening ceremony for the World Athletics Championships took place on Friday night. It went with a bang: or, more strictly speaking, with several bangs, a ballet and a man in motorcycle leathers playing a trombone. And only Eurosport was on hand. The BBC are in Gothenburg too, but someone on their team must have cast an eye down the first-night bill – folk dancing; an appearance by the rock group Brainpool, performing their hit 'Bandstarter'; a nine-year-old girl called Amanda saying hello to the world in three languages – and thought, 'Stuff it. We'll go in on the Saturday morning when Linford's on the track.'

The cost to the viewer at home can be very simply summarized. No David Coleman. David Coleman's opening-ceremony commentaries – fearless explanations of foreign folklore at its most obsure from a man supremely qualified to talk about sport – have taken on a legendary status, frequently yielding at least as much entertainment as anything which succeeded them in the following days. Few who witnessed it will ever forget his elucidation of a particularly opaque Norse dance-saga-on-ice prior to the last Winter Olympics.* Enormous clumps of people in tracksuits carrying flags around for hours on end just cannot be the same without him.

Eurosport's commentary box contained Tim Hutchings and Steve Cram, both of them formerly distance runners of great repute but as yet largely untested in the long-haul which is arena-based Swedish pageantry. Tim and Steve surveyed the scene – which, at the point we went live, featured women in dangerously small dresses dancing expressively with men in dangerously large sailor-suits. 'Massive presence down on the track,' admitted Tim, a little nervously, like a man watching enemy troops gather on the hill above his town. 'We'll try and keep you abreast of what's happening.'

For the next five minutes, Tim and Steve were silent. They were stunned, I imagine – and fair enough. The screen teemed with hundreds of people of all ages, shrouded in monk-like blue robes and doing exercises. It was as if the aerobics instructor Mr Motivator had got loose in a Pentecostal church. At home, we were left to infer what was going on from the captions which occasionally flipped up and from the evidence of our own eyes. If either of these things were to be trusted, we were watching the Gothenburg Symphony

* The ceremony included a tribute to the ancient Nordic tradition of hat-kicking, in which men put a hat on a pole and then kick it. Coleman didn't even flinch.

Orchestra, conducted by Roy Hattersley and with Alexi Lalas from the USA international football team on clarinet. Finally, a horse-drawn carriage entered, bearing what appeared to be the chat-show host David Letterman, and Tim was suddenly back in action. 'The Swedish Royal Family!' he said with audible relief at finally getting a toehold.

And from this moment on, there was no stopping them. 'Choir on the track,' said Tim knowledgeably. 'Simulating the movement of the sea.' 'It's a chance,' Steve added, 'to display the seafaring culture of this city.' As the night went on, confidence increased in bounds, to the point where a woman only had to stand up the middle of the arena wearing a blue leotard for Tim to identify with pinpoint accuracy 'a water-dance where Poseidon is lured into noble contest' – though it's just possible he read that one out of the programme. 'And now a re-enactment of seventy young men starting a fight,' said Tim, introducing one of the more novel, costumed items. 'Well, it is Friday night,' said Steve.

The teams paraded behind flags and placards and shot out rather more quickly than usual. This was because most countries were fielding drastically reduced sides. Steve was able to draw on his own experience to explain the absence of nearly all the big stars. Evidently the 'standing around' can affect your stamina. Also, 'those flags are heavy'. Surely it wouldn't hurt the odd pampered athlete to put in a little extra training for the opening night?

Anyway, the ceremony was a ball, and Tim and Steve took their eye off it just once. We were looking at a picture of the King of Sweden, waving from his seat in the stand. 'The man who took your crown, Steve,' said Tim. This was extraordinary news. Casting back to my schooldays, I could dredge up nothing about a House of Cram flourishing in Europe, nor any memories of Steve appearing on foreign stamps. In fact, Tim and Steve had just spotted, carrying his nation's flag, the runner Abdibele who outpaced Cram in the 1500 metres a few years back. This is the one mild risk involved in Eurosport's team selection. Put two sportsmen together and they will natter. As Tim said, late on in the proceedings: 'You blame me for everything, you do, Crammy.' Cosy.

SPRINTERS FAIL TO GET IN LANE

13 AUGUST 1995

'Oooh, my goodness! It's massive! It's absolutely huge! There's going to be a big smile on *this* lady's face.'

Seven days into the athletics World Championships in Gothenburg, and no signs of flagging enthusiasm from the BBC commentary team, whose remarks have been consistently keen and richly descriptive, though, of course, you really need the pictures to make complete sense of it all. (That was the Women's Triple Jump Stuart Storey was talking about.)

Runners, though, have been losing their way a little. First Jacqui Torrence was disqualified for straying into an adjacent lane in the 200 metres. Then Marion Mutola did exactly the same thing in the 800 metres. As David Moorcroft wisely pointed out, 'rules are rules' and, as he went on to explain, the one offended against here is Rule 141 on lane discipline, not to mention several pages of the Highway Code.

Among those still managing to run in a straight line is the man they're all calling 'that man Michael Johnson'. Day Six belonged to him. But then so did most of the other days, as the American sprinter hoovered up first places and medals like someone with a metal detector, only much faster. The remarkable thing about Johnson is that he effortlessly achieves such speed while wearing a gold necklace thick enough to pass in many British towns for a mayor's chain of office. It may be clear that he's going to win, but is this any justification for letting him wear the medal during the race?

Day Seven, meanwhile, belonged to a non-competitor. If you were the world record holder in the 400 metre hurdles and an injury had deprived you of your opportunity to defend your title at the World Championships, there are any number of vantage points from which you might choose to watch the televising of the event. In the privacy of your own home, perhaps. Or maybe in some darkened bar in downtown Gothenburg, over a string of whisky sours, with Frank singing something slow and moody on the jukebox. The place you probably wouldn't choose would be the BBC's commentary box, with a microphone open in front of you, ready to broadcast your reactions live to the nation. Unless, that is, you are Sally Gunnell.

As Kim Batten smashed Gunnell's world record and stole her crown, Gunnell was positively breathless with pleasure for her. 'Unbelievable!' she shouted. Seconds later, she was down on the track. 'Kim, I just want to say . . .' The conversation could have gone any way at this point. For instance: 'Kim, I just want to say that I am sick to the pit of my stomach.' Actually, what Gunnell just wanted to say was, 'that was unbelievable.' The interview which followed was mostly mutual screaming and laughing. Gunnell was so plain excited about it all, she couldn't even hold the microphone straight: she was flinging it all over the place until the arm of a technician reached into shot to twist the thing into the vicinity of Batten's mouth.

That evening on the highlights show, Gunnell talked smilingly about how the race had rekindled her determination, how she couldn't wait to get back into training the next day. Confronted by shifts of fortune far less significant than this, many of us would have been planning on a good half-year of solid sulking, followed by a month or two of plain bitterness, dispersing eventually into a low-level grudge of indeterminable duration. There was a lesson here.

Also on Day Seven, that man Sergei Bubka, the Russian pole vaulter, won his fifth consecutive world championship, thereby becoming a record holder of records. The television coverage really splashed out for this one, positioning a camera up high beside the crossbar and training another on his family in the stands. Storey pointed out 'his wife Vitalia. I'm sure his son, Sergei, is here too,' he added. And let's not overlook all of Sergei's other friends, relations and anyone else who knows him.

'When I won first one is not so big pressure like now,' explained Sergei afterwards. 'Now when I come into the stadium, I don't have to miss one attempt, I don't have everybody looks for me and my competitors has good motivation, but I'm a little different situation.' 'We know exactly what he means,' said Desmond Lynam, back in the studio.

Looking set to defeat the World and Commonwealth Eccentricity Records is the Kenyan steeplechaser Christopher Koskei, to whom Des referred as 'that man who runs barefoot'. This is, to say the least, brave. Having seen the British runner Alison Wyeth limp off in agony, her heel sliced accidentally by the spiked shoes of a runner on her tail, I wouldn't step out there in anything less than hobnail boots.

An obstacle course of thick fencing and water splashes, the steeplechase is effectively a horse race for which the runners have forgotten to pack a horse. Koskei's other new slant is a hurdling style which involves approaching the barrier side-on and almost flipping himself over. 'Goodness knows what he's going to do if anybody teaches him to hurdle,' said David Coleman. And goodness knows what he's going to do if anybody gives him a horse.

'His hurdling is not textbook,' Brendan Foster confirmed. 'I don't suggest anyone at home practises hurdling like that.' Sound warning, though I'm not sure how many of us at home really were thinking about our hurdling techniques at this point. We were still busy trying to master the pole vault.

CHRISTIE BOUNCES BACK TO CONFOUND DOUBTERS

19 AUGUST 1995

In Gothenburg, Linford Christie was face-down on the cinders while several men in anoraks strapped what appeared to be a packet of frozen peas to the rear of one of his thighs. There are places in Europe where it would cost you a small fortune to arrange a scenario like that, but if you're Linford and you've just crashed out of the 100 metres in the World Championships, the service comes free.

At that point, the future looked pretty bleak for Britain's sprint champion and European and Commonwealth tantrum medallist. The combination of defeat and injury, mixed in with Linford's much-publicized disenchantments with athletics authorities and the press, suggested that the next time we heard from him, he would be running a Will Carling-style motivation agency out of Knutsford.

A week, though, is a long time in a top-flight hamstring

clinic and blow me if Linford wasn't back on our screens for the Weltklasse event in Zurich, brought to us by ITV. And blow me again if he didn't win.

This was no cheap and cheerful, post-Gothenburg side-show, either. The Weltklasse – which, as Jim Rosenthal pointed out, twice, means 'World Class' – had attracted just about every big name in contemporary athletics by the novel but undoubtedly effective means of writing them all giant cheques. So Linford was lining up against Donovan Bailey and both the other World Championship medallists who danced past him in Sweden while he lay on the track having his wounds tended.

For the occasion, Linford elected to wear what can only be described as an all-in-one Mars bar wrapper. The next day's newspaper pictures of his bare-chested victory lap (sadly not featured on the television coverage) would reveal that, underneath, he had thoughtfully painted the Puma logo on to his left pectoral – an astonishing new development in product endorsement. Even nude, Linford wears Puma. If this ever catches on in a big way, the racing driver Damon Hill, who is not short of sponsors, is going to be spending six hours every morning just doing his make-up.

In the race, Donovan Bailey was out-powered. As a staggered Alan Parry put it, 'he had to take bridesmaid's place to Linford tonight'. The blushing bride himself then granted a trackside exclusive to Jim Rosenthal. Actually, there was no blushing. The chilling defiance of the look which Christie wore directly after crossing the line had softened slightly, but he was still, even in victory, doing his now traditional bear-with-sore-head act.

'Pleased?' Rosenthal asked. 'As long as I can shut up the doubters,' Christie said, 'the people who've been giving me hell.' As he said this, he was struggling to be heard above the sound of hundreds of German fans, singing his name in unison. We can only imagine how hellish that must feel.

'I'm going to start thinking about me,' he told Rosenthal, 'about running for me and the people around me.' Surely this put-upon schtick is wearing really thin now. Linford enjoys public goodwill of a kind normally reserved exclusively for the Queen Mother on her birthday. And she, to my knowledge, has never interpreted all those people waving flags and hankies at her as a massive surge of resentment. Linford, on the other hand, would probably feel persecuted to discover a hole in the middle of his Polo. Maybe he needs this grudge to run against. But you wish he would lighten up now and again.

HANSEN TELLS MAN U KIDS, 'YOU'LL WIN NOTHING'

27 AUGUST 1995

Match of the Day swept back. The new Premier League season came around so quickly, they must barely have had time to hoover the studio. Indeed, Des, Gary and Alan may well have looked at their watches at the end of last season and decided they were better off kipping over on a camp bed. Whatever, they're back and it's as if they've never been away.

I'm not forgetting, incidentally, that there was a *Match of the Day* a whole fortnight ago, covering the Charity Shield match. This, strictly speaking, was the first of the season. But everyone knows that pre-season try-outs are no reliable barometer for anything that's likely to happen over the ensuing year. Chelsea's Robert Fleck once scored in a pre-season friendly, which gives you some measure of the degree to which everything prior to 3.00 p.m. on the first Saturday exists in a Tom & Jerry realm, because he rarely bothered again.

So if, for the Charity Shield, *Match of the Day* had appeared on our screens presented by Dale Winton, with expert post-match analysis from somebody's hamster, nothing could safely be inferred about the form of the programme in the long struggle through the winter months to come.

As it turns out, the programme returns unchanged. There's been no unrest in the stands nor, as far as we know, in the dressing-room, and no one has been screaming at the chairman to get his chequebook out. And accordingly *Match of the Day* goes into 1995–96 with exactly no new, laughably overpriced strikers and precisely zero beautiful but nearly pensionable continentals. Also, no one's had one of those embarrassing bleached hair-jobs. It's still Hansen at the back, Lineker up front and Des in the calming libero role which bore fruit during his spells at Wimbledon (tennis) and Gothenburg (athletics). Why change a winning formula?

Des pointed out that Hansen and Lineker were 'worth around £20 million a pair at today's prices' but he added – reassuringly from the licence-payer's point of view – that they would 'continue to provide analysis for a free copy of the *Radio Times*.' Just a thought: if Gary Lineker does *Match of the Day* for a copy of the *Radio Times*, then presumably you can get him to do the after-dinner speech at your work's Christmas party for little more than last month's *Marie-Claire*. Have a word with his agent.

Looking frisky early on, Hansen suggested on Saturday that Chelsea's Dutch genius Ruud Gullit, recently signed from Italy, might do well, when under pressure, to 'play the percentages' – in other words, hoof the ball into the stands on a safety-first basis. This remark drew a laugh of disbelief from Lineker. But then it is the function of Hansen to supply bones for picking. On Wednesday, he was on especially corruscating form, dismissing an entire Manchester United side with one, crisp sentence: 'You can't win anything with kids.'* One fears what the effect of these words might be on the morale of the kids themselves. Luckily the programme goes out at an hour when most young players will be tucked up in a nightclub.

One mild objection: we're still not shot of those daft noises overdubbed on to to the progamme's opening music – bogus cheers and thuds – all of which suggest a slightly desperate half-hour in the sound effects department. The noise which accompanies the shot of the ball hitting the back of the net, for instance, is clearly someone whipping back a shower curtain. This is one of the all-time great TV themes which is being drowned out here. (Though musicologists may care to notice how, when the tune stops and starts again half-way through, the drummer misses the beat completely. It's late enough to be Ringo. Or even Robert Fleck.)

On Wednesday, *Match of the Day* ran directly into the documentary look-back series *Match of the Seventies*. Here was an opportunity to lament the passing of time and the collapse of all one once held dear – except it didn't work out like that. For one thing, you realized how much *Match of the Day* has improved. Now that cameras are everywhere, it

* Manchester United and their kids, of course, went on, over the next few seasons, to win every trophy known to man and a couple of others. Punditry is a tricky game. But also a forgiving one. Hansen did not lose his job.

can genuinely cover the day – all the goals, all the incidents. Drawing on the days when *Match of the Day* was two games and bust, *Match of the Seventies*, though great fun, doesn't actually have the capacity to tell the story of the season.

In the programme dedicated to 1974–75, for instance, Derby won the league but if Dennis Waterman hadn't told us near the end, we'd never have known, apart from a couple of goals and some documentary footage of the club's dinner-dance. True, one of those goals was accompanied by Barry Davies's voice-wrecking explosion of excitement – 'Interesting . . . very interesting . . . oh! Look at his face, just look at his face!' – words which, for people of a certain age, are embedded in the mind as firmly as the chorus of any song. But this was above all a clash in which the present came off best. Terrace aggro, horrible Admiral strips, no Dutch geniuses on the books of Chelsea . . . How could one not prefer now?

COLOMBIAN GOALIE WITH CRIMINAL RECORD TAKES FLIGHT

10 SEPTEMBER 1995

In the future, people will say, 'Do you remember where you were the night Higuita pulled off the scorpion?' And people will reply, 'Of course. I was watching it on *Sportsnight* with Barry Davies.' (Some will reply: 'I was watching it live at Wembley,' but given the pathetically small attendance, they will almost certainly be lying.)

It was the start of England's international football season, an occasion of almost complete insignificance. Croatia had pulled out, pleading a slightly more pressing fixture at home in the form of a civil war, and in stepped Colombia. The night could so easily have degenerated into a basic hair story. For one thing, there was the matter of Paul Gascoigne's rug: he'd promised to ditch his relatively recent blond, light-bulb look and one feared the worst – some sort of rapper's crop with the image of a pint of lager razored into it, perhaps, or maybe an unwittingly offensive tartan dye-job. In fact he went for a back-to-basics black rinse, so recently applied that, when the rain came, one was slightly surprised not to see it running in rivulets down his neck.

The Colombian players, too, are big believers in hair. During the pre-match warm-up, Barry Davies, our commentator for the evening, pointed out Valderrama, 'a man who hasn't changed his hairstyle in ten years of international football'. Later, when Davies said 'Valderrama – beautifully curled', it took a moment to be clear that he was referring to a pass, rather than the man's appearance generally. Davies somewhat presciently also recommended that we keep an eye on Higuita, 'the eccentric goalkeeper', a portly figure with a shoulder-length cascade of glossy black ringlets who looks like King Charles sponsored by Umbro.

And with that, the game was underway. It was a credit to Terry Venables' young but fast-maturing English side that they managed to adapt swiftly to Colombia's tenaciously possessive style and also to remain undistracted by the overriding impression that they were in fact playing against the rock group Aerosmith. Everything seemed to be shaping up well when, half an hour in, Higuita hit the launch button and made the rest of the game a formality.

On reflection, these were perhaps not the ideal conditions in which to attempt unassisted flight. There was soft but consistent rain and an early-September chill in the breeze, both of which could have contrived to make things tricky for lift-off. But as the ball floated goalwards, Higuita watched it all the way, before springing forwards, flipping up his legs and pinging it back off his heels.

The expressions on his face were a joy to behold: not simply the enormous delighted grin he wore as he landed, but also, just seconds later, a completely straight-faced and unperturbed look, as if the incident had never happened – a sign, if not of outright madness, then certainly of the possibility for richly interesting moodswings.

Barry Davies couldn't believe his eyes. 'Unreal!' he said, from somewhere inside an astonished laugh. 'A character in every sense,' he added. 'It's amazing they managed to keep him in jail for four months.' This was a reference to Higgy's recent arrest on a kidnapping charge. (Simply in terms of criminal records, the Colombians made the home side look flat-footed and flair-less. The best England could field was Tony Adams – drunk-driving – and Dennis Wise – altercation with cabby and cab, case dismissed.)

'Goalkeepers are crazy,' Des Lynam said afterwards, 'but this one . . .' And words failed him. 'All goalkeepers are crazy,' Jimmy Hill told Des just a couple of minutes later. 'But this one . . .' And then words failed him, too. With the benefit of time, we can more clearly articulate the significance of that giant leap. Higuita will go down as the first man in history to make the table football game you find in pubs appear to have any relation whatsoever to the real thing.

'Obviously,' Terry Venables told Ray Stubbs in the tunnel afterwards, 'the only thing we was short of was goals.' Obviously, any sentence beginning with the word 'obviously' is about to say something obvious. Tel went on: 'We're on target for where we are, I think.' This too was hard to dispute. But not until David Seaman can pull off a scorpion can England be expected to be taken seriously as an international footballing force in the fullest sense.

Before the match, Frank Bruno, the new heavyweight champion of the world (or one of them, at any rate – politics have rendered this sport confusingly fractured) dropped in to the *Sportsnight* studio to chat to Des about his victory over Oliver McCall last weekend. Frank, in a magnificent blue suit, admitted that it had been tough but reckoned he had survived by refusing to get wound up by his opponent's tactics, not least of all what Frank called 'the verbal things he was saying'. 'I had to duck and dive, bob and weave, grab, y'norrowamean? Waltz him, show him me Ginger Rogers steps and everything, y'norrowamean?' Des asked Frank to show the championship belt to the camera. 'Cheers, nice one, Des,' said Frank. 'You've got it upside down, by the way,' said Des.

Frank then thanked as many people as he could think of, including his wife and family, God, all of his fans and – incredibly sweetly – the man from *Sportsnight* who had sent him the fax asking him to come on the show. 'Very nice,' said Frank. Shortly after this, Frank thanked his manager for getting the fight shown on Sky. This possibly wasn't an entirely tactful thing to say while sitting inside the BBC sports department, but nobody seemed to mind. No one says verbal things quite like Frank.

BOWLS GETS YOUNGER; KIDS TV GROWS UP

2 OCTOBER 1995

A question troubling the nation: exactly how interesting is televised carpet bowls? What is the pleasure in watching a large black object arrive slowly beside a small yellow one? And how much of your time would you be prepared to give this spectacle? Two minutes? Ten? Or the full four hours or so on offer daily from the BBC?

Some would argue that in contrast with, say, white-water rafting, indoor bowls was short of moments of genuine exhilaration. What can you say about the adrenalin-content of a game whose crisis point involves a man getting out a tape measure? But the BBC knows what it's doing here. After all, it has had enormous success with another sport where coloured balls are positioned fastidiously against a green baize background. And the championships had something of snooker's inexplicable, dangerously hypnotic charm. You tuned in on Sunday for the preliminaries and the next thing you knew it was Thursday afternoon and Hugh Duff was putting out the reigning champion, Mark McMahon.

You know you're getting old when bowls players start looking young. Whatever happened to the gnarled, pipe-smoking bowling journeymen of yesteryear? They seem to have been all but eradicated by a new, floppy-fringed, fresh-faced generation. That quarter final between Duff and McMahon could just as easily have been an audition to replace Robbie Williams in Take That.

Not that the audience in the Guildhall, Preston, saw it quite that way. The cut-away shots to the crowd presented a tranquil scene. Most of the people looking on were old enough to be the players' grandparents. Refreshingly, there were no police on horseback in attendance. One of our commentators this week felt compelled to commend the crowd to us. 'Good audience,' he said. 'They've learned the etiquette of the game. Not to move before the end of a set. And to keep quiet while the bowler's on the mat.' Of course, these feats of discipline are much easier to pull off if you happen to be asleep at the time.

There was evidence to suggest that the afternoon audience at home, on the other hand, was wide awake – though not necessarily attending strictly to the matter in hand. During this week, the camera has alighted regularly on one Maria Ward, a lady seated prominently just beyond the bowlers' shoulders. Maria Ward is evidently the recipient, via the BBC, of fan mail – and all by just sitting there and smouldering quietly.

In many ways, the BBC's coverage of the entire event has taken the Maria Ward approach – nothing flashy, just patient attention with suitably understated commentary from, among others, John Bell and David Rees-Jones. That said, John occasionally applied himself to the electric pen device which enabled him to illustrate the likelihood that, for example, Hugh was going to bring his bowl towards the jack either down the left-hand side of the carpet or down the right. This was only useful if you were troubled by the thought that Hugh might be going to try and blast it into position off the decorative flower beds.

Doutbless Duff and McMahon and the other players will shortly find themselves invited as guests on to *Live and Kicking*, the Saturday morning children's programme on BBC1. After all, nearly everyone else in sport passes this way. This Saturday alone, the programme welcomed the WBC champion and panto veteran Frank Bruno, the triple-jumper Jonathan Edwards and Oliver Skeete, the man frequently touted as 'Britain's only Rastafarian showjumper', though not in fact a Rastafarian at all.

Live and Kicking has pop music, cartoons, hordes of children in the studio and many games involving shouting and the wearing of knee-pads and helmets. Yet sports people seem happy to give up their time for the opportunity to be interviewed by the irrepressible Emma Forbes. 'The most important thing for me,' said Jonathan Edwards, 'is to please God and glorify him.' 'Great!' said Emma.

Skeete, meanwhile, was on the 'Famous For Five Minutes' slot – a reference not to himself, but to a young girl called Amie who was about to take a pony round Wembley Arena. In a long but as yet undistinguished career, Skeete has found himself hoisting major showjumping silverware on precisely no occasions. Mostly he is famous for appearing gamely on a Channel 4 documentary last year, doing none too well in some minor event somewhere on a horse apparently on loan from a local brewery.

So it was with some consternation that one heard Skeete inform Amie, 'Don't worry. I'm with you all the way.' Having Oliver Skeete with you all the way would be a bit like setting off into the desert in a car with Mark Thatcher. But this was a moment to cherish the wonderful, unconditional trustfulness of childhood: Amie was seen beaming warmly, rather than vomiting nervously into a handkerchief. In the event, she got four faults and a refusal, a personal best for her, as it would have been for Oliver Skeete.

Bear *Live and Kicking* in mind. In the future, when every sporting event worth considering has gone pay-per-view, the only chance that most of us are going to get to watch the nation's top athletes in action will be in circumstances such as these: alongside Bobby Davro, operating the gunge-bucket on Saturday morning TV.

PAUSE FOR THOUGHT ON *A QUESTION OF SPORT*

23 OCTOBER 1995

'It's more than just a programme,' the snooker player John Parrott said, firmly. 'It's an institution.' He was referring to *A Question of Sport*, the BBC1 quiz game, which, ahead of a new series, allowed itself the luxury of a fond look-back over its first twenty-five years. A careful comparison with other, established national institutions reveals that Parrott was, if anything, understating the case. Not crumbled by scandal, or frozen by indifference, *A Question of Sport* looks in better health by miles.

We've now had a quarter of a century of the 'What Happened Next?' slot, of mystery guests and of David Vine or David Coleman saying, 'Home or Away?' And in that time, only the haircuts and the theme tune have changed. And some of the haircuts haven't altered to the point where you would notice without squinting very hard.

The programme seems conceived as a direct smack in the face to popular theories of business viability. How do you stay competitive in the fast-moving, shark-infested waters of the nineties? You change, you evolve, you keep moving. Actually, no you don't. You just get the old picture-board out again and see if anyone can recognize Nigel Mansell when he's covered in soot.

True enough, the theme tune spent a large part of the late

1970s underwater and bubbling madly in a token gesture to the age of the synthesizer. But it had begun life on an extremely rickety piano; an allusion, perhaps, to the Victorian era of self-generated family entertainment, a theme the programme has maintained in its production standards ever since. Heroically immune to the advance of technology, *A Question of Sport* is still thrilled to pieces about the advent of the pause button – the gimmick which enabled the 'What Happened Next?' slot. Part of the programme's homeliness arises from the feeling that there is nothing here you couldn't stage yourself with a few old *Shoot!* annuals and a pair of scissors.

Deeply nostalgic sequences from old editions showed Emlyn Hughes, Mr Touchy-Feely, attempting to keep his hands off an important guest, HRH the Princess Anne. And there was a clip revealing Linford Christie laughing. I rewound the tape to check, and this really was the case. (Christie, of course, gave up laughing some time ago as a protest against being so popular.)

And here was a flushed and sozzled Paul Gascoigne, attempting to keep his mind on the game's intricacies. 'Paul,' Coleman said. 'Home or Away?' Gazza was speechless with perplexity: or rather, speechless with advocaat, which Ian Botham had been feeding him in the green room before the show. Minutes passed as he wept with hopeless mirth. Eventually, he resorted to writing 'Home' on a piece of note-paper and holding it up to the camera, like someone in a kidnap attempting to get a message to the outside world.

Apparently, Botham had told Gazza that advocaat wasn't alcoholic – a detail which tells us a lot about Gazza's gullibility, but also quite a bit about Ian Botham's sense of humour. You could speculate that Botham was more of a physical comic than a verbal one – less Woody Allen, more locker-room japester, the kind of person who enjoys filling his teammates' jockstraps with putty, and so forth. The programme now routinely sets Botham in opposition to Bill Beaumont, who wears permanently the expression of a man who has just discovered that a choc-ice has melted in his back pocket. (It was probably put there by Botham.) Some analysts might feel that to look back to the days of Hughes and Willie Carson was to look back to a livelier age, when the programme was more chipmunk than sloth.

But to look back was also to revise slightly the common conception that *A Question of Sport* is really only a display module for overheated knitwear. It's more than that. It's a display module for stupendously ambitious shirts as well. It must be something they put on the invitations: 'Please come looking as if you were in a supermarket when a bomb went off on the cake ingredients shelf.'

One mystery went unsolved. Why does nearly everybody study the picture board (on which hard-to-identify portraits are concealed behind numbers) as if it was chess, deliberating long and hard before deciding, 'I'll go for Number Four, please, David.' What are they thinking about in these vital seconds? Is there some tactical dimension here which the rest of us are missing?

FOOTBALL'S FOREIGN INVASION – PEACE AT LAST

6 NOVEMBER 1995

At the end of what critics were united in calling 'a disappointing week' for British football in Europe – one in which it became apparent that the finest talents the Premier League can currently muster would struggle against a Latvian farmers' XI – the documentary series *Football Fussball Voetbal* (BBC2) took a long and langorous look back at glorious British European campaigns of the past. The words 'salt' and 'wound' came to mind.

The idea of *Football Fussball Voetbal* is to travel thoughtfully through post-war European football on a region-per-week basis. This might seem a lot of ground to cover in the time but it's a good deal more lingering than the average American coach tour. *Football Fussball Voetball* is also unique in contemporary television, in being a programme about football which at no point features Kenneth Wolstenholme, or anyone else for that matter, saying, 'Some people are on the pitch . . . they think it's all over,' a set of words once deeply evocative but now desperately in need of a close-season break.

The British edition was written and presented by John Motson which meant there was little point disputing any of the factual information, as wild as it seemed. Did British clubs really appear in a European final for eight consecutive years, starting in the 1960s? Did Newcastle United really once win a European trophy?

One did wish, though – albeit nervously, and with all necessary respect – to take up with Motty his assertion that the early-to-mid-sixties was a time 'when Anfield reverberated to the sound of the Beatles'. Strictly speaking, wasn't that the Cavern?

A sequel to this programme follows later in the series, dealing with British clubs in Europe in the 1980s and 1990s. (Rumours that the BBC are considering scaling the edition down and running it on a Sunday afternoon, back-to-back with a couple of Bugs Bunny cartoons, are probably exaggerated.) This one was mostly black-and-white territory, drawing on the days when 'babe' meant 'Busby' rather than *Baywatch*. When Tottenham fans ran on to the pitch at the end of a game, the Newsreel reporter could conclude, 'No wonder the fans went wild!' Try that now, and you get banned from the ground for life.

Few tips were forthcoming about getting over what everyone is calling 'the present malaise'. Clips from training sessions revealed that Brian Clough and Jock Stein went a long way in Europe by being terrifyingly rude to their players, but doubtless our present day managers have already thought of that. And Peter Osgood's revelation that, following a major binge in a Greek Hilton, a substantial portion of Chelsea's triumphant Cup Winner's Cup team of 1971 was, in fact, badly hung over at the time, never really looked likely to solidify into a major FA initiative.

That said, in cricket, Ian Botham's self-commissioned solutions to the national side's problems don't always seem so far removed from this, his manifesto appearing roughly to be: 'Make me manager of the England cricket side and I will lead us on to glory, via compulsory golf outings and frequent karaoke yard-of-ale nights at the Dog and Feathers.' So maybe Ossie's got a point.

Bill Shankly was shown insisting on the distinction between being beaten and being defeated, a distinction now largely lost to us. These days 'being defeated' is something the fans suffer; 'being beaten' is all that the manager pretends it amounted to in the next week's programme notes. Perhaps it would go some way towards beginning a British regeneration in Europe if our managers learned to admit defeat.

Gloom and post-mortem washed over into the weekend. Gary Lineker was so upset about the situation, he went out and had his hair flattened, appearing on 'Football Focus' (*Grandstand*, BBC1) wearing a slight variation on the currently modish French-crop look, as seen on teenagers, Paul Gascoigne and blunt crayons. (If you're keen on Gary's version, just ask your hairdresser for 'a European malaise, please, Bobbi'.)

It took a storming *Match of the Day* to clear the air. This was, as Des Lynam suggested, our opportunity to become Euro-sceptics all over again. The top four clubs playing against each other, and both matches getting shown on *Match of the Day*? Now, this really was like the old days. We're inured by now to Sky Sports disrupting the schedules, holding games over to Sunday and Monday and messing with the drama of the league (with the league's full consent). But Sky had clearly trusted their match selection for this weekend to someone in a blindfold wielding a pin. As a result, they had taken Blackburn and Everton out of the frame, and virtually nobody cares about them anyway. It was an old-style Saturday afternoon, followed by an old-style Saturday night.

As if that wasn't enough, *Match of the Day*'s cameras were also in Middlesbrough for the debut of Juninho – 'a diminutive little fellow' according to Lineker. And not all that tall, either. Ray Stubbs, as excited as only Ray Stubbs can be (he goes all the way up to Emlyn Hughes on the excitement meters), alerted us to a shot of Juninho's mother and father, 'watching proudly'. Actually, they looked to be huddling together desperately in an attempt to get warm. That wasn't pride on their faces, it was icicles.

Still, their son set the place alight and viewers of *Match of the Day* were forced to a cheerful conclusion. Bergkamp, Cantona, Ginola, Juninho – there's nothing wrong with the English game whatsoever.

MURRAY DOES ADELAIDE; DRIVERS MAKE HAND SIGNALS

NOVEMBER 1995

It was the last Grand Prix of the season and no one was more excited about it than Murray Walker. No one ever is. On BBC2, in the middle of the night, he spoke to us from Australia.

'Welcome to Adelaide,' Walker said. 'Adelaide SA,' he added. 'Sensational Adelaide,' he further clarified. 'We've seen the massed bands, we've seen the pipers, we've seen the choreographed "Adelaide, You're A Star" display . . .'

It was beginning to sound as if we had joined the party a little late. All we were seeing at home were the usual mechanics milling around on the grid and a long shot of a completely unexplained, handwritten sign reading 'Helen 4 Yosser'.

But even agonizingly early on a Sunday morning, Murray Walker will get you involved. Consider the moment when David Coulthard took the unusual step of crashing on his way into the pits. The written word can only hint at the noise made by Walker at this point. It combined surprise, amazement and dismay and sounded a little like someone saying 'organ' while sneezing.

Down in the pits, an unseen Barry Sheene trapped Coulthard for an instant response – to the crash, that is, not to Walker's noise – and was rewarded with the phrase 'that's racing'. Except that, strictly speaking, racing is exactly what it wasn't; it was turning into the pit-lane. Jonathan Palmer predicted that Coulthard was going to find this embarrassing, looking back. 'Embarrassing is one word,' said Murray Walker. 'Mortifying is another.' There was no arguing with that.

It began to look a little less embarrassing for Coulthard – and perhaps even less mortifying – as the race wore on and other drivers, attempting the same simple manoeuvre, found themselves in trouble. There was talk of dust and oil down there, though, as Jonathan Palmer pointed out, all those who got into a mess in this place did seem oddly reluctant to take some of the obvious precautions – like slowing down, for instance. Perhaps the Adelaide circuit designers would have done well to follow the example of town councils across Britain and to have inserted some traffic-calming devices. It was nothing which a couple of sleeping policemen and an orange bollard couldn't have sorted out.

Most of the big guns were out of the race before the halfway mark, leaving only Damon Hill and a bunch of parrot-coloured stragglers. The former champion Alan Jones was on hand in the commentary box to give us the Australian perspective on all this. Alan didn't speak for quite a long time, until a collision between Jean Alesi and Michael Schumacher prompted him into action. 'What was Alesi thinking of?' Murray Walker wondered aloud. 'I can hazard a guess,' said Alan. 'He was thinking, "You're not going to get past me, you arrogant little Kraut." That's what he was thinking.' An awkward silence descended for several seconds after this.

Adelaide provided an emboldening conclusion to Hill's season but also a big and sunny finish for Murray Walker's. Walker's performances get no less impressively vigorous with the years. He is in his seventies now, but his acceleration (from nought to oblivion in absolutely no time at all) remains as sharp as ever. When the coverage suddenly slings him a random shot of someone twirling into the barriers, he is ever ready with an appropriate 'Worrgh!' or a swiftly applied 'Yaioww!'

True, he has his well-worn gimmicks, including making words out of syllables. 'Fan Tastic!' he will shout. Indeed, it's quite possible that there are people out there who, knowing Grand Prix racing only through Murray Walker, are firmly under the impression that Sen Sational is one of the lesser-known Danish drivers.

But to listen to him is to realize how urgency has many shades. For example, there is the urgency of an air-traffic controller during a computer blackout: 'Michael Schumacher is not, I repeat not, closing the gap on Coulthard.' Then there's the urgency which generates instant newspaper headlines: 'Damon Hill fastest in Adelaide!' And there's the urgency of a parent reading to a child from a particularly high-octane fairy story: 'And now, guess who is leading the Australian Grand Prix!' Walker has all of these and more.*

* There is an obvious opening for Murray Walker as the voice of children's literature on audio tapes. 'By. The. Hair. Of. My. Chinny. Chin. Chin. I. Will. NOT! Let. You. In.' And so forth. It is extraordinary that his people have not thought of this.

Even with Schumacher out, the action kept on coming. We were watching Frentzen struggle with Blundell on a corner, the pictures arriving from the camera on board Frentzen's car. Often these juddering remote-controlled images seem of doubtful illustrative use – unless you're keen to see tarmac go past at 170 m.p.h. – but not this time. Suddenly a grubby glove filled the screen. It was Frentzen, offering Blundell that time-honoured motorists' gesture – the finger. 'Oi oi oi,' shouted Walker. 'That is not very polite.' It was time to hear from Alan again. 'That's not very easy, either – turning right with only your left hand on the wheel like that.'

We watched Olivier Panis hobble over the line in a cloud of steam, his car having decided to do a Flying Scotsman impression several laps from the close. Panis, happy with these rare points, will be hoping to book himself into a non-smoking car for next season. And Hill, returning in triumph, even managed that tricky turn into the pits, offering the crowd what Palmer referred to as 'bootfuls of throttle'. According to Alan: 'Damon was really doing the four-wheel version of a motorbike wheelie to celebrate his victory, which is great because it's showing his character.' Fans of Alan – and, indeed, of Murray – will be delighted to know that next season opens in Australia. It cannot come too soon, or too early in the morning.

HURDLING MADE EASY; STEVE DAVIS MADE DIFFICULT

12 DECEMBER 1995

The documentary series *Peak Performance* (Channel 4) asks the question, 'What drives an athlete?' And it comes up with some pretty specific answers. On Thursday, for instance, the programme crisply informed us that there are 100,000 muscle fibres in Allen Johnson's left leg alone.

Johnson is an American sprint hurdler and *Peak Performance* spent a large part of its thirty minutes lingering over his muscles – measuring them, analysing them, or just plain staring at them. And very fine they were, too. Clearly, this was partly an excuse to show oiled pectorals before the 9.00 watershed. (When the trembly voice-over, courtesy of the actress Zoe Wanamaker, alerted us to Allen's 'massively developed hip-flexers', one was tempted to check the room for minors.) But it made the programme admirably literal in its approach. Unimpressed by psychology, *Peak Performance* was prepared to stick its head under the bonnet and talk mechanicals a while.

That said, some of the deeper secrets of sprint hurdling were reluctant to emerge. 'You're trying to run as fast as you can,' Johnson explained. 'And every few steps, you lift your legs up.' Armed with this insight, we went out on to the track, where Johnson was perfecting a bouncy motion known as 'rotary running'. (This is not to be confused in any way with 'Rotary dinner'.) Basically, the idea seemed to be to minimize your time in the air and to hit the ground running – familiar tactics for anyone who has ever travelled with carry-on luggage only and fought for a seat near the front of the plane.

Johnson needs to shave just 0.07 seconds off his time to take the World Record at the Olympics in Atlanta next year and he's so serious about this that he's taking advice from the enormous Jeff 'MadDog' Madden. When we first encountered MadDog, he was leading out on to a pitch the American football team for which he does most of his best work. His chest alone was roughly the size of a washing machine and somewhere near the top end of it lay a giant medallion reading 'MADDOG' and featuring a snarling dog's head in gold.

The voice-over pointed out that Johnson 'could lift MadDog with one of his legs'. But only, presumably, if he didn't mind having it torn off in a fury immediately afterwards. MadDog is the inventor of a muscle fitness system entitled 'Explosive Power', the mysteries of which we never quite got to the bottom of. But if Allen makes the record next year, it may be because MadDog is behind him, in more senses than one.

Out of the UK Snooker Championships (BBC), Ronnie 'TameDog' O'Sullivan continued to do his bit for the profile of his sport by cropping up early on Thursday evening on *New Gamesmaster* (Channel 4). *New Gamesmaster* – should it have escaped you – is a loud and fast computer games consumer show, aimed at the demographic group often referred to as 'kids of all ages' – i.e. students. The programme test-drives new computer games, in which, almost invariably, armoured or robed figures are seen beating the pixels out of each other with sticks, and offers a low-down on the latest gadgets and hardware.

(Sample critical comment: 'This Pamela Anderson of a console . . .')

Ronnie – heralded by our presenter, Dominick Diamond, as 'top snooker bloke' – was on board to check out a new computer pool game, in competition with a member of the studio audience. Actually, 'on board' isn't quite right. Just to make things unnecessarily difficult, Ronnie was playing via modem from a remote location in a lavishly upholstered sitting room.

'How ya doin?' probed Dominick, back in the studio before the match. Ronnie said he was, 'All right. Not bad.' Dominick reminded Ronnie that he had won £285,000 in prize money so far this season. 'That's an amazing amount of money, isn't it?' Dominick said. 'All right,' Ronnie said. 'Not bad.'

Ronnie's opponent Melanie, fifteen, looked relaxed in a T-shirt with a dog on the front. We returned for their nail-biting head-to-head after some commercials. Dominick, clearly reluctant to let the cash theme go, asked Ronnie, 'Make any more money in the break?' Ronnie said he hadn't.

The commentary, from Dominick and someone suitably unexcited from a computer magazine, was a moving tribute to the gentle art of the legendary snooker commentary duo Lowe and Virgo. 'Tricky!' said Dominick, as Ronnie doubled one in. 'The sort of shot that gets you glassed in Woolwich,' said the bloke from the computer magazine.

Ronnie did all right. Actually, he did better than that; he did not do bad. Melanie fluffed tragically on the Nine ball. Over in leather pouffe land, Ronnie fisted the air jubilantly. 'Not the most difficult opponent you've ever faced, Ronnie,' Dominick said. 'No,' said Ronnie, graceful in victory. 'The easiest.'

Meanwhile, on *A Question of Sport* (BBC1, Friday), Steve 'really quite interesting, when you think about it' Davis continued his public transition from blank-faced, barely-sentient cue-maestro to all-night, hellzapoppin party animal and righteous man of mirth. He joshed; he laughed; he quipped; he recklessly took the 'Away' question, to the dismay of his team captain. He even warmly ridiculed the slightness of his own physique (though, in a recent and highly unpredictable tabloid kiss-and-tell scandal, at least one source has paid eloquent tribute to Davis as a massively developed hip-flexer).

In short, he was on course to steal the show. But then, prompted by David Coleman, he mentioned a new book he's been working on. It's about chess. The makeover is not quite over.

ATHERTON'S EXCELLENT ADVENTURE; CLARK'S FRANK EXCHANGE

11 DECEMBER 1995

For viewers, it was a week of long hauls. In South Africa, valiantly securing a Test Match draw for England, Mike Atherton batted for what seemed like the best part of a month, though it turned out to have been a mere 645 minutes when measured. Afterwards, Charles Colville, Sky Sports' Mr Cricket, addressed the England chairman, Ray Illingworth. 'What about that Atherton innings?' Charles said. 'Was it the key to saving the day?'

Immediately after this performance, a rumour was rife that Colville is about to be offered the front man's job on a specially commissioned series of in-depth historical documentaries, where he will pose crucial questions such as: 'Geoff Hurst's 1966 hat-trick: was it good news for England?' and 'Bjorn Borg: did he ever really settle at Wimbledon?'

Ninety goalless minutes of Lyons v. Nottingham Forest in the UEFA Cup proved no less gruelling, though they were inadvertently enlightened, towards the end, by a BBC oversight. It would surely by now be one of the first rules of football broadcasting: don't position a microphone anywhere near a manager while the game is in progress, unless you have the luxury of going back afterwards with a bleeping machine.

It's well known that managers, though unerringly given to harmless 'parrot' and 'moon' formulations in post-match interviews, are fluent for the ninety minutes of play in the kind of language which rappers get into trouble for. The point was made forcibly in the famous documentary about Graham Taylor's management of England (*An Impossible Job*) and was underlined more recently during a deep-background programme on Birmingham City, for which a microphone was tucked inside the Umbro coat of manager Barry Fry. The soundtrack for the resulting footage sounded – once the bleeps had been deployed – more like an unavailable telephone number than a television programme.

On Tuesday, as the tension mounted, with Forest going all out for a nil-nil draw, the cameras cut repeatedly to where Frank Clark, the Forest boss, was standing on the touchline in a dark coat, his serious face frequently lost behind a man-size handkerchief. A nearby microphone started to broadcast his increasingly anxious instructions. This was flirting with disaster, and lo and behold . . .

'Play the fucking thing short!' Frank shouted, as audible through the pitch-side microphone as if he had snatched it up and attempted to use it as a megaphone.

'Play the ball short is what they're saying on the Nottingham Forest bench,' said our commentator John Motson, obligingly translating from the obscene. Still, Nottingham Forest clung on and stayed in the competition, so for once the phrase 'English manager embarrassed in Europe' had only a strictly immediate resonance.

More need for a bleeper, or even a blackout button, during *Love in the Afternoon* which visited 'TV's eccentric racing tipster' John McCririck and his wife, Booby, at home. This was in the 'Lovestyles of the Rich and Famous' slot. (*Love in the Afternoon* has the high production values and fearless item-scheduling that one associates with the best afternoon television.)

So, how does a romantic evening pan out for John and Booby? 'She brings me champagne and smoked salmon in bed,' John said. 'I may service her afterwards if she's fortunate.'

Call me controversial, but looking on over the years at McCririck's purple suits, his care-in-the-community hats, his solid tonnage of gold jewellery, his enormous voice and windmilling arm gestures, I have often wondered, just quietly, whether he wasn't after some kind of notoriety. On this new evidence, it turns out that under that loud, showy exterior, there lies another loud, showy exterior. In the space of approximately three minutes, McCririck managed to claim for himself the 'magnetism of maleness', to commend his wife for having 'quite a nice chest' and to maintain that 'a woman wants a man to tell her what to do'.

Booby – to whom, surely, a nation's hearts go out – seemed quiet, but was just biding her time. 'John went to public school,' she remarked eventually. 'They were brought up that way.'

1996

SID FINDS THE POWER IN ESSEX

22 JANUARY 1996

Sky Sports are beaming us live coverage from the WDC Darts Championship in Essex and everybody is shouting about it. 'Sky bring you the very cream of the milk!' shouted the legendary commentator Sid Waddell. 'Darts of the highest calibre!' shouted John Gwynne, beside Sid – and beside himself, too – in the commentary box. 'Darts of outrageous proportions!'

Deafening stuff. In the quarter finals, hot favourite Phil 'the Power' Taylor took on Keith 'Suffolk Punch' Deller in front of what Sid called 'a knowledgeable crowd' at the Circus Tavern in Purfleet. 'He's Phil Taylor!' Gwynne warned us. 'A man who can make you eat your words!' But what a meal that would be, in the case of John and Sid, who talk of players 'nursing in' the darts and 'clattering in the ton forties'.

'Taylor is into that treble 18 cover like a fox on speed!' shouted Sid, more than bearing out the prediction in the listings magazine *Cable Guide* that he would be 'suitably fired-up' for the occasion.

Just occasionally, Sid will go for a major darting analogy – a sort of rhetorical 180 – but just clip the wire with the third dart and have to settle for a ton forty. This happened on Saturday, when Phil Taylor starting coming good. Sid shouted: 'When William Tell was playing in the Swiss Super-league, he was hitting the apple. This player is hitting the middle of the apple.'

This was OK Sid, but it wasn't vintage Sid. Vintage Sid came later, as Taylor took the third set: 'He's nicknamed "the Power" – someone must have put 50 pence in the meter!' (It only works if you shout it.) In the words of the MC, 'Un-undred-un-eye-tee!'

At one point Sid, not unreasonably, took a moment to rue his own non-appearance in the New Year Honours list; he was, as he put it, 'without a gong' for yet another year, unlike 'Whispering' Ted Lowe, the BBC's voice of snooker, who received an MBE. Clearly this was a just reward for years of quiet, meditative table-side appraisal. But as soon as someone decides it's time for shouting to get its due, Sid's knighthood is as good as wrapped.

On a more meditative level, Sid and John have been wondering whether the awesome form of Phil Taylor warrants him a place right up there with the darting greats. Gwynne only wished we could see an encounter between the Power and Eric Bristow 'when the Crafty Cockney was in his heyday'. Sid mused, 'Maybe, John, there's a darts Valhalla, so we all end up in the sky sometime, sitting sipping mead and watching the great ghosts. Might happen.' Might happen? Must happen.

DARTS ON ITS METTLE AT THE BIKINI LINE

12 FEBRUARY 1996

Everyone in television wants a piece of the sports action at the moment, even the cable station L!ve TV. Tremendously underfunded, L!ve has a studio high in the Canary Wharf tower and several cameras, but nothing very much in the way of what you might call programmes. Cynical detractors are already calling it Sh!t TV.* The station can't really muscle its way into the multimillion Premiership football market or trump ITV's Formula One motor racing bid. But Kelvin MacKenzie, the former editor of the *Sun* newspaper and now the brains behind L!ve, has found a way to fight for a corner on his own terms: *Topless Darts*.

In *Topless Darts*, two women stand on a beach in Australia wearing only bikini bottoms and play each other at darts. Or sort of. Rules differ from the conventional Topped Darts in a number of crucial ways. For instance, there's no descent from 501, checking out on a double, or anything complicated like that. The winner is, more clinically, the first to hit the bull. Curiously, this always happens after two minutes, which is the length of the 'programme'. Also, it's not clear that the darts we see hitting the board (shown as an insert in the top corner of the screen) bear any relation to the darts we see leaving the hands of the competitors.

You don't need to be Eric Bristow to realize that the women are selected for reasons other than a natural darting acumen and a smooth throwing action. Indeed, *Topless Darts*

* Following some underwhelming viewing figures, L!ve ceased broadcasting in 1999. Many of us still miss it very badly.

is one of the only places you will ever see a dart thrown underarm.

The show ends when the triumphant darter waves her arms above her head and pulls on a L!ve TV T-shirt. Tuning in last week, I found myself mulling over a thousand imponderables. Why were nearly all the women called Michelle? Were these beaches on which the sun never shone, or was the video tape in the cameras just too cheap to register it? And how much was Ian the commentator getting paid?

Ian, who keeps up an analytic patter for the entire two minutes, confessed to us on Thursday that he wasn't coming to us live from oche-side on the beach, but in fact was in Canary Wharf, hunched over a monitor. Clearly Ian has the saddest job in television since the person who cleaned up after that famous urinating elephant in *Blue Peter*.

You could argue that *Topless Darts* is offensive to women, though actually it's not clear that something so innately feeble could ever gather the strength to offend an entire sex. It may, though, just about be offensive to darts, a sport which has suffered more than its share of abuse and which has laboured so hard to polish up a modern, go-ahead image. And now this. Darts deserved better.

HOLE FOUND IN GEOFF BOYCOTT'S KNOWLEDGE

19 FEBRUARY 1996

It may yet prove richly significant that the first image Sky Sports beamed back from the cricket World Cup in India was of an England player receiving treatment after tripping into a fence in training. It was shown to us last Sunday evening, just ahead of live coverage from the opening ceremony. Not so much as a ball bowled – indeed, not so much as a flag waved or a dance danced – and England were already flat on the grass.

If England ever do rise to the occasion out there, we can be pretty sure someone will crick his back on the way up. Two games in, the team's injury average is significantly more impressive than Mike Atherton's batting figures and the chairman Ray Illingworth is frantically phoning home for spares. And even those who are as yet free of medical problems are said to be wearied by the travel schedule. And then there's the fact they've played so much damn cricket recently. Touring cricketers who like neither touring nor cricket – that can't help much.

As England eased stiffly past the United Arab Emirates, Sky was forced to play Doctors and Nurses again. Craig White departed with a wrenched stomach. 'He's strained an intercostal muscle,' Charles Colville informed us impressively, though, given the travelling, it may well have been an intercoastal muscle. 'We're not going to kick him on the bus tomorrow, but he'll be going soon,' said Illingworth, with the charm and sympathy for which he is famous.

As if that wasn't enough, with the score at fifty-seven for one, Neil Smith threw up and retired woozy. This was a shame, not least because we at home had been getting thoroughly acquainted with Neil, thanks to some deep background information from our commentator, Tony Lewis. 'Senior viewers might remember Neil Smith's father,' Tony said. 'This is Neil Smith, his son.'

Still, breeding alone will not necessarily spare you an attack of heat exhaustion and Smith walked slowly back to the pavilion, looking as if someone had lightly poached his head. It might just have been the sun, but when the cameras caught Atherton giving Smith a leery grin, Geoffrey Boycott, alongside Lewis in the commentary box, was suddenly confident it was curry.

'Everyone laughs a bit when someone is unwell in India and Pakistan,' Geoffrey said, 'but it's no laughing matter, I can tell you.' There is, it's already apparent, no limit to the things Boycott can, and will, tell us during this World Cup. Only a week has passed, but even now Tony Lewis is casting around competitively for things Boycott might not know.

'Do you know what Dukanwala means, Geoffrey?' Tony asked yesterday, as the UAE bowler of that name completed an over. 'No,' admitted Geoffrey. 'It means shopkeeper,' Tony said triumphantly. 'For the first time in the tour,' he added for our benefit, 'the man is speechless.'

But no he wasn't. 'Have we got a chimney sweep playing?'

Generally, one is grateful for Boycott's grim reasonableness. He gets smartly to the point, even if he does, on occasion, seem to be involved in a one-Yorkshireman mission to reverse the English language ('A good cricketer all round is Neil Smith' and so on). You do wonder though, about the selectors' wisdom in offering him spells alongside the altogether more excitable Tony Greig.

It was Greig's duty in Ahmedabad to build us up for the first ball of the tournament and he spoke in a suitably throaty growl: 'A buzz round the ground for that opening ball. This is exciting stuff, Geoffrey.' Back came Boycott: 'Yeah, you always get that.' The cost of Boycott's unsurprisableness may well be a certain loss in pressure. ('A golden, flaming meteorite has just crashed down on the outfield. Amazing scenes, Geoffrey.' 'Yeah, well, it happens, Tony.')

But nothing, it seems, is going to stop Greig having a good time. So far he's already had to combat the opening ceremony in Calcutta (the usual baffling pageantry) and a post-match cheque presentation at which someone had omitted to supply the cheques. 'Oh well,' said Greig. 'We'll do that later.' Perpetually delighted and entirely undimmed by either the travel or the cricket, he's already shaping up to be Commentator of the Tournament, if he can only avoid injury.

When he described a Graham Thorpe catch in the New Zealand game as 'a minor miracle!' he risked, perhaps, straining a Pentecostal muscle. But this was his outstandingly committed description of the moment when Atherton ran out Hick and the umpire took the precaution of consulting the video monitor:

'That's well fielded, there's a mix-up, this could be close, this'll be out, he's got him, it's all over, oh give him out, go on, I reckon that was out by miles!'

And it was.

EDDIE WARING; THE RUN OF HIS LIFE

29 JANUARY 1996

So, finally, after all this time, after all the questioning, after all the sifting of evidence, the matter finally came to its dramatic head last week. Eddie Waring: guilty or innocent?

The case was heard during BBC2's *A League Apart*, a history of rugby league on the occasion of its centenary, written and presented by Michael Parkinson. Roughly, it went like this: was Eddie Waring a saint who spread the word about rugby league far and wide? Or was he a sinner who created a northern stereotype, distorting the game for ever in the minds of soft southerners?

Speaking for the prosecution (in the Marcia Clark role, as it were), the author Geoffrey Moorhouse hoped to establish the existence of a trail of patronizing caricatures of northern people leading directly to Eddie Waring's commentary box. We, the jury, heard tapes on which Waring could be distinctly heard saying, 'Oop and under!', 'early bath!' and 'by 'eck!'. We were also shown a cloth cap, found on the premises and believed to be Waring's.

For the defence, Alex Murphy, a former rugby league player and the Johnnie Cochran figure here, argued that Waring was only a force for good – that he would not, could not and did not bring this gorgeously fluid game into disrepute. Anyone who said a word against Waring, Murphy warned us, would 'get no change out of me'. In other words, if the cloth cap doesn't fit, you must acquit.

It could be argued that Parkinson (as Judge Ito) let the accused off lightly. He did allow the showing of a clip of Waring making a guest appearance on *The Goodies*, but opted to exclude much of his potentially incriminating work on *It's A Knockout*. On the other hand, the programme included an early photograph of Waring in an enormous three-piece suit, looking like Al Capone. It was a tough call. Finally, one was inclined to plead the Fifth.

A League Apart led us from the sport's roots right up to Rupert Murdoch's reorganization of the game into a Super League. Here was a whole batch of considerations to take into the live coverage of England v. Australia in the 1995 Rugby League World Cup, which was on BBC1. But before the game got under way, there was the opening ceremony to contend with – a dispiriting affair, caught awkwardly between the sport's earthiness and a marketing man's vision of its future.

There was a dance routine from a small troupe of boys

and girls in navy blue tracksuits. And there was a musical interlude, featuring Carol Decker ('the former lead singer of T'Pau, making her welcome return to the live arena', according to the announcer in the stadium). And then out came Diana Ross, of all people, in a gold cloak, waving like a newly-wed from the roof of a vintage Rolls. Eventually she alighted on the hallowed turf and set off towards the centre-spot to make like an aerobics instructor. Never mind whether the pitch would take a stud; would it take a stilletto?

You had started to wonder what Diana Ross was actually doing here, in a half-filled Wembley Stadium at a quarter to three on a dreary October afternoon, when she let you know exactly. 'We are being watched by 250 million people,' she said, in a pause between numbers, 'and I want to introduce to you my new album, *Take Me Higher.*' (Doubtless there was other stuff she had been going to say – about her determination to stand by this traditional English game, with its important role in the binding of northern working-class communities; about the role in its history of Eddie Waring. But she must have forgotten.)

When England and Australia finally got down to it, the BBC threw us all the statistics it could find – possession, territorial advantage, penalties, even 'Average Pack Weight', which is a label one normally only expects to see in Sainsbury's. But there was still space to manoeuvre for our commentator Dave Woods. He is so worked up on occasions that he has more information to impart than a single sentence will comfortably bear. After Paul Newlove powered through for an extraordinary final try, Woods screamed: 'He may weigh over fifteen stone, but this boy has pace from Bradford.' Still, Woods did more to kindle an enthusiasm for the game than any amount of old Diana Ross songs.

Are television viewers really going to buy into rugby

league? There's certainly the allure of a higher-than-average physical grief quotient. Saturday's match alone offered us a torn hamstring, two substantial head wounds and what our pitch-level reporter referred to as 'a problem with a right eye socket'. The game even features what is referred to as 'the blood bin', where players go to staunch their cuts. So, yes: given the current appetite for programmes featuring casualty departments, rugby league could be the biggest thing ever.*

BRUNO GOES PAY-PER-VIEW; BRITAIN NOT QUITE READY

18 MARCH 1996

So, in the end, £9.95 bought you a little over five minutes of muddled tangling, a brief but deadly flurry from Mike Tyson and the sight of poor old Frank slumped like a plastic sack against the ropes, while the referee prised his gumshield free.

Before the fight, Sky Sports' commentator Ian Darke, ring-side in Las Vegas and positively trembling with anticipation, offered us his opinion that we were about to see 'probably Britain's biggest sporting moment since 1966 when England won the World Cup'. That's a tough call. It was, at least, one of the shortest. And certainly, from the television watcher's point of view, the most expensive.

Sky was claiming in the region of 500,000 pay-per-view takers, which, at £9.95 per head, is a very nice region. Still,

* Alas, the revolution has yet to take place. At the time of this printing, *ER* is still more popular than rugby league. So is *Casualty*. So, indeed, are programmes in which animals get ill.

in television terms, that's not much more than the kind of audience Channel 4 generates with Czechoslovak cartoons – small fry, definitely, by comparison with the sixteen million who might watch the FA Cup Final in a good year. If this really was one of the great British sporting moments, 'the fight of the century', 'a fight for the greatest prize in sport', or any other of Sky Sports' windy formulations, it's a shame a high percentage of the British population was necessarily asleep right through it.

Pay-per-view: it all sounds very simple, but don't be fooled by those smooth hyphens. A week ago, I phoned Videotron, the company who supply cable television where I live, to place my order for Frank and Mike. Getting past the engaged signal at Videotron is, I have learned, a major test of sporting endurance. It's best to block out some time, pack a lunch and go at it solidly for a day.

But I got there eventually, as the shadows were beginning to lengthen, when a woman brightly informed me that Videotron, uniquely among cable suppliers, were unable to bring Frank and Mike into their customers' living rooms. She said there hadn't been time to fit the machinery. If I already felt cheated at having to fork out extra money to see this fight, I now felt doubly so at not being able to.

Plan two: friends with a satellite dish. Dish-owners simply had to dial a number in the Sky subscribers' magazine, though two of us discovered you could eke out this work to last the best part of an evening, what with the dialling, the being told to hold and then, after a couple of silent minutes, the line going dead on you.

In a while, frustration levels were high and rising. It would not be long, I could tell, before one of us – or both of us at the same time – was wrenching the phone from its socket and smacking it against the mantelpiece until it shattered.

But finally, there came a voice we had not heard before, a recorded voice. It said, 'Please wait while we register your order goodbye beep.' And the line went dead.

It surprised us that a financial transaction with Rupert Murdoch could be quite so abrupt. It confused us still more that the apparently successful completion of our call should sound like a malfunction. I called the special pay-per-view Helpline, queued for a while, was rung off a couple of times, called back and eventually got through to a real, live Sky Television woman. 'If we get to the bit where the line goes dead, are we on?' I asked. She didn't know. She said she had never heard the recorded message.

Still, the pictures did arrive and you couldn't say they weren't thorough. We watched Tyson and Bruno arrive at the arena; we hung out with them for a while in their dressing rooms, where Frank was shadow-boxing and where Tyson was being shouted at by a member of his entourage. And in the immediate build-up, the cameras took us star-spotting. There was Jack Nicholson, having a drink. There was Don Johnson chatting to Eddie Murphy. There was Jack Nicholson again, raising a thumb. At one point, a ball of tumbleweed was seen bowling along the aisle. It was Bob Geldof. With Jack Nicholson waving, just away to the left.

Can we blame Frank's preparation in any way? Was there anything he didn't do? It's hard to feel so, though, in retrospect, perhaps the red and blue dressing gown in which he advanced to the ring was a minor mistake. It looked like something a garage-owner might throw over a petrol pump which isn't working. Contrast Tyson's altogether more frightening ragged, black, sleeveless, sideless jumper – sackcloth and ashes, via Nike. It was all over before it began, really; and certainly, not long after.

We all owe a debt of gratitude to L!ve TV, whose determination to cover Sunday morning's fight was undiminished by a complete absence of sound and pictures. L!ve, you will know, is the low budget cable station which cares so much about the needs of its viewers, it has introduced a nightly dose of topless darts. We could rely on L!ve, then, to turn its sensitive moral scanners on to the injustice at the heart of pay-per-view and, lo and behold, in their pathetically underpopulated studio in Canary Wharf, they put on a simultaneous mock-up of the fight, with two actors taking their cues from the commentator, Eric Guy.

In the background, a man was feeding ten pounds into a fruit machine, in order to bring us that authentic Vegas flavour and also, we were told, to remind us of the money we were saving by watching L!ve. As for the fight, the actors spent most of the time pointlessly clinging on to one other. Just like the real thing, then. But like it, hate it or send it up, pay-per-view is now officially with us.

THINGS THAT GO BUMP AT AUGUSTA

15 APRIL 1996

'Quarter past six in the evening here at Augusta,' Peter Allis said one day last week, 'and it really is a treat.' They simply cannot contain their pleasure out there at the US Masters, one of the few television programmes which seems to be broadcast live from Paradise.

Take Steve Rider's BBC studio encampment. Not for Steve the leaky greenhouse of outside broadcast legend, nor some big-windowed cattle shed hastily erected above the venue, with members of the crowd intermittently pressing their noses against the glass and trying to say hello to their mothers. Steve speaks to us against an uninterrupted background of tranquil fronds, gentle trees and hilariously rare flowers. You wouldn't be surprised to see a flamingo float into the space behind his shoulder, or perhaps a unicorn, or even a lion offering a lamb some milk and honey. Even the lawnmowers, shown briefly at the close of play on Friday, seemed to have been choreographed by a ballet director. Small wonder that Steve has adopted, near permanently over the last five days, the relaxed, dreamily amused expression of someone undergoing a foot massage.

That said, for the players, Paradise is a little more thorny than it appears at home. 'If you look ahead,' Allis pointed out, 'you can see all the ridges and bumps and, er, things which go to make up the 14th.' This seemed an especially poignant summary of the treacherous nature of that Augusta course: even if you survived the ridges and the bumps, there was every possibility that you would come up hard against a completely devious and utterly unforeseen Thing.

Against this eventuality, players were resorting to ever wilder tactics. Scott McCorren had abandoned a putter and was using instead what seemed to be one of the larger extensions from a chimney sweep's brush. And Greg Norman had developed an entirely new repertoire of pre-shot mannerisms: Greg now shakes his left arm, hokey-cokey-style, just prior to gripping the club and then, with his feet, does a kind of miniature square dance – although he may just be trampling down a Thing. Norman's hat, meanwhile, suggests his continuing interest in playing Crocodile Dundee in any future addition to the series. He looks as if he might just be about to whip out a knife and skin the nearest available lizard/flamingo/unicorn, ready for char-grilling back at the clubhouse.

Tips on tactics for the rest of us have been in short supply.

Dave Marr, Rider's sidekick, resplendent in a yellow tank-top and blue shirt combination, announced this week: 'I would teach anybody who was going to play golf – figure it out for yourself.' You've been a great help, Dave.

Back in the real world (or thereabouts), the news last year that Ilie Nastase was pursuing the job of Mayor of Bucharest was perhaps the most alarming political development since Stevie Wonder announced he was standing for Mayor of Detroit. But Wonder eventually abandoned the idea, whereas Ilie has put on a suit and tie and a very serious long coat, and is pressing full steam ahead. The foreign affairs programme *Correspondent* (BBC2, Saturday) caught up with him on the campaign trail.

Apparently, Nastase was last year literally jolted into an awareness of his mission by Bucharest's tremendous potholes – or what we in Britain would call 'craters'. Other problems facing the city include cockroaches, rats and stray dogs – hardly unusual, as urban blights go, except that in Bucharest it's often difficult to tell the three apart. The place was falling apart, Nastase smartly realized and, as he put it, 'I have an art of leading.'

Polls put Nastase way ahead right now, but it's been a struggle. In Romania, those with an art of leading have historically also had a certain skill in feathering their own nests. The public suspicion which would greet Nastase anyway is doubled in his case: he has, after all, spent the best part of the last thirty years in the south of France or on the tennis circuit, places in which the realities of post-communist social disorder are, shall we say, slow to intrude.

Then there's the potential political liability of his past as an umpire-abuser and a clown. In a market, Ilie was seen getting some stick from a garlic salesman who loudly voiced the reservations he had about Ilie actually running the tram-lines, rather than simply larking about in them between points.

A spokesman for Ilie's main mayoral rival raised a reasonable question mark over the former international heart-throb's concentration levels: given that Ilie used to have a problem keeping still on his chair at change-overs, how was he going to cope with the rigours of two-hour council sittings on gripping topics such as drainage renewal?

But this was a question which answered itself. Doubtless Nastase will think of something: wrapping the mayor's medallion round his forehead, for instance, or performing a skit with some stray heraldry and his copy of the minutes. He'll be fine.*

SNOOKER: THE DARK SIDE

6 MAY 1996

'Goodness!' David Vine said, looking flushed as we returned to him in the studio. 'You think this is a quiet sport . . .' We do. Or rather, we did until last week at the Sheffield Crucible, when snooker – the game of guile and hush – cut up all rowdy on us. Partly it was background clamour: above the gentle click of cue ball on colour rose, according to rumours from behind the scenes, the thump of player's fist

* Nastase never did make it to Mayor of Bucharest. But he did get to partner Hank Marvin at the annual Cliff Richard Pro-Celebrity Tennis tournament in Birmingham, which must have been ample consolation. See page 336.

on tournament official. But even down at table-side, things were noisier than ever.

The new gimmick for the players is vigorous self-encouragement, regularly in the form of a throaty 'Come arn!' accompanied by a radical muscular spasm and usually terminating in a brandishing of the forearms. It's nothing Jimmy Connors wasn't doing twenty years ago, but it's taken all this time for such graphic displays to seep through snooker's thick cloak of decorum. Now, on a regular basis, the sport offers us the slightly disarming sight of men in black tie gripped by brief convulsions and shouting like the possessed. Normally you would need to go to Oxford during the ball season to see that.

Mostly we have Peter Ebdon to thank, the loudest of the 'Come arn' artists, the man least likely to celebrate a break or crucial set victory by returning blankly to his mineral water. But he's not alone in perfecting what Vine refers to as 'controversial outbursts'. A few days ago, incredible to relate, we even saw Steve Davis have a go. Davis is the closest thing snooker has to a Queen Mother figure. I thought we could rely on him to maintain a serene face even in the event of an explosion in his own trousers. Something is terribly awry when Mr Interesting begins behaving like a model in a Nike commercial.

Maybe the pressure has finally got to him. It's certainly hit Ronnie O'Sullivan recently, though, ironically enough, for as long as he's in the vicinity of the table Ronnie remains a strangely beatific presence – 'so casual, but so wonderful', as the BBC's John Spencer remarked. The problems seem to start when he gets backstage, but there the cameras do not take us. Snooker must be about the only remaining sport whose television coverage remains concentrated in the arena, with the dressing rooms and practice areas and corridors chastely curtained off.

But maybe this is just as well, given that one of O'Sullivan's recent alleged misdemeanours involved his relieving himself against a wall not strictly erected for that purpose. That was always going to be the kind of story you were happier to find leaked from the studio.

The actual snooker, incidentally – when you could get to it through the hubbub – was worth making a noise about. How does one account for this game's ceaseless televisual allure? Spencer did his best: 'It's the only sport I know,' he said, 'where the crowd are on the edge of their seats while the top players are missing shots.' Strictly speaking, this didn't rule out tennis, or football, or, for that matter, any spectator sport involving top players, crowds, seats and shots. Still, it was worth a try.

Fans of Eric Hall, the bristle-headed football agent and professional cockney, will be on the edge of their seats when they learn that Eric is safe and well and currently fronting his own show on L!ve TV, Britain's cheapest cable station. Eric, we all know, has never actively sought publicity for himself and it's nice, for once, to see one of sport's quiet men acknowledged and rewarded.

True, *Sport L!ve* on a Saturday afternoon is not exactly *Grandstand*. Eric seems to know this. 'Colin,' he called out to his producer at one point, 'you sure Des Lynam started this way?' Colin's answer was inaudible, so the question remains: did Des ever – as Eric does now – host a phone-in gameshow involving tapes of old greyhound races?

Unlikely, somehow. What happens is, Eric gets a caller to nominate a colour. Then he gets the producer to run the tape of the old greyhound race. If the dog wearing the nominated colour wins, so does the caller. (What the caller wins, I have no idea: in the brief period during which I was able to watch the show nobody won.)

A random element enters the proceedings by dint of the fact that, sometimes, Eric doesn't hear the callers too well. (Don't blame Eric: knowing L!ve's budgets, there's probably a quantity of string and old tin cans involved somewhere along the line of communication.) For example, breaking the ice on Saturday, Eric asked Ian from Romford to name his favourite song.

'Bread of Heaven,' said Ian.

'What of Heaven?' asked Eric.

A ride over the Badminton horse trial course would have been smooth by comparison.

TARBY IN GAME-SHOW CRUNCH; ENGLAND IN CHINA

27 MAY 1996

To stay in the hunt for the PGA Championship at Wentworth, Nick Faldo had to deal with a shot which had bounced off a marker post and landed on a spectator's plastic bag. But he should complain: over on BBC1, Ronnie Corbett was having to bring his shot wide of the ornamental pool and past the motorized rabbits in order to keep Emma in the frame for the safari holiday and cash prize.

On *Full Swing*, a new Saturday evening quiz game, celebrities chip golf balls around on a virtual golf course and a studio set made out of Astroturf. Meanwhile, Jimmy Tarbuck asks contestants to tell him what the initials VAT stand for. The programme presents the surprising juxtaposition of cutting-edge technology and jokes invented some time in advance of the plough and honed ever since on the pro-celebrity golf tour. 'Would you call yourself a hooker?' Tarby asked Tim Brooke-Taylor. It's like golf, really, only slightly less bizarre.*

No time for any nonsense before the European Cup final (ITV). Just a couple of minutes for Bob Wilson to say hello and get the pre-match views of our panel, Glenn Hoddle and John Barnes, while also accustoming viewers to Barnes' interestingly radical tie – a bow on which the bow appeared to have spun off on the way to the studio.

Juventus or Ajax? It was a tough game to call. Barnes – wrongly, as it turned out – said he was tipping Ajax on account of 'their win in Panathinaikos' in the previous round. There was weeping in the streets of Panathinaikos that night; and they weren't too happy about it in Athens, either.

Out in Rome, Brian Moore and Kevin Keegan talked their usual good sense, but frequently at the same time as each other, something they may need to look at on the training ground ahead of the Euro '96 tournament. Moore thought he detected, at one point, 'a slight turn of the pendulum Ajax's way'. Time to get that pendulum checked, as well.

At half-time, the ceaseless fun and laughter which is the Barnes/Hoddle double-act was necessarily curtailed to make room for an important report from Gary Newbon. Having drawn a straw so short it would probably qualify under EC

* Somehow *Full Swing* never quite made it into light entertainment's top drawer, alongside perennials like *The Generation Game* and *Stars in their Eyes*. Maybe the courses were, in the end, too difficult.

regulations as a grain, on the night Ajax played Juventus in Italy, Newbon was in China, on tour with the England team.

No one seems to know why England have gone there, with the European Championships coming up, though money might have something to do with it. Whatever, there was plenty of controversy for the fearless Newbon to get his teeth into. He spoke to us from the 'controversial pitch' (it looked like an airport runway which had gone slightly to seed) and then engaged Terry Venables, the England coach, in a conversation about the 'controversial decision' to slog all this way in the first place.

'We've got to think a lot more modern than what we have,' Venables said, before pointing out that in 2002, the World Cup will be held 'in this part of the world'. England were there now, he said, 'to find out what it was going to be about'.

It was a relief to hear this and to have banished once and for all those nagging thoughts that the trip to China had nothing to do with football and everything to do with cash, politics and powerful agents. Absolutely not, as was now clear: two weeks prior to a tournament in their own land, England had flown halfway round the world to face weak opposition in preparation for a competition more than six years away, which may or may not be held in one of two countries (Japan and Korea) quite near the one they were staying in. As Venables might say, you can't think a lot more modern than what that is.

The question is, will Glenn Hoddle, when he ascends to Venables' seat, be able to keep up these astonishing standards of far-sightedness? Somewhat worryingly, on Wednesday night England's manager-elect was having a more local difficulty with the rules of the game. As Ajax v. Juventus moved into a penalty shoot-out, discussion in the studio turned to the new 'golden goal' idea, which will be used to decide matches in Euro '96.

Under the golden goal rule, in a form of sudden death, the first team to score in extra time wins the game. Hoddle ventured the opinion that 'that's OK if it was fifteen minutes, ten minutes. If it goes on for forty-five minutes, you can't plan for that. What happens if both teams stay in their own half? The fear factor when it comes to that level, that could easily happen. And that would give everyone a headache.'

What Hoddle somehow didn't seem to have grasped is that, even with golden goal in operation, the game still goes to penalties after half an hour if no one has scored. As such, then, a forty-five-minute, headache-inducing stalemate is not a realistic prospect. And even if Bob Wilson hadn't explained this just seconds beforehand, you wouldn't need to be a logical genius to work it out. A potentially indefinite sports spectacle would be tricky to get past police, for instance, or health and safety officers, not to mention the person responsible for switching the stadium lights off. Still, Glenn has some time now to clarify this matter for himself, and he's the kind of guy who will get there eventually.

One of the other excuses offered up to explain the China trip was that it would remove England to a place remote enough to discourage the nation's disruptive travelling supporters from jumping on a plane (prior to jumping on the locals). Some chance. Fifty-eight minutes into the game, shown live on Sky Sports, a muffled tapping was heard, as of a fan's finger on an outside broadcast microphone, and then a slightly distorted but distinctly English voice said: 'One two. One two. Hello, mum.'

Soccer hooliganism had reared its terrifying head yet again.

GRAHAM TAYLOR CONFESSES: 'WE'RE NO GOOD'

3 JUNE 1996

On *Fair Game* (Channel 4), Greg Dyke asked: 'Has the job of managing the England football team been rendered untenable by the attentions of the tabloid press?' He didn't consider the alternative question: has the job been rendered uninhabitable by previous residents?

'You're in a no-win situation a lot of the time,' Graham Taylor said, apparently oblivious to the thought that 'no wins' might have contributed to his problem at least as much as the *Sun* did.

It was interesting to see this dilemma tackled in an investigative series which is itself no stranger to sensationalism. Dyke held up to the camera the blazer worn by the England manager. 'There's not a kid in the country', he said, 'who doesn't dream of wearing this and leading the team out on an international day at Wembley.' Manager fantasies? That would explain why you see so many kids wandering around in replica FA blazers.

Surely the only dream children have, with relation to the national side, is the traditional one of playing for it – with, perhaps, a modern subsidiary dream about joining Gazza for a post-match round of Flaming Lamborghinis (the England squad's cocktail of choice on their tour of the Far East).

Now out of the fray, Graham Taylor was able to consider England's history as a world footballing force and tell Dyke: 'We're not very good: those are the facts.' This clear-eyed honesty might have helped him at the time. The standard tone of the England manager in recent years has been beleaguered self-justification. You heard it again in *Fair Game*, from Bobby Robson, all these years later: 'Travel on a Monday, one day to recover, play Wednesday night; we got a 1–1 draw in very hot, sticky conditions against a Saudi Arabian team who weren't dummies. Came back as a plonker.'

And then the shrug of disbelief. Anyone so determined to justify himself against the odds cuts a figure ripe for satire. Would the papers have been able to hit home so directly if the managers hadn't made themselves such open targets?*

QED, the science series on BBC1, had an alluring title: 'How to win Grands Prix'. It put you in mind of those tempting self-help manuals – *Improve Your Swing, Master Italian in Three Hours* – and in a way, its claim proved to be equally lavish. I concentrated hard throughout, but somehow don't feel I'm anywhere nearer joining Damon Hill in a shower of champagne on the podium at Imola.

Still, there were compensatory pleasures. The programme sat in with the Benetton team through the winter, as they prepared for the current Formula One season. This was a triumph of access in itself. Motor racing mechanics are a notoriously furtive bunch. Ask these people a simple question such as: 'Is it true you'll be using a steering wheel in '96?' and you get back only a dark smile and a tap of the nose. Clearly, though, one wasn't going to be able to take notes during the broadcast and then go directly into the garage and bolt together something capable of troubling Schumacher's Ferrari.

What the programme communicated most clearly were

* Greg Dyke's performance on *Fair Game* was so good that in 1999 he ended up in control of the entire BBC.

the atmospheres in which this peculiarly absorbed labour takes place, from chilly dawn testings through to the steamy Australian pit lane. And to the old question, 'Is it the driver doing the work or the car?' *QED* eloquently demonstrated the obvious, but perfectly satisfactory answer: it's both.

Stirling Moss came on at one point to try to describe what it takes to drive one of these things. 'It's just like if you're flirting with a girl,' he explained. 'If you feel she's about to clout you, you back off a bit. If you think that you're doing rather well, you push on. Same with a car.'

One wanted to press Stirling for more information. Like, how do you handle the trickier bends? And what if the girl turns out to be someone else's wife? But he had already gone.

For two months on Channel 4's *The Greatest*, presenter Gordon Kennedy and his panel have battled with the impossible task of comparing athletes from different eras and different disciplines. And they have done so uncomplainingly and, frequently, in the face of considerable public indifference, so we owe them our deep thanks.

Cynics, referring, presumably, to the programme's unswerving allegiance to the old-fashioned 'marks out of twenty' approach, have alleged that *The Greatest* was to rigorous and plausible sporting debate what *Romper Room* used to be to political analysis, but this, surely, was too harsh. In a fittingly moving and triumphant finale, certain to have melted the most flinty of hearts, the athlete Daley Thompson came out tops over the footballer George Best – a rare instance of something failing to go George's way in this, his half-century year, and an even rarer instance of something going Daley's.

But let no one dispute this verdict: the people have spoken. Or rather, the people in the studio have pressed their Yes/No remote response pads while the people at home have rung their verdicts in at the usual up-tempo charge-rates. That the winner should be someone actually cited in the programme's end credits as a consultant on the series is one of those happy and heart-warming coincidences that lift all of our spirits from time to time.

That he should also be the author of the book tied in with the series, and currently available from a shop near you – well, that's just the kind of wonderful magic which only television can bring us. Congratulations to everyone involved.*

EURO 96 OPENS; DRAGON SLAIN BY PLUCKY SAINT

10 JUNE 1996

Not worried about the obvious jokes, the Football Association chose to open the Euro 96 tournament by taking us back to the middle ages. At the centre of the Wembley pitch, ahead of the match, sat the tallest jousting-style tent ever seen. It was hard not to be curious about what it contained, but Bob Wilson, ITV's anchorman, did his best. 'It promises to be spectacular,' he said, 'even entertaining, but you never really know with these opening ceremonies, do you?' True

* Strangely, four years later, despite this massive vote of confidence, when BBC viewers named Muhammad Ali the Sports Personality of the Century, Daley Thompson barely got a mention. Sport can be cruel like that.

enough. But these days, no self-respecting sporting occasion can get under way before several hundred local schoolchildren have stood in a circle, and the first yellow card of Euro 96 must be shown to Wilson for failing to enter into the spirit.

In the studio, Jack Charlton wasn't exactly playing the part of cheerleader, either. Wilson wanted to know if the prematch scenes cast him back to the glorious summer of 1966, when Charlton played his part in England's World Cup-winning side. 'Not particularly,' said Jack.

The tent, tugged down by Sir Stanley Matthews, proved to contain a giant replica of the Henri Delaunay Trophy. As John Motson might have remarked: 'It's delightful, it's delirious, it's Delaunay.' Previous experience of opening ceremonies led one to be mildly fearful that Diana Ross would burst out of it in a shower of hair. But the trophy just sat there and shone. I'm still mildly suspicious that something went wrong, that a catch failed to spring and that Diana is in there even now. But there wasn't much time to ponder this on Saturday; as if by magic, during a commercial break, the cup was gone.

Mick Hucknall and Simply Red arrived shortly after with a gospel choir to deliver 'We're In This Together', the official anthem of Euro 96. It's a nice enough song, but it could be said to lack oomph. Indeed, it's the kind of thing you can imagine a group of people slowly beginning to sing when trapped in a lift shaft. 'We're in this together, forever,' the lyric says, though that may prove to be wildly optimistic in the case of England, who, on Saturday's evidence in the draw with Spain, didn't look like being in it much beyond the qualifying stages.

During the second verse, realizing that the nation's attention was probably wavering, the ITV production crew sensibly threw in a long and lingering crowd shot featuring my *Daily Telegraph* colleagues Paul Hayward and Henry Winter. Extraordinary the elation you feel, spotting someone you know on the telly. Extraordinary, and also pathetic.

By then, St George had brought down a dragon just outside the penalty area. This was a smart historical event to re-enact. Even in these sensitive times, it was politically uncontroversial in a way which other recreations (The Battle of Britain, for example, or Agincourt) might not have been. Unless, of course, you happen to be a dragon.

If only the ITV coverage had been as tactful. Their presentation couldn't have been more partisan if Bob Wilson had appeared with a pair of Union Jack boxer shorts on his head. How feverishly nationalistic were ITV? Put it this way: the England team sheet was screened against a picture of that famous football venue, the white cliffs of Dover.

Also, ITV's theme tune is 'Jerusalem', a direct smack, one feels, at the BBC's controversial use of 'Ode To Joy' by the boy Beethoven. The significant difference is that 'Ode To Joy' actually goes well with clips of football; 'Jerusalem' does not, even in ITV's slightly souped-up, synthesizer arrangement. And it's going to sound odd coming ahead of the channel's coverage of, say, Turkey versus Croatia.

Up in the commentary box, Brian Moore abandoned all pretence of objectivity. It was one thing to refer to the England team as 'we'; surely it offended against the simplest rules of politeness to refer to the Swiss side as 'them'. ('Their throw,' Moore said, at one point.)

Moore is a tremendous commentator, capable of great changes of pace and seemingly effortless strings of phrase. But these days, he's not so much required to commentate as host a ninety-minute conversation with Kevin Keegan. 'He'll be disappointed with that, Brian.' 'I agree with you there,

Kevin.' Inevitably, the pair bump into each other a lot and have to keep disentangling themselves. 'Sorry, Kevin,' Moore said. 'You were saying?' That was gracious of him, but frankly, I would have been happier to hear him say: 'Shut up, Kevin, I was commentating.' In the Moore–Keegan set-up, the notion of an authoritative single voice talking to you at home, helping you understand, is all but obliterated. In fact, the television viewer gets to feel doubly alienated. Not only are you not there, you're also reduced to the status of an eavesdropper on someone else's chinwag.

We're barely into Euro 96, but controversy already surrounds the substitution boards, held aloft on the touchline to let players know they're being replaced. UEFA have abandoned the traditional cards with numbers on in favour of a hand-held electronic scoreboard. If anything, the numbers on this are slightly less visible – certainly in direct sunlight. At one moment of confusion, Switzerland nearly managed to take off England's Tony Adams, which would have been a tactical coup on their part, and one with far-reaching consequences for football in general. I was with Keegan in feeling this new UEFA initiative represented unnecessary meddling. Presumably, come the 2002 World Cup in the Far East, when you want to pull a player off you'll have to do it over the Internet.

Still, the business with the baffling board does at least explain why Terry Venables took off Steve McManaman. Nothing else does. Except that McManaman was the only player on the pitch who looked like swinging the game England's way, and you wouldn't want to break with tradition, would you?

ENGLAND V. GERMANY, ITV V. BBC – IT'S WAR

28 JUNE 1996

When the BBC play ITV, the world surely trembles. On Wednesday, England versus Germany brought our top two terrestrials face to face, football-wise, for the first time since the World Cup semi-final in 1990. Ahead of the game, liberal voices were raised, urging the media to play down the conflict but, let's face it, it's ITV and BBC we're talking about here. This is war.

Des Lynam was first to loose the bomb doors and push something damaging ITV's way. Closing out the afternoon coverage of France v. the Czech Republic, Des pointed ahead to the evening's big one. 'I'd be surprised if you didn't watch it on the BBC,' Des said. 'Frankly, I'd be disappointed.'

Boom! A direct strike! In one wily sentence, Des had manoeuvred the cold matter of channel selection into the realms of the intimately personal. Now the choice was: tune to the BBC or let down Des. And how could anyone be prepared to disappoint Des, after all he's done for us?

With the smoke still clearing, ITV's Bob Wilson brushed the soot from the shoulders of his tunic and bravely recommended his team members. 'Jack Charlton, 35 England caps. John Barnes, 78 England caps. Kevin Keegan, 63 England caps.'

Not for the first time in this tournament, ITV were playing the patriotism card. The problem is, at the top level of television punditry, international experience for the home nation guarantees nothing. Consider the BBC's Ruud Gullit, analyst of the tournament by a mile, and he's never represented England at anything.

Later, Des resorted to more conventional BBC weaponry, promising a screening which was 'live and uninterrupted'. Actually, the BBC's coverage is only 'uninterrupted' if you don't count Jimmy Hill as an interruption. But then, truth is the first casualty of war, followed shortly afterwards by ITV's viewing figures.

You'd have to look at it coldly and say ITV were outplayed in all areas of the field. During the penalty shoot-out – won, inevitably, by the Germans – the combined audience was calculated at 26.2 million, a staggering 19.8 million of them tuned to the BBC. The average viewing figure across the game was 17.4 million with the BBC and 6.2 million with ITV. We're talking a 3-1 victory for Lynam, Barry Davies and company here, and ITV have a lot of thinking to do, close season.

CLIFF SINGS; PLUS THAT DUKE OF KENT BALLBOY INTERVIEW IN FULL

8 AUGUST 1996

Astonishing images from Wimbledon on the last Saturday: skies a colour one can only describe as blue, dotted with strange white fluffy things, and the light full of weird, golden stuff. 'Sunshine,' concluded John Barrett in the BBC commentary box. It's at times like these that you fully appreciate having an expert like Barrett around. Not all of us have memories going back that far.

The second week had been nothing but grey skies. Rain brings down upon Wimbledon all manner of crises and miseries. It's frustrating for the spectators, impossible for the players and sheer hell for the commentators. 'Why, they even ran out of fudge in the sweet shop,' Barrett told us on Saturday, in the tone of one about to compose a letter of complaint to the club secretary.

Yet here we were on the last Saturday with the tournament, amazingly, back on schedule and the women's final about to begin. The only evidence of the lousiness of the preceding days was British Summer Time's gift to Steffi Graf – what Barrett unhesitatingly diagnosed as a 'nasty cough'. Or as Virginia Wade put it, removing the matter properly to the realm of tennis, 'Steffi keeps getting into this coughing situation.'

What we had to worry about was the chance of this coughing situation developing into a fully-fledged ear, nose and throat concept, leading eventually to a play-hindrance scenario. But it didn't pan out that way. Steffi walked off with the silver tray and the cheque for £353,000 – 'not that she'll be thinking about it,' Barrett promised us. And Arantxa Sanchez Vicario (try saying that with a mouthful of fudge) was in the role of pugnacious bridesmaid all over again.

This year, for the first time in television history, a microphone was able to pick up the magic which is the Duke of Kent's end-of-tournament ballboy interview. This happens annually, as the Duke and Duchess make their way to the trophy presentation through twin lines of Wimbledon's most underrated servants, but its contents were a mystery until Saturday.

'Did you enjoy being a ballboy?' the Duke asked, before immediately answering himself: 'Frightfully hard work.' Then, further down the line, he stopped in front of another one: 'Did you enjoy being a ballboy? Frightfully hard work.' What one really wanted to hear was a ballboy returning the question: 'Do you enjoy being a member of the Royal Family? Frightfully hard work.' But they're too well trained.

Earlier that morning, Todd Martin (crazy name, crazy guy) had an open door into the men's final slammed in his face by MaliVai Washington (crazy name, crazy city). 'Now there's a change in the pendulum,' said David Mercer, not the only commentator recently to have been thrown by a malfunctioning pendulum. Indeed, is there any chance he bought his pendulum from ITV's Brian Moore? During football's European Cup final recently, Moore detected 'a slight little turn of the pendulum Ajax's way'. It's time this pendulum was pulped or replaced by a more reliable electronic light meter.

The only performer at Wimbledon consistently in a position to take advantage of the weather was Des Lynam. The wetter it got, the drier Des became. On Wednesday he guided us through some images from Court No 1, where Wimbledon's uniformed stewards were leading portions of the drenched crowd in time-passing mime games and renditions of 'Singing In The Rain'.

It would have been easy to capitalize sentimentally on these pictures. Only Lynam would have had the necessary calm to insinuate that being caught up in the middle of all that might have been like finding oneself trapped in a holiday camp staffed by the army. The camera alighted on one of the most active stewards. 'He's a household name,' Des said. 'In his own household, at any rate.'

Shortly, in what was to become front page news, a professional household name would appear on the Centre Court, wearing one of John Barnes's checked jackets. It was Sir Cliff Richard and – great news – he was holding a microphone.

Astonishingly, the BBC were on the scene right at the beginning of this unplanned moment. You'd think someone had tipped them off or something. Still, they definitely hadn't been given a set list. 'Hope he doesn't do "Summer Holiday",' Des said. 'What about "Summer Holiday"?' suggested Sir Cliff, out on the court.

How popular is Sir Cliff? Put it this way: many people phoned the BBC late on Wednesday to complain that his impromptu appearance had not been listed in *Radio Times*. Even allowing for the fact that some of these calls may have come from people who would have liked to have known when Sir Cliff was on so that they could go out and miss him, this is a remarkable testament to the fifty-five-year-old singer's enduring appeal, particularly among the bewildered.

Later Sir Cliff popped up to the BBC booth for a bit of post-gig smooth talk with Sue Barker, whose outfits this year have provided us with nearly all of Wimbledon's brighter moments. Sue and Sir Cliff had their names linked some years ago, before Sir Cliff decided to release himself as a single. But the old chemistry still bubbles. On Wednesday, he told Sue he was sorry she hadn't been up there on the Centre Court among the women players who pretended to be his backing singers; Sue was, after all, 'a better dancer than Pam Shriver'. The flatterer! No shortage of fudge in Cliff's sweetshop!

A shame, you reflected, that the pair never got it together when they seemed to share so much. Not just a love of tennis, but a taste for clothes made out of their mums' sofas. It would have been a marriage made in Debenhams.*

* At the beginning of the year 2000, Cliff Richard became the only popular male vocalist to have had Top Ten hits in three different centuries. Or something like that.

ATLANTA OLYMPICS IN FRAGMENTATION DEVICE SCENARIO

29 JULY 1996

On CNN, the Atlanta incident looked like an episode of *E.R.* Within minutes the news station had its logo ready: 'Olympic Park Bombing' boxed in red and black. And to go behind it, it had its footage of ambulances leaving the scene rendered in black and white and slowed down. Quicker off the mark than any 911 response unit, CNN will make a news item into a story.

Somewhere in the flood of analysis there was a trickle of information. Woody Johnson from the FBI confirmed the use of 'an anti-personnel fragmentation device'. And before long someone called Martin Vitch, introduced as 'a security expert', was without irony telling us how, with a few nails and a piece of pipe, we could all build our own. These kinds of events make most of us go quiet. Television, of course, has its hours to fill.

Some time later, and an entire world away on Lake Lanier, Steve Redgrave and Matthew Pinsent got on with performing their now world-famous trick in which a rowing boat seems to develop an engine. The surge with which they took off prompted the BBC's Gerald Sinstadt to jump in feet first. 'One doesn't want to go overboard too soon,' he shouted, 'but this is remarkable.' In rowing, of course, one doesn't want to go overboard ever, if at all possible.

The medal ceremony took place on a floating platform made from planks of wood. Women in large white hats, bearing trays of flowers and medals, entered from the mainland via a little bridge. Seen from above, it looked like a slightly stilted production of *Madam Butterfly*. Except, of course, the tunes weren't so good because, for the first time at the Atlanta Olympics, the organizers were required to dust off their tape of the British national anthem.

One can only imagine the desperate rummaging through an official Olympic cupboard which must have preceded this moment. The tape would have been in there somewhere, under the Syrian national anthem, probably, not to mention a bunch of old James Taylor albums and a CD of Icelandic folk songs for use in emergencies.

Redgrave's victory was a joy to see, but for compressed viewing pleasure, the two hours after midnight on Saturday will be hard to match: Gail Devers trying to compose herself for the 100 metres semi-final while the crowd was going nuts about her boyfriend's record-breaking triple jump; Jonathan Edwards struggling to make a legal leap but holding on; Linford Christie qualifying for the 100m final, and then disqualifying for it.

So great were the various tensions, they could not even be dispersed by the graphs which appeared on the screen after each of the 100m heats and which were worryingly reminiscent of old homework exercises. These graphs seemed to have something to do with speed and time or, possibly, the boiling point of potassium hydroxide. I imagine they came courtesy of our American broadcasting hosts. Certainly the BBC's Stuart Storey didn't have much time for them. 'One or two statistics for you,' he said. 'Totally meaningless.'

But Storey did have a moment, amid the excitement, to explain one of Atlanta's more tremendous innovations – the self-raking sandpit. Yes, without intervention from human hand, the triple-jump sandpit levels itself off and moistens itself up. Astonishing. Apparently, for Sydney 2000, they're working on a pole-vault bar which automatically replaces itself when dislodged.

As Christie settled, David Coleman, without whose trembly voiced preliminaries these events would be approximately one eightieth of the fun, attempted to keep calm. Christie, Coleman reassured us, was 'a man who knows himself and knows the event'. No danger, then, of him suddenly putting on a dress and running off into the self-raking sandpit. 'And when Christie looks around this field, which he won't . . .'

Who could blame him? All the finalists seemed, as the camera panned, to be in various phases of gibbering and twitching, only Frankie Fredericks and Christie came across as people you might open your front door to on a dark night.

Ato Bolden was hoping to distract the rest of the field by wearing a pair of Elton John's glasses. Made from radically angled pieces of red and clear plastic, they looked like an architect's model for the arrivals hall at Stansted Airport. It's a close call between Bolden's shades, Michael Johnson's Aladdin-style golden slippers and Devers' fingernails for the Atlanta Games' most fearless act of accessorizing.

And then came Christie's cock-ups. Machines said he was too fast away. Twice. It was all down to a pressure-pad, as Daley Thompson explained in the studio. 'What happens is, it goes off in the starter's ear.' Looking at the replays of the second false start, Christie seems to be disputing the charge before anyone has even charged him with it. If you're intending to protest your innocence at a later stage, this tactic is, in the precise meaning of the term, a schoolboy error.

Impossible not to share Christie's frustration, though. 'He'd rather have died with his boots on, as it were,' said Thompson. Not that Christie was going to let a small matter like being disqualified affect his salute to the people. No medal for him. But surely he should be awarded some kind of commemorative gong for becoming the first athlete to award himself a lap of honour after a race in which he took no part.

'The Americans said they were going to be one-two-three,' bragged the winner, Canada's Donovan Bailey, seconds after the race, with the sweat still pouring off him. 'What happened to that?' It's always rewarding to see a sprinter retain a sense of dignity during a moment of triumph. And one day at the Olympics, maybe we will.

A SET-TO AT THE PING-PONG

2 AUGUST 1996

A party game for deep in the second week of the Olympic Games: think up the phrase you're least likely to hear coming from the commentators out in Atlanta. 'It's gold on the track for Great Britain,' would have to be a contender, obviously. So would, 'And the American sprinter Michael Johnson bursts out laughing.' (Johnson is the athletics world's Mr Seriousness.) Or how about, 'Extraordinary scenes here at the table tennis'?

'Extraordinary scenes here at the table tennis,' said Tony Gubba. We were watching the women's final, China versus Chinese Taipei, a grudge match if ever there was one. Imagine Liverpool versus Manchester United, only with added tanks. And suddenly, just when you thought these Games were out of surprises, we had a world and Olympic first on our hands: crowd trouble during the ping pong.

'A major kerfuffle,' shouted Gubba as the security guards

went in. 'I've never seen scenes like this,' he added. Unfortunately, neither have we, even now. The cameras remained prudishly locked on the players until the incident had passed – except for the moment when they showed us Juan Antonio Samaranch, the president of the International Olympic Committee, looking suitably unamused. The host broadcaster let us down badly here. People will talk for years about the great table tennis riot of 1996 and we'll have nothing to remember it by.

There was further controversy in the yachting where the Brazilian Robert Scheidt lived up to his name by appearing to orchestrate a false start which deprived Britain's Ben Ainslie of a chance to boat for gold. Meanwhile, it was Dougie Donnelly's doubtful privilege, in the thick of all this, to commentate on the indoor volleyball. It can have been no comfort to Dougie that the play offers next to nothing to commentate on. 'Very tall Italian team, in fact,' he said, doing his best to sound keen.

Elsewhere, everyone is suddenly gripped by their own expertise. 'You've got to keep it low, you've got to keep it tight,' Tony Gubba said at the table tennis, correcting one of the finalists on a slightly wild return of serve. At the football, meanwhile, Nigeria took Brazil to extra time and first-goal-wins. 'You're never quite sure how to play this Golden Goal business,' Garth Crooks said, his confidently knowledgeable tone unswayed by the fact that, in his distinguished career as a player, he has been called on to play out a 'Golden Goal' scenario exactly never.

It's happening to us all, though, as the days go by and the hours of viewing mount up. You think there's anything you can tell me now about 400 metres hurdling? You think there's anything I need to learn about attacking the bar, pole-vault-wise? In the sitting room at this stage, everyone's a fully paid-up, gold medal-wearing double decathlete.

SUMMER OF SPORT IN DISAPPEARANCE MYSTERY

12 AUGUST 1996

Next time someone complains that there is too much sport on television and wouldn't it make a change to have a comedy programme or a nice film now and again, ask them where they were on Tuesday 6 August 1996. On that date there was – and these words come with difficulty, choked by a mixture of anger and disbelief – no sport on television whatsoever. None.

Obviously, I am referring to the four terrestrial channels here. The dedicated sports cable channels would not dream of letting down the nation like this. They realize a public commitment to quality coverage of quality sport is not something you enter seemingly seriously, only to drift away at will. Just because it was Tuesday 6 August 1996, Eurosport was not going to pull the plug on its truck racing and tractor pulling.

Would that BBC1, BBC2, ITV and Channel 4 had even a scintilla of this basic regard for human rights. But no. Right in the middle of the so-called 'Summer of Sport', with Euro 96 and the Olympics and Wimbledon, when viewers have come to expect at least fifteen hours daily of uninterrupted live coverage, a three-hour highlights package and at least one of those funny, slow-motion clip compilations set to the latest single by Oasis, the terrestrials made the arrogant and baffling decision to blank out sports altogether.

There was no warning, no apology, no explanation. Where the television listings had for so long contained directions which were easy to understand – 'Olympics' and 'Olympics Continued' and 'Loads More Olympics' – on Tuesday there were weirdly named programmes such as *Watchdog* and *The News*. And out of nowhere, our screens filled with people who were neither Desmond Lynam nor wearing kit. Who were these so-called 'presenters', and what right did they have to be there?

Take Carol Vorderman, for instance, allowed on Tuesday to host something called *Out Of This World*. Here is a woman who has never gone under the 12-second mark at 100 metres, who was unseeded and finished absolutely nowhere at Wimbledon this year, and who has not once pulled a tight hockey international out of the fire with a late assist. So what is she doing on television during the 'Summer of Sport'?

Or consider George Melly, granted air-time for the gratuitously sport-free *Seven Ages of Man*. He might have a bit of jazz form, but his record in any of the established Olympic events is abysmal. Yet suddenly on Tuesday, it's OK for him to pop up on our screens and present a programme.

And what of the sports addicts, whose habit has been so liberally encouraged over the last three months? No counselling was on offer, no phone lines put in place. The addicted will have been left craning into the distance beyond on-location news reporters, hoping to catch sight of an adjacent cricket match; or sitting through *Dawn to Dusk Safari*, about elephants journeying across Botswana, in the hope the elephants would stop off en route for a circus-style kick-about.

We had thought we would never again go to bed sportless.

How wrong we were and how betrayed. Normal service resumed grudgingly at 3.20 a.m. on Wednesday on ITV (*The Big Match Replayed*), picked up slightly that night with *The European Match*, but did not really settle into the blanket coverage we have come to expect until Thursday, when the Test match started. The Test match has been going on ever since – hours and hours of it, which is good. And some of it has even been mildly entertaining, not least the debates between bowler and umpire about the shape of the ball. 'I actually prefer this to synchronized swimming,' said Richie Benaud on Saturday. Me too.

What happens is this: every two overs or so, the bowler will approach the umpire and, in a debate which harkens back interestingly to mediaeval times, try to convince him that the ball is flat – this in order to try and take advantage of a new one. The umpire then produces a measuring tool, rather like an elaborate bottle-opener or a Swiss device for removing stones from Boy Scouts. With this tool, the umpire demonstrates beyond doubt that the ball is, in fact, round. The bowler then goes away until the next time.

It doesn't sound like much, I know, but after about the fourteenth time, it takes on something of the hypnotic charm of one of those cathedral clocks where little figures come out and chime the hour.

Talking of little figures, a new Channel 4 documentary series, *Filthy Rich*, pulled off a major journalistic coup this week by getting an interview with the notoriously publicity-shy Eric Hall. The bristle-headed, cigar-smoking football agent is a fiercely private person, as anyone will happily attest who has witnessed his sports phone-in programme on L!ve TV, his regular appearances on quote-duty in the national press, or his cameo in every documentary programme made about football in the last five years.

Filthy Rich was interested in Hall on the grounds he is rich (though how rich we never learnt) and rich by underhand means (certainly far enough underhand for the programme to fail to illuminate them). Among a host of character witnesses, Lawrie McMenemy called him 'a lovable rogue'. 'Lovable' is a word people use exclusively to describe those whose company they cannot stand. Hall, meanwhile, took the opportunity further to drum home his catch-phrases ('monster monster' and '-ish', added to words and sentences to qualify them) and also, rather sweetly, to sing to us. 'If I were a rich man,' he sang, 'dubba dubba dubba dubba dubba dubba dubba do-ish.'

The scene at the launch party of a football-themed bar in London, where Hall rubbed shoulders with the disgraced Arsenal manager, George Graham – well, Hogarth himself could not have done justice to it.

BECKHAM FROM THE HALFWAY LINE

19 AUGUST 1996

So that's Goal of the Season dealt with: it was Goal A, David Beckham for Manchester United against Wimbledon. Beckham was just inside his own half at the time and physicists agree that he was so far away from the goal that, theoretically, it should probably count as next season's Goal of the Season as well.

Trevor Brooking, on *Match of the Day,* advised us to 'drool over the bit of skill' which was easy, if a touch indecorous. But astonishingly, no one suggested that Beckham should be fined for precociously deciding football's most important issue, one normally up in the air for nine months.

We've had the goal; I suppose now we'll just have to concentrate on the actual season.

Desmond Lynam, the only Briton really to shine at the Olympics in Atlanta, was back to the routine, domestic task of having his ear bent by Alan 'Handsome' Hansen, and looked entirely happy about it. And Hansen himself has intelligently used the brief close season to take his wardrobe into a whole new beige phase, though doubtless that will be as shortlived as all the other phases before it. (Imagine the expense, for Alan Hansen fans, of keeping up with the replica strips.)

Many wondered whether the BBC's flagship football programme would take advantage of the Bosman ruling to bring on board a play-making foreigner. In fact, the temptation to look abroad has been resisted – unless you count the person responsible for translating Ravanelli's post-match interview into English. *Match of the Day* has rarely had recourse to subtitles – though it did come under pressure to use them when Kenny Dalglish was in management. This season, as the number of Premiership players with English as their first language dwindles into single figures, we can expect it to resemble a Buñuel film season on BBC2.

Say what you like – and in whatever language you like – but the tide of change sweeping through English football meets a reliable sea wall in the form of Hansen. This time last season, to the astonishment of Gary Lineker who was sitting beside him, Hansen was recommending that Gullit, of all people, would do well to 'play the percentages' rather than go in for any of that fancy stuff. On Saturday, watching Liverpool trying to craft their way out of trouble, Hansen maintained: 'If you're in doubt, just launch it,' a comment Des Lynam liked so much, he wrote it down.

That said, a certain continental playfulness does seem to

have entered even Hansen's style. Of Ravanelli's hat-trick performance, Hansen remarked: 'He scored three goals but what else did he do?' Then he laughed loudly. Many of us will remember, with a shiver, the days when Hansen said those kinds of things and meant them.

Out on the pitch, John Motson – never knowingly under-briefed – was able to raise a germane reference to a small refereeing incident in a pre-season tournament; and Tony Gubba was positively bursting to tell us exactly how small Middlesbrough's Juninho is, referring to him as 'little Juninho', 'the little Brazilian' and, classically, 'the little Middlesbrough player'.

It was Gubba who raised an important technical matter regarding Ravanelli's shirt-over-the-head goal celebration. After he'd done it for a third time, most of us had noticed an inherent design fault with the performance: he can't see what a berk he looks. But Gubba introduced a further, legislative matter: 'You're not actually supposed to bare your chest in the Premiership this season,' Gubba said, without further elaboration where we sorely needed some.

Who made this decision? On what grounds? Does the rule apply only to the Premiership, or can you expose your chest as much as you like in the Nationwide? And what about cup games? Surely this was an issue which should have been discussed right at the top of the programme.

The new season came a day earlier to Sky Sports, where chests are not so much exposed as routinely beaten, with the principal aim of drumming up our enthusiasm. Clearly, in the case of Friday night football from the Nationwide League, they've got a big job on their hands, one which had ITV sweating last season. Remember poor Ian St John, who smiled until his facial muscles ached but still never quite convinced us that his spirit wasn't poised directly over a deep lake of disappointment and despair.

At the start of Friday's coverage of Manchester City v. Ipswich – a game which, according to presenter Russ Williams, was 'vital for both sides, especially Manchester City' – a montage of key Nationwide figures was shown over a pumping soundtrack. There was Jim Thingummy. Oh, and Bob You-know-who-I-mean. And wasn't that Alan Whatsit who used to play for what d'you call 'em?

Sky's bold notion for 96–97 – 'Sky Sports biggest-ever football season' – is to fill almost every minute of the day with top class, live action. Or failing that, a match from the Nationwide. To make room for all these exclusive broadcasts from the homes of Birmingham and Wolverhampton Wanderers (to name just the big ones), they've had to find an additional channel, Sky Sports 3. If you're not interested, at least it's all out of the way.

HAMED ROCKED BY SNIFFLE

2 SEPTEMBER 1996

'Not to brag, or anything like that, but I've definitely mastered my sport.' Who else but the boxer Prince Naseem Hamed, talking to Sky Sports. Not to be rude, or anything like that, but what a jerk.

Hamed, from Sheffield, defeated Manuel Medina from Mexico in a performance which seemed to disappoint his fans but which, in all other respects, fully underscored everything we know about him: his brashness, his crassness, his absence of humour. Hamed's triumphal 'I've got you on the run' leer, directly after a punch connects, is the ugliest sight in sport this side of a Dominic Cork wicket celebration.

All of which only makes Hamed the perfect product for Sky Sports. So easily does he acclimatize to the channel's emotional temperature, they should really incorporate his head into the logo, like Mickey Mouse with Disney. 'His entertainment value, in and around the ring, is unquestioned,' according to Sky's boxing compere Paul Dempsey, prompting two questions: does Dempsey need to be so willingly uncritical? And is that really entertainment?

Never knowingly undersold, Hamed has been known to make his way across the floor of the arena to the ring perched on a giant golden throne, borne aloft by shining minions. This time one gritted one's teeth and wondered what now? The Queen Mother's landau pulled by a team of unicorns?

But Hamed has abandoned all that, or so he said. 'I wasn't comfortable with the situation,' he explained to us before the fight. 'I wasn't myself.' So it was back to basics. 'Just an ordinary walk to the ring,' noted our commentator Ian Darke, 'which is how many say it should be.' But those many don't include the Sky production team, who decorated the beginning of Hamed's 'ordinary walk to the ring' with a blizzard of graphics in fancy colours and fonts, bearing important messages such as 'one and only', 'undefeated', and 'sultan of sting'. You have to trust Sky to have done their homework on the demographics, but I must say it surprised me to see a programme which began at nine in the evening targeted so specifically at six-year-olds.

Now that Hamed is committing himself to making a small entrance rather than a big one, it's left to his shorts to do the talking. I don't think the Irish compere was trying very hard when, in his pre-fight introduction from the centre of the ring, he gestured towards Hamed and referred to 'gold trunks, black trim'. This was a bountifully fringed garment of the kind made popular by Latin-American cabaret acts. Also, if we're being accurate, it was the trunks which were black and the trim which was gold. But let's not be hard on the compere. In a development which might apply metaphorically to boxing as a whole, these days you can't see the trunks for the trim.

Manuel Medina had been described by Darke as 'the biggest challenger to Naseem so far'. Darke also pointed out that Medina 'hasn't been stopped for seven years' and, during the fight, referred to 'this durable Mexican'. I took this to mean Hamed would do well to beat him. At the end of the evening, though, Barry McGuigan in the studio described it as 'a humiliating and deflating night' for Hamed, the attitude seeming to be: what took him so long to knock this Mexican chump out of the way?

In the ring afterwards, Hamed told Darke what kept him: 'I'm not making no excuses whatsoever, but I had a cold before the fight. But, end of the day, no excuses.' This cold was shocking news. And no less shocking when – end of the day, no excuses – Hamed mentioned it thrice more inside the next thirty seconds. When, before the fight, Sky showed their two-and-a-half-minute, rock-video-style interview with Hamed, concerning his preparations, all broken into segments with graphic titles – 'Attitude', 'Entrance', 'Knock-Down' – there certainly hadn't been one marked 'A bit of a sniffle'.

Darke wondered if Hamed would now fight Wayne McCullough. 'End of the day, he's hiding in Las Vegas,' said Hamed. In fact McCullough was in the crowd, where Darke sought him out. 'I've been waiting for the last year to fight him,' said McCullough. Enter promoter Frank Warren. 'Gimme the mike, gimme the mike,' said Warren, who then shouted that only the day before at the weigh-in he had offered McCullough 'a million pounds' to fight Hamed. The conversation then developed as follows: Oh yes he did. Oh no he didn't. Oh yes he did.

Warren wears black tie for these occasions, as is traditional, but if it's his intention to get involved in this kind of post-fight pantomime on a regular basis, maybe he should come dressed as Puss in Boots or Widow Twanky. Maybe everyone involved in televising this stuff should, as well.

FIVEBELLIES TO THE RESCUE

23 SEPTEMBER 1996

One of the most crucial aspects of successful team management is substitution: knowing who to put on and when, thinking on your feet, being able to act decisively in the event of a sudden injury. Which is why the production team on the satirical quiz show *They Think It's All Over* are, collectively, manager of the month for September after Thursday's tactical switch which saw Paul Gascoigne, who pulled out of the show at the request of his manager at Rangers, replaced by his mate, Jimmy 'Fivebellies' Gardner.

Clearly this was a brave and imaginative choice. Many of us hadn't even realized that Fivebellies was available for selection. The man had precious little small-screen experience, apart from a few cameo roles in news footage of his best friend getting drunk/suntanned/married. And also, on the occasions when he had been given an outing, he hadn't always impressed the critics with a commitment to verbal invention, such as might sustain one in a programme devoted largely to unscripted humour.

One's fears, inevitably, were that what was possibly a launch-pad could so easily turn into a graveyard in which Gardner, and his future career in television, would suffer an undignified burial: Fivebellies and a funeral.

On the contrary, however, Fivebellies rose up and shone. True, he didn't speak very often. Mostly he just sat there while the others bounced jokes off his considerable target area. Certain kinds of joke need a butt, and this week the butt belonged to Fivebellies.

And when he did say something, it was unintelligible to the untrained ear. 'Jimmy might have got the rest of that question right,' said Nick Hancock, the presenter, 'but I couldn't understand him.'

Furthermore, his audible remarks – at one point he seemed to be accusing hairless comedian Lee Hurst of having no hair – were not, perhaps, notable for the flash of a rapier. The thing was, he managed to smile throughout. His earrings and his bleached crew cut took it in turns to sparkle. He was a permanent beacon of good humour. He was also able to answer a question about Prince Charles and a camel – proof, Fivebellies immediately argued, that 'Geordies aren't stupid'.

And all in all, by comparison with his mate Gazza's fabled appearance on *A Question of Sport* – the time when Ian Botham convinced him the drinks in the green room were non-alcoholic, so that Gazza eventually appeared teary-eyed with mirth and with his tongue apparently glued to the bottom of his mouth – Fivebellies was positively Olivier as Hamlet.

His teammate, the comedian Rory McGrath, thought it appropriate, for some reason, to mention that famous edition of *Have I Got News For You* when Roy Hattersley failed to show up and was replaced by a tub of lard. McGrath himself has just come off the touchline to stand in on some commercials for British Telecom while the company looks for a long-term replacement for Bob 'It's good to quit' Hoskins, so may be assumed to know what he's talking about when it comes to trying to impress important people in injury time.

It's interesting to note that Gary Lineker has gone from high-profile commercials to a slot on a quiz show; whereas Rory McGrath has gone from a slot on a quiz show to high-profile commercials. Fivebellies take note: what a boundlessly fascinating and limitlessly rewarding thing a career in television can be.

ALLY AND JOHN CHALLENGE PRINGLE TRADITION

7 OCTOBER 1996

So farewell, then, Bill and Ian. And a big hello to Ally and John, new team captains on *A Question of Sport* (BBC1). McCoist and Parrott began their reign last Tuesday, replacing Beaumont and Botham. And what happens next? Nothing for ages, if previous form is anything to go by.

This is the first tactical team switch we have seen for eight years and only the second time in a quarter of a century of Homes and Aways that both team captains have been changed at the same time. Beaumont had been in the seat since 1982 – and had not really smiled since 1985. Botham came on board in 1988, replacing the reliably energetic Emlyn Hughes, who had lasted five years in two separate stints, an unmatched achievement on the show, and the more remarkable when you recall how Hughes used to play as if the legs of his trousers were on fire.

The programme seemed to go through a comparatively disturbed period during the mid-1970s, when Fred Trueman and Brendan Foster failed to last out a year. Otherwise, a place on *A Question of Sport* is as close as broadcasting gets to academic tenure. Potentially, the new boys should be looking to host the millennium special.

Initial signs last Tuesday were that McCoist and Parrott will play a slightly more active version of the game. Then again, beside Beaumont and Botham, two large sacks of garden waste ruffled by a gentle breeze would look active. But the drift seems to be away from elbows on the desks and plump cheeks cupped resignedly in large hands and more towards a kind of eager, edge-of-the-seat joshing.

Both used the early, limb-loosening picture board round to fire off a mild warning insult at the other. 'I'll go for John's highest break against Stephen Hendry: eight,' said McCoist. 'I'll go for Ally's favourite shirt number: twelve,' replied Parrott. It's not exactly the Two Ronnies, but these are early days.

The single weak area was the failure of both new boys to indulge in the show's traditional Pringle frenzy. Controversially, both favoured cotton over the surely, by now, obligatory man-made fibres in noisy patterns. McCoist wore a blue polo shirt with a lined collar. Parrott had on a pale blue shirt which was plain. I repeat, plain.

We'll be looking for more commitment in that department later in the season, but last week it was left to Coleman to fly the flag for shocking knitwear – or rather, to wear that flag, which comes in several shades of blue and speckled with sundry circles and triangles, with a navy blue shirt underneath. This was more like it. Young people today: no respect for the past.

There's more money than ever sloshing around in football at the moment. 'How can you cash in?' asked *Pound for Pound*, BBC2's financial advice programme. 'Mug a chairman,' was the obvious answer, but *Pound for Pound*, which bravely attempts to make things like personal pension plans and building society loan schemes look televisually stimulating by employing rock music and presenters in polo neck sweaters, was rather more interested in the trade in football club shares.

As the programme made clear, with six clubs presently listed on the stock market, we're now past the stage where a fan might buy a single share simply for the fun of framing the certificate and banging it into the wall above the fireplace; a Thatcherite version of the team photograph.

Yet the pathology of the football fan still comes into play, even in the world of high finance. No Manchester City supporter is likely to buy shares in Manchester United, even though United's pieces of paper represent, by some way, the shrewder investment. 'Dirty money,' one City fan called it, affronted at the mere suggestion of investing in the home of Ryan Giggs.

It's not yet determined whether football shares represent a reliable punt. The general conclusion seemed to be: if you really must bother, invest in Manchester United rather than, say, Oldham Athletic. But try selling that idea to the average Oldham fan.

Meanwhile, one evening on CNN, the screen filled abruptly with American baseball umpires, many of them extremely large and all of them extremely angry. One of their number was spat on by a player recently, and they're mad as hell. Someone called Ken Kaiser, sporting some of the biggest jowls west of Bill Beaumont, said, 'Sooner or later, you're going to be in an English soccer situation where you don't like the decision, you shoot the official.' Unless I've missed a few referee fatalities recently, this was something of an exaggeration. But small wonder our national game is having trouble taking off over there.

SPORTSNIGHT – THAT STRAIN AGAIN

28 OCTOBER 1996

Goodnight, *Sportsnight*. The BBC has announced that the programme will run until May 1997 and will then enter the garage for a complete engine strip-down and a remoulding of the bodywork. Then it will re-emerge, at a different time of the week (possibly at flexible times) and be given a new name to indicate a radical and absolute break with the past. Something like *Sports Tonight*, perhaps.

Some anxieties have been voiced about the collapse of an institution and the end of an era. The programme certainly has a distinguished history. But even *Sportsnight* replaced a predecessor (*Sportsview*, which ran for thirteen years until 1967) and the idea that the programme has come to occupy an immovable slot on a Wednesday night is a sentimental illusion. Recently, as various tilts and shifts of the sports calendar – most of them initiated by broadcasting – have unbalanced Wednesday night's position at the centre of things, *Sportsnight* has found itself slipping off to other nights of the week in any case.

Yet a certain chill does accompany the announcement of *Sportsnight's* end, one which has at its source, I would hazard

– and even if only subconsciously – the question mark now hanging over the future of the *Sportsnight* theme tune.

Nobody doubts the BBC's pre-eminent position as a provider of signature music for sports programmes. *Match of the Day*, *Ski Sunday*, the cricket one, the showjumping one, the golf one . . . And even if the bidding wars go badly against them over the next few years, there are those who firmly believe the channel could boldly relaunch themselves on the back of the slogan: 'The BBC: next to no sport, but some cracking theme tunes.'

Sportsnight, needless to say, is up there with the best. The teleprinter-style staccato motif, the blaring horns, the rattling crescendo – not for nothing is this the longest running theme tune on the BBC after *The Sky at Night*. At the top of the programme it's a rallying cry. And at the end it serves as an alarm call. Only last Wednesday, in fact, it awoke me from a deep, sofa-based sleep I had fallen into during the snooker.

In short, it's a stomper (and I commend to anyone the full-length version of the track, available on the album *The A–Z of British TV Themes from the Sixties and Seventies* – rarely off my turntable – which includes some interesting introductory electric guitar work omitted from the televised extract).

We owe the *Sportsnight* theme to Tony Hatch, composer of the truly astonishing 'Downtown' (a smash hit for Petula Clark in 1964) as well as the deeply moving themes from *Neighbours* and *Crossroads*. Now based in Australia, he spoke last week of his willingness to resell the *Sportsnight* theme if the BBC decided they had no further use for it. And if you think Hatch isn't capable of such a clinical and cold-hearted deed, then you obviously don't remember the episode of the television talent contest *New Faces* when, as a reliably unimpressed member of the judging panel, Hatch awarded a singer called Malandra Burrows nought out of ten for star quality. Malandra Burrows was eight years old at the time.

Of course, the question remains whether a television theme tune has any resale value. It's not as if there exists a vigorous transfer market for opening numbers. Then again, ITV's sports department don't seem that fussy about second-hand goods these days. Having lost in quick succession Formula One motor racing and the FA Cup final, the BBC cannot now stand back and allow a commercial intruder to nip in and steal the theme to *Sportsnight*.

Dosh, Channel 4's matey financial affairs programme, called upon betting expert Angus Loughran (Statto from *Fantasy Football League*) to assist in 'the *Dosh* Gambling Challenge'. Herein, three teams (dentists, taxi drivers and women hockey players) were given £300 and sent, respectively, to the casino, the horses and the dogs to see who would come out better off. Statto went with each team to offer insight and guidance.

The result: everybody lost. The dentists came back with 27 pence, the cabbies with £62 and the hockey team with £140. The conclusion: if you go to the dogs, you might lose less than if you go to the horses or to the tables. On the other hand, you might not. Thank you for that, *Dosh*. And thank you, Statto.

WOKING GRIPPED BY CUP FEVER

18 NOVEMBER 1996

Ah, the romance of the FA Cup – a world where astonished giants drop to their knees, where underdogs can turn kings, where dreams burn bright and reality is eclipsed, and where

Nick Collins of Sky has to sound enthusiastic while saying: 'OK, so let's see how Woking line up.'

Non-league Woking were at home to second division Millwall on what Richard Keys in the studio called 'another cracking FA Cup night from Sky Sports'. You've got to credit Sky for being there at the start (most people's interest in the Cup won't click on until the big teams enter for the third round in January) and for lugging their cameras to these tiny grounds and offering whole hours of detailed attention and exposure to matches for which the terrestrial channels have neither the money, time, nor even, one suspects, the inclination. But that doesn't mean you've got to like the way they do it. People have remarked before on the disparity between the noise and pace of Sky's coverage and the actual status of the event being covered. And there's no better place to see that disparity thrown comically into relief than Woking on a chilly Friday.

The early rounds of the Cup may well be about minnows but unfortunately it's a condition of presenting sport on Sky that you have to speak as if the fattest salmon you've ever seen is, at that very moment, thrashing around at the end of your rod. So, maybe we were at Kingsfield Sports Ground on Friday and maybe there were only five and a half thousand in the crowd, but there was nothing to separate the vampy tone of the coverage from the tone applied to any game on Sky's Premiership calendar. The computer graphics clattered on to the screen, a melodramatic Celine Dion song played during the pre-match goals compilation and the presentation team talked it up and then up some more. If the first round is, as Martin Tyler lustily insisted, 'where the FA Cup really gets into full swing,' then what does that make the third round?

Much of the pre-match chat between Keys and Ray

Clemence, his studio guest, centred, quite rightly, on Woking's Clive Walker. Walker is thirty-nine, but continues to prove fast and dangerous. Still, that might not lead you to say of him, as Keys did: 'He's quality and he's got a touch and no matter how old you get, that never goes, does it?' This was desperate hype and desperate nonsense. Ask Bobby Charlton.

Clemence, incidentally, had some enlightening predictions to offer concerning Woking's tactics under their manager Geoff Chapple. Ray reckoned Chapple's side would 'go out and try and score more goals than the opposition'. Ray added: 'He's always had that theory of the game.' Chapple himself, meanwhile, did Sky proud with his pre-match soundbite: 'The few million viewers tonight won't be disappointed with non-league football.' We await the publication of Sky's figures to find out exactly how few million viewers that was.

Keys also did his bit to get us excited by Woking, the town. 'Not a footballing hotbed, you would think,' he said, 'but in recent years Woking [the team] have started to turn it into one'. I'm not entirely sure I know what a 'footballing hotbed' is, though it sounds like something involving George Best, a magnum of champagne and a Sunday tabloid. But I do feel fairly confident that one's excitement about and interest in an FA Cup match involving Woking has to do with the fact the town is explicitly not a 'footballing hotbed' and that talking about the place as if it was just months away from turning into Milan only has the effect of diluting the fabled FA Cup flavour until you can't taste it any more.*

* The match ended Woking 2 Millwall 2. But plucky Woking sneaked the replay 0–1, with a ninth minute goal from plucky Clive Walker. They then pluckily disposed of Cambridge United in the second round and even more pluckily drew with Coventry City, away from home, in the third. But they went down to a plucky 1–2 defeat in the replay.

NEW DAWN FOR ENGLISH RUGBY; SUN FAILS TO PENETRATE

25 NOVEMBER 1996

Normally when people talk about sticking something where the sun doesn't shine, they can be assumed to be talking both crudely and metaphorically. Yet this is the sadly literal fate of English rugby when it's at home at Twickenham. Those mountainous new stands bulk impressively in the sky but, of an afternoon, they make the playing surface a grim, tanning-free zone.

And though Saturday was, as Steve Rider on *Grandstand* (BBC1) pointed out, generously sunny for the time of year, and though an aerial view of the ground did occasionally show a strip of golden light bathing the lucky people in tier 17, row X, down there on the pitch it looked as grey and bleak as overcast Warsaw.

Unpromising conditions, then, for a new dawn. Yet this – as everyone in and around the studio seemed roughly to agree – was what England managed to 'usher in' with their victorious performance over Italy. True enough, the Italian side weren't exactly stuffed to overflowing with rugby's legendary names. They also 'lacked height' according to the experts – though to the uninformed observer, they only 'lacked height' in the way that Jo Brand could be said to 'lack girth'. But there were faces and figures in those blue shirts which one would have hotly feared to meet up a dark alley – or on the pitch at Twickenham, which amounts to the same thing.

What about that huge one, for instance – the dead ringer for Frankenstein? To much scorn from Nigel Starmer-Smith and Bill Beaumont in the commentary box, he was twice penalized for recklessly tackling people around the neck, though it may be he was quite innocently hoping to get his hands on a spare bolt.

'New' was the word most exercised in the studio, before, during and after the game. It tended to get attached to words such as 'blood', 'direction' and 'approach'. Someone even referred at one point to 'New England', an allusion presumably to the political notion of 'New Labour'. This may well be an analogy it is not helpful to pursue. After all, if the England rugby side had sacrificed principle for popularity to the same degree as the Labour Party, they would now be playing football.

On the contrary, the brand of rugby promised us in the pre-match interviews was one in which feet were intended to feature as little as possible. 'Rugby is a game that should be played in hand,' said Tim Stimpson, one of the five 'new boys' afforded the luxury of a hope-raising BBC pre-match video sequence which showed them charging around in glamorous slow-mo, steaming like horses during a cold training session and speaking to us from a variety of cosy, home-style locations. All of them received a further hearty endorsement from Rider's studio guests, Jon Callard and 'big' Dean Richards. (There wasn't much room in that studio. In fact, Richards had to leave one of his ears out in the corridor.)

We heard early on, too, from the new captain. Phil de Glanville may sound as if he ought to be a minor character in *The Merry Wives of Windsor*, but he 'gives good pre-match', as they say in broadcasting. Phil's predecessor, Will Carling, found there was nothing about the role of England captain which prevented him striking up a friendship with the wife of the heir to the throne. Alas, it's Phil's personal tragedy that he comes into the Carling role just when Windsor has run right out of wives. But perhaps he'll think of some other way to distinguish himself in the job.

Out on the pitch, there was significant action very early on when one of the Italian forwards answered in the affirmative the age-old question: is it possible to sing a national anthem while wearing a gumshield? Here was a challenge 'New England' disappointingly backed out of, but they certainly gave the anthem some stick. The camera panned past these beacons of hope for English newness: Chris Sheasby; Simon Shaw, six feet nine and no relation of Sandy, clearly; Andy Gomarsall, clutching the badge on his shirt, the sentimental fool; and Adedayo Adebayo whose name appears to have been lifted directly from the lyrics for *The Sound of Music* ('High on the hill was a lonely goatherd / Day-ee Adedayo Adebay-ee-o').

Seconds later, Mike Catt christened the new-born side by missing a penalty kick so simple, you'd have backed a blindfolded Sandy Shaw to secure the points. 'Kicking was always going to be England's Achilles' heel,' Starmer-Smith reassured us. Next time around, Catt sensibly elected to use his boot rather than his Achilles' heel, and the rush of points had begun. What's more, not long after that, the floodlights came on so we could actually see some of them.

A sportsman in no need of greater illumination, Damon Hill took time to make a guest appearance on *TFI Friday* (Channel 4), a chat show presented by the shy and retiring disc jockey and media mogul, Chris Evans. In its own way, this is a more dangerous thing to do than tailing Michael Schumacher into a corner at Monza.

Unscathed, however, Hill popped up again on Saturday

morning, this time as a guest on the rowdy children's programme *Live and Kicking* (BBC1). That's more dangerous than going into the same corner with Schumacher, only this time with your engine on fire.

Why is Damon taking these personal risks right at this point? No obvious reason suggests itself. It's surely pure coincidence that the nation is poised over its *Radio Times* coupons, ready to nominate the BBC Sports Personality of the Year for 1996. One unimportant trophy, expressive of a negligible thing like popular approval, couldn't possibly be of any interest to Damon who is, in any case, a man of integrity and way above such political baby-kissing.

CHANNEL 4 LOCKS INTO GRIDIRON

2 DECEMBER 1996

It was Week Thirteen of the American football league season – unlucky for some, including the Washington Redskins, who lost at home to the San Francisco 49ers during what's known as 'sudden-death overtime'. (This may sound like a novel pay-and-productivity deal struck by workers at a funeral parlour, but in fact it's just the NFL's equivalent of football's 'golden goal' ruling.)

Lucky old Gary Imlach, however, who, in his role as Channel 4's Mr Gridiron and Englishman abroad, chose this most inauspicious of weeks to ignore the established thespian advice on working with children – and got away with it. Linking an edition of *The American Football Big Match* from a variety of locations inside a Washington supermarket, Imlach was obliged at one point to address the camera while wheeling a shopping trolley containing three kids down a capacious aisle (imagine New York's Sixth Avenue made out of cereal boxes).

It was not clear where Gary got these children from and we can only hope he returned them afterwards. Almost certainly they had been bribed with confectionery to sit still and let Gary say his piece. So, inevitably, as the camera rolled, the small boy spotted his moment and went into an extended impression of Mick Jagger after swallowing a chilli. Gary, amazingly, didn't bat an eyelid. What a professional.

Then again, if you've seen what Imlach has seen and been where he has been in the course of his NFL coverage, then it's going to take more than an upstart tot to throw you out of your rhythm. Sure, a sizeable part of Gary's job looks enviably like tourism: at the top of the programme (and again on the round-up show, *Blitz!*), when he's not hanging around in supermarkets, he's generally to be found in the vicinity of some famous American landmark or other.

This makes the burden of his role look roughly comparable with that of his channel-mate James Richardson, the presenter of the Italian football magazine show, *Gazzetta Football Italia*. A significant part of Richardson's onerous duties includes the drinking of cappuccinos in dinky Milanese pavement cafés and the skimming of the Italian newspapers for stories about George Weah.

But it's not all sunbathing for Imlach. Not one of television's bigger physical presences, Gary is nevertheless obliged to interview people who are – routinely, given the nature of the sport – seventeen times larger than he is. This week he was down on the touchline with ex-Redskin and former 49er Charles Mann. By standing on tip-toe and stretching – sort of the ascent of Mann – Gary could just about get his Channel-4-endorsed microphone within reach of his interviewee's navel.

Selfless efforts on our behalf pretty much characterize Channel 4's NFL coverage, an admirable service which manages to condense a lot of information without seeming abrupt and contrives to be ritzy and American-flavoured without becoming embarrassingly wishful. It helps that for match commentary we hand over to qualified Americans: but then American football without the sophisticated chatter of American voices would be unthinkable.

Generally, commentator Pat Summerall gets to speak in any gaps left for him by his co-commentator, John Madden. Madden is so garrulous he makes Ron Atkinson seem a little shy. He is also one of international television's most committed believers in the on-screen marker pen – that device which enables pundits to unpack the tactical significance of what we've just seen by scribbling all over it. Not content with illustrating incidents from the play, Madden even underlines details on the statistics cards provided by the producers. By the time he's finished ringing players, noting dates of birth and drawing sundry lines of longitude and latitude, the screen looks like a doctor's prescription. Somehow, though, you end up with the medication you needed.

Sportsnight (BBC1) sent Sue Barker to profile the jockey Frankie Dettori, a sports-broadcasting task attractive and cheerful enough to rival those of Imlach and Richardson. Dettori has the kind of energy and charm which leaps into cameras and emerges at the other end, in your sitting-room, seemingly undiminished. Nothing seems to wow the nation at the moment like a bit of broken English, as so many foreign footballers are discovering. And as many home-grown footballers have discovered in the past.

Sportnight's cameras also joined Frankie on Newmarket Common at whatever that ridiculously early hour is when horse people start going about their business. Even at dawn – and a foul and rainy dawn, at that – he proved irrepressible. 'Good morning!' Frankie told the camera. 'My name is Michael Fisher. The weather forecast today is lightly breeze.' I almost went out and backed him to be right, which is not an urge one always experiences after hearing Michael Fish.*

ITV WITHIN REACH OF SILVERWARE

9 DECEMBER 1996

Congratulations to ITV on finally qualifying last week for the quarter-finals of football's European Cup after all those fruitless years. Ever since the channel started covering the competition, the English interest has taken a dive at an unattractively early stage, along with the viewing figures, it being a mysterious but nevertheless immutable broadcasting law that the delight of a Juventus, an Ajax or a Paris St Germain in full flow does not magnetize the punters in anything like the same quantities as the prospect of watching Roy Keane.

So, as Manchester United pushed past Rapid Vienna, a curse was laid to rest and, in scenes of unbridled joy nationwide, television executives and advertising people alike took to the streets to link arms in celebration or to drive around in their cars sounding their horns and waving their wallets out of the windows on sticks.

* Michael Fish once told the nation that an approaching hurricane was nothing to worry about. See also Alan Hansen's allegation that Manchester United would never win anything with kids (page 54).

Let no one say ITV did not work hard for this victory on the night. It was five degrees below zero out there in Vienna and, in a cruel oversight, the designers of Rapid's stadium had omitted to incorporate glass-fronted broadcasting booths anywhere in the ground, leaving Bob Wilson, our presenter, standing out in the cold and praying that the slightly numb feeling at the tip of his nose was not frost-bite.

Beside him, Terry Venables somehow kept his face thawed by smiling bravely, while Glenn Hoddle had taken the sensible precaution of binding himself several times around with leather. It must have taken the best part of a day to unwrap him. Despite the odds, there was a moment during the half-time chat which was not cold but, rather, straightforwardly cool. A few minutes earlier, Peter Schmeichel had flung himself across the goal to palm away the ball in a manner which – as Bob, Terry and Glenn agreed – bore some comparison with the famously 'impossible' Gordon Banks save from Pele during the World Cup in Mexico in 1970. 'Let's have a look at that,' said Bob; and blow us all if the clip of Banks did not appear on our screens so we could make an instant comparison.

By live outside broadcast standards, this was a piece of showbusiness to rival that bit in David Copperfield's magic show where he flies. How did they do that? The faintly troubling thought occurred that Wilson actually carries around in his pocket a video of great goalkeeping moments, just on the off-chance.

In truth the explanation was more prosaic. The broadcast from Vienna was linked to the London studios, where the late-night highlights programme was being assembled, so someone back there was packed off to the library to look under 'B' for Banks and the clip was, as they say, 'spun in' from home. Still, it looked good at the time, mostly thanks to Wilson who, by not remarking on the moment's unusualness, made it appear the most natural thing in the world to be instantly cross-referring to an incident from a game played a quarter of a century ago.*

Match of the Day (BBC1) offered the second of what many of us hope will be a long series of post-match interviews with Chelsea's most recent Italian signing, Gianfranco Zola. As with most of the people who talk to the programme these days, English is not Zola's first language. (Rumours of a sponsorship deal between *Match of the Day* and Linguaphone are as yet unconfirmed but definitely plausible.)

With Zola in particular, the English is, as yet, very much at a blueprint stage. There are lots of hugely endearing pauses and smiles. 'The team today didn't win the game,' he informed us on Saturday. 'I am going to be very happy . . .' And then the interviewer completed the sentence for him: '. . . when the team does win.' Cue huge laugh to finish with from Zola. Next week on the programme, the nippy frontman goes to a market and buys some fruit.

* This kind of cross-reference rapidly became the norm, particularly on Sky Sports. In April 2000, when Chelsea's goalkeeper Ed De Goey thumped the ball against Dwight Yorke of Manchester United and then watched it balloon over him and into his net, within half an hour Sky's studio team was having a good laugh at De Goey doing pretty much the same thing against Southampton a couple of years previous. That's the miracle of digital archiving for you.

A WIFE ON THE OCEAN WAVES

16 DECEMBER 1996

Modern Times (BBC2) brought to our attention an obscure but deeply enthralling rivalry from the dangerous and expensive sport of powerboat racing. On the one side stood Cliff Smith from Littlehampton, who runs a small refuse business, the turnover of which has halved in the last decade, and who is reduced, on occasions, to scrounging engine parts from other competitors; on the other, Charles Burnett III, American heir to a food and drink fortune worth $2 billion. 'It's wonderful to be able to think you don't have a structured life,' said Charles, as we watched him driving round the grounds of his mansion in England in his own tank.

Charles accused Cliff of 'making obscene gestures' during races. Cliff, who generally seemed not to approve of what he called 'hoo-hah Henrys', thought Charles should shove off to Dubai. Charles took Cliff's Isle of Wight Needles Trophy away from him, which didn't seem to diminish Cliff's antipathy. But in many ways, the programme was most remarkable for the performance of Cliff's wife Sharon who, far from offering her husband unwavering support, talked instead to the camera about how irritating she found the whole business.

When Cliff got back to the harbour after his unsuccessful attempt to snatch the Coast Classic at Cowes, Sharon greeted him warmly as follows: 'A waste of time and a waste of money. We've come here all weekend. Twelve minutes out there and you're back here again.' Cliff said he wanted to work on the engine for a while. 'You can fiddle about with that at home,' said Sharon. Behind every successful male powerboat racer, there's a woman who can't understand why he bothers.

Behind every Sunday League football referee, meanwhile, there's an entire nation of men, women, children and animals who fail completely to grasp his motivation. What possesses anyone to take on willingly a role associated in the public mind with Stalinism and the worst excesses of Pol Pot? You'd say the same about traffic wardens, but at least they get paid.

These grave matters were pondered in *Oi! Referee*, a short and funny film by Paul Whittington for the *Lloyd's Bank Channel Four Film Challenge* (Channel 4). Charlie Cooke's first duty is to check the pitch over for broken glass and dogs' shit. After that, the teams come out and then life gets really miserable.

In the event of a violent insurrection, Cooke had his plan of action worked out: abandon the game; call the police; lock himself in the dressing room until the police arrive; issue a summons against the guilty parties. A sound scheme, though if I had been him, I would perhaps have been concerned about the possible distances between the pitch, the phone and the dressing room.

On *Match of the Day* (BBC1), Robbie Fowler celebrated one of his several goals for Liverpool against Middlesbrough by running to the side of the pitch and picking up and brandishing an outside broadcast microphone – one of those elongated gadgets which looks like a ground-to-air missile in a sock.

This first use of broadcasting equipment in a goal celebration sets a troubling precedent. How long before a player commandeers a camera? Chaos would ensue for the viewer at home. Executives should meet now to draw up some means of nipping this one in the bud. It's one thing when television interferes with sport; it's quite another when sport interferes with television.

CRICKET FAILS THE SLEEP TEST

30 DECEMBER 1996

Directly after Christmas, the television companies examine the viewing figures and then declare their triumphs or mumble their excuses according to their performances in this most crucial period of the broadcasting calendar.

But revealing though these statistics frequently are (and this year they indicate with especially poignant clarity the ascendancy of the Trotter family from *Only Fools and Horses* over the Royal family from Windsor), they seem to me to veil the truth. For no figure is ever declared for the number of people who set out to watch a certain programme but within minutes – worn down by unusual quantities of food or unusual quantities of relatives – fall asleep. Tempting though it is during the festive season to imagine a nation actively united around its sets, it may be that Christmas is just a cosy version of the 1960s: tune in, drop off.

Certainly if you have been following the second Test in Zimbabwe, you will recognize this seasonal discrepancy between the hours the television is on and the hours the viewer is conscious. Some may trust their Yuletide naps to repeat screenings of *Casablanca* or the Christmas edition of *A Question of Sport*, but for me, it's English cricket every time. Nothing gets me away sooner, or for longer.

If ever there was an argument for removing sport from terrestrial television and making it subscription only, here it was. In fact, Friday's play should have been available by prescription only: something to calm the nervous and distressed. One could only pity the Sky Sports team, up to their necks in this sluggishness. Amazingly, Charles Colville is still looking spritely. On Saturday, he managed to find in the crowd the holidaying actor Peter Vaughan.

'So, you're not in panto or anything like that?' Charles asked brightly, adding: 'It's a busy time of year for people of your profession.' A tribute to the elasticity of the interviewer's art, this question was potentially doubly insensitive: a) for its implication that Vaughan might be the kind of actor to do panto; and b) for the brave way it tackled head-on the possibly touchy matter of why Vaughan might not be working while the rest of his profession was.

Vaughan – with an amiable absence of ego for which, I think it is fair to say, people of his profession are not famous – looked away into the distance and calmly pointed out that, no, as a matter of fact, he'd never done panto. Not – he might have added – until now, at any rate.

Back on earth, the BBC are to be congratulated for producing the first documentary about Euro 96 which didn't see the tournament solely through the eyes of policemen. Up until *Euro 96; When Football Came Home*, television had made three retrospective efforts on behalf of Euro 96, each of which began by accompanying sardonic and crisply shirted officers on tube trains to Wembley and ended later that night with the cameraman foolhardily standing under a shower of bottles in Trafalgar Square. Given that the tournament was remarkable for the extent to which levels of violence failed to rise to predicted heights, this seemed perhaps an unfortunate emphasis. It was good, then, to be reminded where the real heart of Euro 96 lay: in David Baddiel and Frank

Skinner singing 'Three Lions on a Shirt'. Oh, and also in some football.

On the subject of heart, the quest to find *The World's Strongest Man* got underway on BBC1. The judging criteria seem refreshingly simple: either you can lift that giant log eighteen times in a minute or you can't. So pick from one of a select squad of barn-scale musclemen, including Nathan 'Megaman' Jones, Vladimir 'Dynamite' Tourtchinski, and defending champion Magnus Ver Magnusson (no relation to the presenter of *Mastermind*, apparently). Magnus has a girlfriend called Asda, which sounded about right.

The arduous task of presenting this competition from Mauritius ('white sands, turquoise seas, all drenched in sun') fell to Philippa Forrester and Paul Dickenson. Philippa was careful to name-check the hotel where the competitors, and perhaps Philippa and Paul themselves, were staying and near which some of the competitions took place ('the exotic Cocoa Beach hotel, which normally finds people relaxing'), but given that advertising is forbidden on the BBC, we may have to put this down to journalistic rigour on her part.

The risks inherent in these trials of strength should not be underestimated. As Paul said: 'It was a terrible moment for everybody last year when Nathan's arm was broken in the arm-wrestling.' Thus far we've seen the competitors carry some implausibly heavy kegs across a dyke and pull a string of saloon cars thirty yards with a rope. The competition continues. In heat five, the decider, they'll all be required to sit through a tape of a day's cricket from Zimbabwe. That should sort the men from the boys.

1997

BRISTOW AGONISTES

6 JANUARY 1997

To the Circus Tavern, Purfleet, with Sky Sports for the World Darts Council championship – our chance to experience once again the magic which is Sid Waddell. Sid's darts commentaries, served at great volume, are a courageous mix of classical allusion (Rod Harrington manages to hit the bull's eye 'good as Jason and the lads finding the fleece') and something more straightforward ('Rodney is busting his pips here').

In one of his more fanciful moments last week, Sid promised us the tournament would deliver 'a tungsten Terpsichore', thus becoming the only person ever to use those two words in the same sentence, and the only commentator to evoke the Ancient Greek muse of dancing in a darts context.

Sid's critics anxiously wonder whether he isn't becoming a parody of himself. People in the audience now hold up to the cameras paper plates on which they have written Sid's name along with various encouraging remarks directed at him or predictions regarding the imminence of his death by overexcitement. Hard in such circumstances for Sid not to play up to the role.

But as a week of Sid in Purfleet revealed, it's too early yet to write off this endlessly inventive performer. How can you not warm to someone who can survey the smoky bedlam of the Circus Tavern and announce with relish: 'The sound of the tungsten, the smell of the crowd'?

On the Sky Sports darts team, antique phrase-turning is not just Sid's province. At Purfleet they were playing for £45,000 and a large glass globe. 'It is a handsome bauble, you'll agree,' said Dave Lanning. That line could have come straight out of Shakespeare. Unlike the trophy, which seemed to have come straight out of Sainsbury's Homebase.

The tournament's major narrative strand was the passage to Saturday night's semi-finals of a resurgent Eric Bristow. Bristow 'dominated the sport' during the 1980s, but for the best part of a decade has suffered a cruel bout of 'dart-itis', forcing him to yield his throne to newcomers such as Phil 'the Power' Taylor and Dennis 'the Menace' Priestley.

Yet Sid mentioned that Eric had 'prepared himself thoroughly' for this one, by going down the pub a lot (to practise, you understand). And though Sid conceded that Eric was 'no longer in his first pomp', he still found him capable of 'an effect on the audience, like Rasputin used to have on the birds a long time ago'. So maybe a surprise would be in store.

Bristow's first game of the week was a group match against Bob Anderson – a stiff challenge for the man they call the 'Crafty Cockney', but as Sid said, 'Eric's been in darting rucks as big as any.' Sid pointed out Eric's 'praying mantis style' – the lightest of grips on the dart, the little finger daintily aloft. 'You can trust darts players with best porcelain,' Sid said. 'As long as you put the right stuff in it.' Eric promptly triumphed. 'This has been a historic day for darts,' Sid concluded.

On Tuesday, it was Gary Mawson's turn. Sid spotted slight signals of distress in Eric's body language: 'Pas joyeux, as Eric would have it.' And, indeed, Eric lost. But he still qualified from his group, thanks to some complicated mathematics. 'Bristow has legs in hand,' said John Gwynne. 'If you see what I mean,' he added.

By Friday, Sid was wondering if some greater honour beyond darts might await Bristow, who is already an MBE for his services to the sport. 'They made Dick Whittington mayor of London,' said Sid. 'Maybe Eric's on some secret list.' Meanwhile, in the quarter-finals, Bristow took on Alan Warriner. At one point, on his way to the board to retrieve his darts, Bristow let out a low, rumbling noise which, to the untrained ear, sounded like a belch, but which, as Sid pointed out straight away, was actually a kind of war cry.

'He's doing the dragon roar which frightened St John,' said Sid. There was a pause. 'Correction,' said Sid. 'St George was the dragon lad. Getting a bit excited here.' Needless to say, Sid's excitement failed to abate as Bristow powered through to the semis. 'Takes your breath away to see this resuscitation of a legend,' shouted Sid. 'What's the melting point of microphone metal?'

And so to Saturday's semi-final against Phil Taylor, which Bristow lost, though only narrowly. This time last year, Sid was considering what might have happened had Bristow, at the height of his power, ever met Taylor at the height of his. On Saturday, Sid's dream of heaven all but came true, though he may be one of the few people on earth who is entirely easy with the notion that one might die and go to heaven, and that heaven would turn out to be the Circus Tavern, Purfleet.

BIRDS OF A FEATHER STICK IT IN THE NET

20 JANUARY 1997

No one would deny that football is indebted to Sky Sports and its millions of pounds in franchise money. Yet I wonder how many people would be prepared to surrender the gains and to retreat deep into the past – yea, even unto the dark days when Gareth Hall was in first-team contention at Chelsea – if it meant never again having to watch a television programme as bad as the Sky *Panasonic Soccer Awards 96*.

Here, before a giant audience at the Wembley Conference Centre, were two hours of gaffes, blunders, blatant plugs and embarrassments. On a night seemingly dedicated to the illogical, Englebert Humperdinck presented the Manager of the Year award and Naseem Hamed, the boxer, receiving a random prize for non-footballing achievement, made the longest acceptance speech.

Andy Gray said, near the top of the show: 'I think we'll have a laugh or two along the way.' Dream on, Andy.

What would you regard as the central footballing event of 1996? Call me old-fashioned, but I would say the European Championships were in with a shout. They took place in England; they caused a bit of a stir. Oddly, however, Euro 96 was a topic Sky's *Soccer Awards* remained quiet about. Astonishing to report, the only person to mention it all night was Pauline Quirke from *Birds of a Feather*.

If you read literally Sky's compilation of clips looking back over the year, then England spent a quiet 1996 contesting a handful of meaningless friendlies. It is just a hunch, but could this oversight have anything to do with the fact the rights to Euro 96 went exclusively to ITV and the BBC, while the rights to England's friendlies did not? People laughed when the BBC were reduced to showing stills of Holyfield flattening Tyson in their *Sports Review of the Year* in December 1995. But at least they had the courage to bite the bullet – and the perspective to allow that sometimes sport goes on elsewhere. As far as Sky Sports are concerned, if it does not happen in front of their cameras, it does not happen. This is televisual Stalinism and if, as Andy Gray rather chillingly put it, 'football and Sky Sports are partners', it is a collusion all of us should be watching very carefully.

Speaking of collusion, on his way through the stalls to collect the managers' award, Joe Kinnear, of Wimbledon, was embraced by Eric Hall, who, pink-suited, had risen like an inflating condom from his seat. It was the kind of scene which used to interest Dante.

Each of the celebrity guests got the chance to express their unswerving devotion to the people's game. There was Neil Morrissey, from *Men Behaving Badly*, an ardent Crystal Palace fan – except he 'hadn't got along there this season, unfortunately'. There was Sean Bean, ardent Sheffield United fan – except he'd 'been in Turkey' of late. There was Engelbert Humperdinck, ardent Leicester fan – or at least he phoned for results sometimes from his home in America.

Best of all, there was Linda Robson, the other *Bird of a Feather* and an Arsenal fan, she said. 'Seen any games?' wondered Gray. 'We try not to,' said Robson. 'I'm not really a fan of football. I'm only here for the wine.'

Shortly after this, Bill Wyman and Ronnie Wood came on and stumbled about a bit in a manner which suggested they too had successfully come in search of refreshment. 'I like any decent football match, me,' said Ronnie.

Wyman, as Anna Walker pointed out, was playing 'It's All Over Now' with the Rolling Stones 'two years before

Kenneth Wolstenholme immortalized that phrase'. Actually, that's not the phrase Wolstenholme immortalized (what he said was, 'They think it's all over – it is now'), but what the hell – a link is a link.

And then there was the business with thirteen-year-old Sonny Pike – a talented kid 'about to sign for Chelsea', according to Gray in his introduction, and here to perform a few tricks. 'I believe there are five or six ways you can get that ball airborne without touching it,' said Gray.

At last, Chelsea fans were thinking, the Messiah we've been waiting for. But no.

'Without touching it?' said a puzzled Pike.

'With your hands,' added Gray.

After Pike had finished flicking the ball around, Gray asked him if he was looking forward to playing for Chelsea. 'Don't even know if I'm playing for them yet,' Pike said. 'If you want to find out who I'm playing for, ask my monster agent, Eric Hall.' The heart sank.

An in-studio penalty shoot-out competition was in progress throughout the evening. Top prize: £50,000 for charity. '£50,000!' glowed Anna Walker. 'Yes, I did say £50,000!' From the standard, 12-yard distance, those football crazy celebs were required to get the ball through a hole in a goal-shaped target. The hole was exactly three-quarters of an inch larger than the ball itself.

'No one's got that £50,000 yet,' said Walker, halfway through. This was not surprising. The task would have troubled Eusebio at his peak. So what chance Zoe Ball? The consolation prize for the celeb who came closest was £1,000. This is known in financial circles as deflationary largesse. I've seen the odds on the shooting-ranges at a fairground tipped more generously in favour of the punter. But then, that's Sky Sports for you: a spiv in a brightly lit caravan, holding a string of flammable cuddly toys and a set of quietly bent rifles.

THE ENCHANTED SHORTS OF LENNOX LEWIS

10 FEBRUARY 1997

THE protracted festival of boxing on Sky Sports was British television's third pay-per-view event. How patiently we now get on the phone; how quietly we now write the cheque. When pay-per-view was first floated, amid angry objections, who would have bet on such an early, fuss-free, knock-down victory for Sky?

Sky's *Night of the Champions* was, to be accurate, twenty-four hours of the champions, or two nights of the champions with a long gap in the middle. But *Night of the Champions* was certainly the snappier title. On Saturday, from the London Arena, we got the Naseem Hamed fight, uniting the WBO and IBF titles but very deliberately excluding the BBC and ITV. And Friday night's Las Vegan farrago between Lennox Lewis and Oliver McCall was ours on the same ticket.

While Britain slept, McCall wept. There was McCall, walking round the ring with his arms down while Lewis tried to make up his mind whether to hit him or not. There was McCall's trainer, George Benton, shaking his head in disbelief. And finally, after five rounds, there was McCall being led away in tears. McCall now may not get paid. Unlike Sky Sports.

In the analytical aftermath, my favourite explanation came from one of McCall's former trainers: 'He's a very emotional guy; he just said forget it.' Schizophrenia, too, reared its heads. 'Oliver McCall is a lovely bunch of fellas,' said Barry McGuigan.

Still, Lennox Lewis wasn't going to let a small matter like the random, mental disintegration of his opponent prevent him from delivering the usual victor's platitudes. 'All the sacrifice was worth it,' he said, but who was he trying to kid? For all the fight amounted to, that glittering title-holder's belt might just as well have been made from cardboard and decorated with Fuzzy Felt.

In what will not go down as one of boxing's more intelligent moments, Lewis was additionally keen to take the credit for McCall's psychic crisis. 'I was just playing with him with my jab,' Lennox assured us, before wondering, in all seriousness, whether his shorts might not have contributed something. The American interviewer expressed confusion. Well, Lennox explained, those bright white shorts might have made McCall 'see me come out as a gladiator in some sense'.

Astonishing: a heavyweight fighter bursts into tears and his opponent credits his own trunks. You could not make this up.

Next day, at the London Arena, simply everyone was there. 'See what I mean about the younger generation being brought into boxing?' said the anchorman John Dempsey as the camera revealed Bob Geldof, forty-four.

You would have to say the delights of the undercard were mixed. On the one hand, Danny Williams dispatched Shane Woollass, an unhappily heavy heavyweight from Doncaster, distinguished by a tatooed left calf and stripy shorts which made it look as if he was struggling to escape from a Punch and Judy kiosk. On the other, Steve Collins effectively dealt with Frederic Seillier, from France. I was sorry to see the Frenchman go, if only because, as someone remarked, he 'doesn't speak a word of English' and 'hasn't had much to say this week'. How unlike our own Naseem Hamed.

Hamed, in one of the night's many entirely predictable bulletins on the topic of his mental health, assured us he was 'cool, calm and collective' – an allusion, perhaps, to the Stalin-style farm to which many of us would love to see him banished. Nicky Piper in the studio called him 'brash, arrogant'. There was a time when those were uncomplicatedly pejorative terms. But that was a long time ago – a time before pay-per-view boxing on Sky Sports.

The wretched thing about Hamed is that he brings out the worst in everyone. There is no sense in which he does not operate as a bringer of sour things. Clearly, to support him is to abandon all scruple. At the same time, the desire to see him smacked to the canvas, to see that leering face damaged, to see his inane swagger reduced to a dizzy tottering . . . well, these are not creditable and dignified things to wish for, either.

Perhaps we would be able to concentrate on the brilliance of his boxing if television weren't so keen to wind him up and watch him spin. It might be useful, for instance, not to have a camera in his suite at the Dorchester Hotel; not to accompany him in his car to the fight; not to visit him like a lovesick fan every ten minutes in his dressing room. 'He almost writes his own rules,' according to Ian Darke, a statement which caused me to gasp aloud. There I was thinking Sky were actively manipulating this carnival of hype, when all along, they were the hapless and unwilling victim of Hamed's contractual dictates.

The reality is, Sky can't get enough of Hamed. After the fight, Hamed gave Darke some lip about how he was going to 'bring it all back to Sheffield' and a section of the crowd roared. 'They like that! They like that!' gurgled Darke. And was there ever a more sycophantic sight than that of Darke then presenting Hamed with a special Sky Sports birthday cake?

Let's leave aside the fact it wasn't Hamed's birthday (it's on Wednesday). Here before our very eyes was the literal enactment of having your cake and eating it. The icing, of course, bore the Sky Sports logo. How thoughtful.

ITALY BEAT ENGLAND; HODDLE UNREPENTANT

17 FEBRUARY 1997

Television's inquest into the English national football team's 1–0 defeat by Italy at Wembley began immediately and went on for days. In fact, the dissection probably continues even now on a sofa somewhere in morning-television land, where hosts and guests alike utter the words 'Zola' and 'Le Tissier' and shake their heads and shrug their shoulders.

Frankly, if you couldn't discuss man-to-man marking and the holding role and if you didn't have an opinion on the fallibility of Glenn Hoddle, there was no place for you on television last week and there isn't likely to be again until this whole World Cup 98 qualifying business is resolved in October. Post-match analysis was pretty much on all channels, at all times.

BBC1 with *Sportsnight*, Channel 4 with *Under The Moon* and Sky Sports, who showed the game live, all got in there on the night; ITV leapt in the day after. Why, even L!ve TV, Britain's cheapest television station, probably dedicated regular, hour-long slots to in-depth argument on the topic –

though the last time I looked in, the channel was busy showing a dwarf reading the weather while bouncing on a trampoline. This from the channel which has brought us *Lunchbox Volleyball* and the Lottery stripper. L!ve's commitment to upholding standards of broadcasting is, we must admit, positively Reithian.

In this gale of coverage, it was ITV who came up with most dazzlingly original idea – a notion so simple, yet so effective, it's amazing nobody has thought of it before. What it is is a discussion show in which four famous blokes behind a desk face a studio audience of other blokes and they all talk about a topic – in this case, football – for an hour. Just what the world needs. I don't like to get into the business of prediction, but I reckon this is a format which could really catch on.

The programme is called *Do I Not Like That* (if Graham Taylor were able to claim royalties on the usage of this phrase, he would probably be as wealthy as Paul McCartney by now) and at least it has Richard Littlejohn in charge, a man with a sharp ear for nonsense and an ability to hustle the conversation along whenever it seems to be hitting the old grooves.

No danger of that, of course, with the snooker player Steve Davis, one of Littlejohn's guests, whose illustrious career at the table had not compromised his ability to turn a keen eye on the Italians. 'I'm not being detrimental to them,' Steve said, 'but they're brilliant at fouling.' Steve's novel solution to his own xenophobia was that 'we should paint our shirts' so that it would clearly show when someone had touched them. 'Umbro [the makers of England's football kit] make paints as well,' he added. I think that might have been Humbrol Steve was thinking of. Still, an interesting idea and we were all grateful for it.

Viewers of *Do I Not Like That* are encouraged to fax in their contributions to the debate and Littlejohn does his best to turn this visually unpromising feature into a televisual device by waving the faxes at the camera, or by folding them in half after he has read them, or, with the really uninteresting ones, by screwing them up and throwing them over his shoulder.

Still, this is a notch up on *Under The Moon*'s phone-in format, on Channel 4, where everyone in the studio just has to sit there attempting to look interested while the caller says his (or her, but normally his) piece. Slightly worrying, perhaps, that these early probes into the exciting future which is interactive telly should produce moments which are, in television terms, about as dead as it gets.

Hot debate continued when the Italian football magazine programme *Gazzetta Football Italia* (Channel 4) offered the other side of the story – lots of Italians jumping up and down in cafés and pausing to assert for the camera their nation's footballing eminence in Europe and their personal sadness at the absence from the England side of 'Gazza Gascoigne'.

Over on *Football Focus* (BBC1), Glenn Hoddle told Ray Stubbs that, with hindsight, he wouldn't have changed a thing – a comment which seemed to have interesting implications for the age-old ideal of learning from experience. And Trevor Brooking, amazingly at this stage, found a word which had not appeared in many other people's post-match analyses: 'Poland'. Not to be dismissed, according to Trevor, raising the dread prospect of England not even making it to a play-off place.

They wouldn't stand for such pessimism at Nike. BBC2's *Branded* went to Oregon to visit the home of the world's most aggressively marketed sportswear and found it to be a campus of cool white walls and splashing fountains. 'It's like a cult,' someone remarked. 'But a good cult.'

The company's muscular optimism even allows them to be upbeat about the fact that their products are stitched and glued together by factory workers in Indonesia – yours, in the present totalitarian climate, for around $2 (£1.25) per person per day. But this is sub-contracting, of course, so it's right out of Nike's hands. 'There are some things we can control and some things we cannot,' said Nike's founder, Phil Knight. Want to build a billion-dollar company on cheap labour? Just do it.

ENGLISH CRICKET FOUND ALIVE-ISH

24 FEBRUARY 1997

And word came from a distant place of a new force which was in the world. And the force was in the world, but the world knew it not. For the world had been misled by prophets.

But now the prophets did stand up with a humble expression, asking to be heard again and saying: 'Much did we gnash and wail and declare aloud our belief that English cricket was about as much use as an three-legged ox. And much did we pelt with insults the lad Atherton – yea, even unto suggesting we would have preferred to have Le Tissier instead. And often did we say of Lloyd that he knew not his passage to the exit of an paper bag.

'But we who have been in darkness – or at least in a selection of well-appointed Holiday Inns, all expenses paid – have seen a great light. For we were forgetting the Test matches against New Zealand, not to mention the series of internationals thereafter which are called "One Day". And in these last in particular, England have truly come good. For they have smote the mighty Kiwis and they shall be known across the land as victors and heroes in the highest. At least until the summer when the Australians get hold of them.'

And the prophets urged: 'Ye who dwell in the land of dishes tune, this Saturday night, unto Sky Sports. For steep though it may be at £14.95 per month, it is your only option. Tune in and witness with your own eyes this new-found confidence of which we have spoken. For verily, the lads are on a roll.'

And those of us with dishes, or whose houses are conjoined by cabling, did so tune in, prompt at 9.25 p.m., determined to see for ourselves this long-awaited new force, and to honour it with our unbroken attention, as long as it didn't mean missing *Match of the Day*. And lo, we saw Alan Mullally bowling a bunch of wides and wondered what the fuss was.

It got better, of course. Much better. Indeed, England in consecutive victory shock. But not before, with an eye, perhaps, on historical continuity, England had made it as tough for themselves as possible by flinging themselves over the ball on the boundary and by incurring so many extra balls from wides, they threatened to make the game the first-ever two-day One Day.

The only good thing about this errant bowling was it allowed those of us at home an extensive opportunity to observe Brent Bowden at work. Bowden is a young New Zealand umpire and looks like Tiny Tim crossed with Brian May of Queen. Perhaps seeking to become the first cricketing official to be given the chance to cross over into ballet, Brent reinterprets the traditional signals to the scorer in his own unique fashion – all fluttering arms and gently bending knees in the manner of Pan's People during a ballad. Often, on slow-motion replays, as the bowler whips past him, you will see Brent smiling and talking to himself. It's good to have him around.

Sky broke to us as soon as they could the bad news about Atherton – out of the game because he was 'feeling his back'. So it was over to Ronnie Irani. Or Heavenly Ronnie Irani, as Paula Yates would probably have christened him. Ronnie's first unenviable task would have been to awaken morale and self-belief in a side forced to wear a new strip which was as close a physical representation as one is likely to see of the phrase 'sad sack'. Mark Nicholas in the Sky commentary box said he couldn't make up his mind whether 'uniform' or 'costume' was the correct term to employ, and who could blame him? Here was an outfit in which a slice of West Ham's away kit had been ironed on to something worn by postal operatives in communist China.

Still, in the end, only the weather threatened to get in the way. What rainfall does for Sky's viewing figures, we can only imagine. Sitting up on the off-chance of a break in the clouds at 3 a.m. would have to be one of television's slimmer temptations. Perhaps this was why Bob Willis was so eager to tell us that the rain had 'already eased' just seconds after it had begun and while the image before us was still of the groundstaff spreading the hessian sheets over the wicket. (I should confess I was asleep with the video running directly the lunch interval started: there is, after all, only so much pleasure a man can take without feeling guilty.)

Once the rain had cleared, the game had to be scaled down to fit the remaining time. This was done by a feat of mathematics which will probably remain, to the lay person, for ever obscure, but which, as I understand it, works roughly as follows: you take the number of half-hour portions remaining; you add the minutes Ian Botham has spent in the last hour talking about improvements in the English bowling, without mentioning that he is the bowling coach; you multiply the resulting figure by the age of the oldest batsman in the New Zealand squad; divide by Dominic Cork's international batting average; and then take away the number you first thought of. Hey presto: England were now chasing 132 runs off 26 overs.

Let's hope they had less trouble with the post-match champagne than members of the Chesterfield football team, who have progressed surprisingly far in the FA Cup.* On *The Frank Skinner Show*, Skinner drew our attention to a clip of the recent after-game jubilation in which a member of the side was clearly trying to open the bottle with his teeth. Not recommended. It's one thing to let the bubbles get up your nose, quite another to let the cork.

JIMMY TAKES THE MICKEY; A FAREWELL TO CARDIFF ARMS PARK

17 MARCH 1997

Figures have yet to be released, but it seems likely that the most effective item during BBC1's night of Comic Relief fund-raising was the skit set in the *Match of the Day* studio in which Alan Hansen flicked a switch and blew up Jimmy Hill.

* Plucky Chesterfield went all the way to the semi-final, where they were pluckily knocked out by Middlesbrough.

Communications experts maintain that the surge of callers, phoning in to pledge money in the immediate wake of this experience, will have delivered an almost crippling blow to the phone network, much in the way that kettles, turned on after the wedding of Prince Charles to Princess Diana, threatened to bring down the national grid.

The sketch certainly went down well with the *Match of the Day* team, who showed it again. Twice. I guess they liked the way it revealed a Hill the nation rarely sees: not the querulous, post-match moralist of legend, but rather someone willing to laugh at himself for being the querulous, post-match moralist of legend.

But it's all very well for *Match of the Day* to celebrate Hill's ability to take a joke. For us at home, it simply gets harder to find a sports pundit whom we can dislike with impunity. Where are we to turn for total irritation if our major patience-baiters are forever revealing themselves to be thoroughly well-adjusted people on the quiet?

Hill's contribution to Comic Relief was bold. But for sheer nerve, imagination and fund-raising ambition, the prize must go to *Channel 4 Racing*. Despite the pressures of compiling their splendid Cheltenham Festival coverage, the team still found time to join in with the Comic Relief mischief. And how!

They enlisted a large man with a booming voice, clothed him in various floppy hats and velvets and tweeds of a kind rarely seen this side of amateur productions of *Toad of Toad Hall*, sprinkled him liberally with jewellery, set him down right in the middle of the crowd, and left him there, shouting and waving, for three whole days!

It wasn't clear how much this particular stunt raised. Indeed, some viewers are said to have complained that they actually lost money by taking this figure seriously as a tipster and backing his recommendations. Astonishing really, in the circumstances, but then whenever people try to do something positive and helpful, there will always be someone griping and whingeing from the sidelines.

For me, I don't think you could have asked for a better embodiment than this of the Comic Relief spirit, in which everyone forgets who they are for a few hours and has a damn good laugh for charity. Apparently the name of the man in the fancy dress was 'John McCririck', though that, too, may well only be a comic pseudonym. But whoever he is, we salute him and wonder whether there might not even be a career for him in this kind of thing.

No red noses were evident when the cameras panned the Welsh and English rugby sides at Cardiff Arms Park (BBC1), though many of the forwards were gamely sporting the traditional rugby variant – giant red ears. Meanwhile, up in the commentary box it was all red eyes. For here we were at Cardiff Arms Park just prior to a major demolition job. And as if that wasn't enough, as soon as the English side had finished with the Welsh, bulldozers were going to come in and knock down the stadium.

Conditions could not have been better. It was, as Nigel Starmer-Smith pointed out, a 'spring-like' afternoon, though, given that it actually was spring, it was hard to feel quite as curious about this as Nigel seemed to. But the weather could not diminish the sadness in the air, nor the sound of sentimental fools sniffling. 'You could say, a farewell to Arms,' Nigel said, only dimly audible now above the rustling of his handkerchief.

Nigel and Eddie Butler tried hard to console themselves with the thought that 'something bigger and better' would be built on the site – not a Sainsbury's or a car park, but another Welsh national stadium. 'The pitch will go through 90 degrees,' Butler explained. Actually, the Welsh forwards got to find out what that felt like a lot sooner than planned.

JIM ROSENTHAL ARRIVES IN PROMISED LAND

24 MARCH 1997

The last time we saw Jim Rosenthal, he was basking in the sunny paddock at the Melbourne Grand Prix. This week, on his way to presenting the Rugby World Cup Sevens, he spoke to us from the prow of a tourist cruiser, puttering gently through Hong Kong harbour. Clearly for Rosenthal right now, it's just one short straw after another.

'England are here,' he said, 'ready to go.' Rosenthal, who is these days modelling a new, slowed-down delivery, could well have been taking Des Lynam lessons. We first noticed this in Australia: 'If you want Schumacher to drive for you [pause, slight nod at camera], it'll cost you a million dollars a time.' In Hong Kong, it was the same story: 'Good to have him on our side for once,' said Jim as Jonah Lomu joined the commentary team.

We certainly needed someone to calm things down. Funny old game, rugby sevens. Someone at some point decided to more than halve the usual number of players, but then never got round to scaling down the pitch. The result is fun-size rugby in a full-size wrapper. Still, it makes for fast television, while allowing script-writers to use the word 'seven' in conjunction with the words 'magnificent' and 'heaven' a lot.

ITV offered us a colourful introduction to the tournament – so colourful, in fact, it threatened to go on longer than the actual competition. We were pointed towards the players most likely to influence the tournament ('the magnificent seven') and warned, presciently, that Fiji could well be the side to take us to 'sevens heaven'.

It is inevitable in scene-setting previews of this nature that, at some point, one of the touring sides will be herded up by the film crew and packed off to the nearest thing resembling a bazaar in order to pat a few children and pretend to buy a rug, preferably from a wizened trader. And on the way back, likely as not, the same players will be steered into a restaurant and made to order something punishingly traditional. Naturally enough, the film crew in Hong Kong picked on England. The imminent prospect of having to watch, say, Chris Sheasby attempting to work his way through a bowl of mashed shark's offal using only a pair of chopsticks, meant one spent a lot of this programme braced as if for impact.

Actually, one's fears turned out to be groundless: we merely had to watch Chris Sheasby get himself fitted for a suit. 'Double-breasted,' said Chris. 'Very chic.'

In general, rather than detain us with shots of the England players going places, ITV chose more imaginatively to show us shots of them wondering where to go. 'Can we get five in one taxi?' pondered Austin Healey, and it was immediately clear that the needs of the touring player will not be properly serviced until someone slims the game down still further and develops a Rugby World Cup Fours.

Western Samoa turned over England in the quarter-finals and the succession of power was nearly complete. Finally, we were down to Fiji and South Africa. Fiji romped home. Still, you couldn't accuse South Africa of failing to tough it out. At one of those moments when television brings you closer to the action than you would necessarily wish, we saw a bleeding cut to the side of a player's eye which was attracting the referee's concern. But then another player stepped in and wiped the cut with the sleeve of his shirt, using the kind of motherly tenderness with which one might clean the windscreen of one's car. This seemed to satisfy the referee, and the game went on.

At its conclusion, Rosenthal wished us a fond farewell. Presumably his next stop is the Topless Volleyball Fours in Bali.

In the light of a recent political scandal closer to home, it was interesting to look again at a moment from the comedy quiz show *They Think It's All Over*, highlights from the second series of which were shown on Saturday night (BBC1). Nick Hancock, the presenter, brandished a copy of *Gary Lineker's Soccer Quiz Book* and accused its named author of not having written it. Then he went further and accused him of not even having read it.

'If you didn't write so much as one question in here,' Hancock told Lineker, 'then you are a charlatan.' Lineker then failed to answer correctly the one question Hancock read aloud, at which point suspicion's finger stopped pointing at him and started poking him in the eye instead. There it was, flagrant as you like: Cash for Questions, in another form.

Lineker tried to restore his reputation by arguing, quite brilliantly, that he had only written the questions, and not the answers. David Gower, on the opposition bench, chortled loudly but stopped when Hancock threatened him with a copy of *David Gower's Cricket Quiz Book*. They were all at it, in other words. Except that, unlike their parliamentary equivalents, the sports people were getting paid not to ask questions – indeed, not to do anything at all. The better deal, surely.

POOR APPETITE FOR BREAKFAST-TIME FOOTBALL

21 APRIL 1997

Eleven-fifteen in the morning: what kind of time is that for a potentially championship-deciding football match? Thank you very much, Sky Sports. 'An early start to a day of reckoning,' said Richard Keys on Saturday, shortly after sunrise at Anfield. Too right. Pictured in the tunnel, the players of Liverpool and Manchester United seemed to be slapping themselves to stay awake.

Eleven-fifteen is all very well for park sides with hangovers; it's no hour at all to demand a performance from high-calibre Premiership players who, as dedicated professionals, will have hangovers which need a lot longer to get over.

When Sky pulled this same trick on Chelsea and Arsenal a couple of weeks ago, players remarked on the queasy burden of having to get up early enough to be able to face, and then digest, the requisite energy-giving meal of chicken and pasta. Let's be clear, it's not easy at home, either, with the Shreddies still going down.

But then, in relation to the Premiership, Sky has worked itself into the position of a Roman emperor at a banquet. It only has to shout, 'Peel me a grape,' and everyone jumps. Well, almost everyone. Sky would point out, in their defence, that the schedule isn't entirely theirs to play around with. Decisions on kick-off times have to be made in collaboration with the local police. But even here, can we be sure the authorities have the good of the game and the convenience of the viewer in mind? Or is something more self-serving going on?

Merseyside police would have been faced with the following stark choice: hold the match in the evening and entertain Manchester United fans in the city all day with the pubs open; or get the job done early and make it home in time for the racing on Grandstand.

'Seldom have two teams needed three points so desperately,' said a voice-over, mid-way through. Actually, this wasn't a reference to Liverpool v. Manchester United at all. We were looking ahead to Sky's coverage of the match between Coventry and Arsenal. This channel has never been reluctant to tout its wares: the average Sky live game contains more trails than Yosemite Park. In the space of one football match, the following events were plugged: Coventry v. Arsenal, Carlisle v. Colchester, England v. Georgia, England U-21 v. Georgia U-21, West Indies v. India at cricket, European PGA golf from Cannes and a night of boxing featuring Naseem Hamed.

You can't blame the channel for wanting to advertise itself at half-time and during commercial breaks. It's the plugs during the game, with accompanying on-screen graphics, that grate. After twenty-eight minutes, just as the game before us was getting interesting, we were alerted to the future delights of the Auto Windscreen final – 'a Wembley occasion', Martin Tyler assured us, hopefully. 'Sure to be a big crowd.' After thirty-five minutes, we were asked to make a date in our diary for Hamed v. Hardy. 'We've got a special pay-per-view event to tell you about,' said Tyler, and your heart sank on his behalf. A commentator as good as Tyler deserves to be able to concentrate himself, and us, on the matter to hand, rather than play street-hawker.

All in all, Sky's football coverage is remarkable for

quantity rather than quality. This isn't just a matter of that irritating phone-in man-of-the-match competition for which votes are canvassed after only seventy minutes of the game (thus in the Coca-Cola Cup final replay last Wednesday, which went to extra time, people were invited to call in their summary judgement on a match which was not to finish for another fifty minutes). It's the way the coverage is in thrall to the replay and the close-up – those natural enemies of a game's flow. The sequence of events following Gary Pallister's goal on Saturday was typical: three replays from different angles, one slow-motion replay of the manager's reaction, then a tight close-up on Pallister. Then finally you rejoined the game when the ball was in the middle of the Liverpool half – and you had no idea how it got there. Odd that a channel so dedicated to football can bring itself to look away so often.

ITV SNAFFLE FORMULA ONE; MURRAY WALKER SNUFFLES

28 APRIL 1997

It had to happen some time, and, in Imola, it did: the revenge of Murray Walker's larynx. Yes, finally, during ITV's Formula One coverage, in its first season since the commercial broadcaster outbid the BBC for the rights, Britain's most reliable voice-box rebelled. Walker sounded as if someone had him pinned by the throat to the back of the studio. You can't say he didn't have it coming, what with all those years spent making himself heard above the loudest noise in sport after a Linford Christie post-race press conference.

'A cold', some experts were calling it. But others, closer to the pit lane, thought Walker might have a developed a Ferrari-style problem with his aerodynamics and were wondering whether a last-minute switch from hard-compound tonsils to soft-compound tonsils hadn't cost him some vital wear and tear.

Still, Walker is nothing if not a battler and the show went on. It was a Punch and Judy show, chiefly. Murray sets 'em up; Martin Brundle, his co-commentator, knocks 'em down. Like the moment when Murray offered a heart-felt tribute to the talents of the rookie driver Ralf Schumacher, brother of Michael. 'It's amazing how quickly this man learns circuits,' Murray said. 'How difficult is that?' 'It's not difficult at all,' Brundle said. Cue noise of Walker getting clobbered with a truncheon.

This is turning out to be Brundle's most active season since he drove for Benetton in 1992. He is prone, it's true, to the occasional tabloid moment, which someone in ITV's garage should maybe have a word with him about: Brundle's way of registering that Heinz-Harald Frentzen and Michael Schumacher were looking good in Saturday's session was to say: 'The Germans have got their towels on the front of the grid.'

Yet one remains agog at the way Brundle can talk one through a qualifying lap and spot fractions of a second being dropped in the merest twitch of the steering wheel. He has given a new lease of life to those blurry images from the on-board cameras above the driver's helmets. Previously, these were mostly of use to bored and broke students, who could press their faces close to the screen and enjoy the resulting buzz. Under Brundle, who can read in these pictures instances of late braking and sloppy steering, they become valuable conveyors of information. 'Yes, I think this could be provisional pole,' he said, as we watched the back of Frentzen's gloves complete a speeding lap. And it was – by 0.3 seconds.

We have been keeping a careful eye this season on Jim Rosenthal's presentation positions. Having the production on-site was one of the innovations ITV boasted about when they announced their plans for Formula One, so it's worth having a look at where they end up. In Brazil, they were directly under the flight path of the helicopter shuttle. It is hard to concentrate with Noel Edmonds going up and down outside your window. And it wasn't much better in Argentina, where Rosenthal and his chums seemed to be in a box which one of the cars had come in.

Blessed relief for them at Imola, then, where it appeared that someone had loaned them a warehouse for the weekend. In the process of crowing with triumph at this up-turn of fortune, ITV handed us a landmark moment in televised sport: the first aerial shot attempted within the confines of an outside broadcast studio booth. I don't think the blimp was involved, but I could be wrong.

Over on *Grandstand* (BBC1), where Formula One used to be, touring cars now were. I suspect I am not alone in finding the sight of Jacques Villeneuve in a Williams more exciting than the sight of some bloke in an Audi. I can, after all, get the latter in my street fairly regularly.

But these days, *Grandstand* must take what it can and make do. Later in the show, an overrun at the snooker forced Steve Rider – once hotly tipped for the ITV Formula One job – to issue the following poignant apology: 'We've lost the time we originally allocated to our world championship curling coverage.' What a total professional Rider is. He brought to this sentence a tone of nicely judged sobriety which carefully included the possibility that someone, somewhere, was actually going to be disappointed about this.

This is a strange phase for *Grandstand*. The time may not be far away when someone on the show has to apologize that, owing to an earlier delay at the 65-and-over badminton from Framlingham when the shuttlecock got lodged in the church hall rafters, there will be no time to show the scheduled chocolate egg hunt from the beer garden of the Dog and Forget-Me-Not at Epsom. And when that moment comes, the programme is going to need Rider more than ever before.

How peculiar, though, the fates of television's sports jockeys. Rosenthal is out there in the sunshine cultivating his new role as TV's Mr Smooth; Rider is back in London, cancelling the curling.

GEORGIA NOT ON SKY'S MIND

5 MAY 1997

To Wembley with Sky Sports for the World Cup 98 qualifier, England v. Georgia. Bit of a dark horse, Georgia. And there's nothing like Sky Sports for leaving you in the dark about a dark horse.

Isn't it remarkable how little one actually learns from television on these occasions? As usual, guests are invited along to the studio who know next to nothing about the opposition and probably have not understood the fee for their services to include some homework the night before. To secure the rights to an international with Georgia, and then to get Joe Royle and Ray Wilkins to do the expert analysis, is, in a way, to decide in advance that the opposition do not much matter.

Royle did find it in his English heart to praise the ability of Georgiou Kinkladze, the one Georgian an English audience would have known something about, but added: 'There are question marks to the product of that ability sometimes.' Everyone in the studio nodded sagely, though this sentence might just as well have been in Russian for all the immediate sense it made.

'I don't think we should ever forget our values,' said Wilkins. 'We do cross a good ball.' He pursued this line of thinking as the Georgian side lined up for the national anthems. 'Just looking there at the goalkeeper,' Wilkins said, 'he's not the tallest man in the world, the goalkeeper.' But what does it say about the degree of Wilkins's insularity that he can't even be bothered to look at the team-sheet and discover and use the goalkeeper's name?

In the absence of useful knowledge or insight, we were served perfunctory estimates of the Georgian team's 'state of mind' – which told us nothing about Georgia but everything about the speaker's unshakeable and almost touchingly old-fashioned belief in the sheer privilege of playing England at Wembley. As Wilkins put it: 'If they're not looking forward to this one, they won't look forward to anything.'

Later, England's manager Glenn Hoddle looked back. 'On another night,' he told *Sportsnight* (BBC1), 'we would have been ahead before.' Hoddle's reluctance to deal with the matter at hand grows ever more startling. Almost anything he says after a game can be reliably paraphrased as follows: 'If it had been a completely different match, it would have been a completely different match.'

It took *Sportsnight*'s multinational talents – Jimmy Hill, Alan Hansen, Ruud Gullit – to lend the game some perspective and the opposition some respect. When a match offers a clutch of z-filled eastern European surnames and a pair of twins, Barry Davies is your commentator.* The coverage stooped only once to gimmickry and may not attempt it again: the moment when Ruud Gullit turned up his nose at being asked to score the game out of ten was one for the archives.

On the subject of gimmicks, I timed Naseem Hamed's procession to the ring on Saturday (lasers, smoke, dancing – the usual tedious non-event) at six minutes, which meant it lasted four times longer than his fight. Worth £14.95 in pay-per-view fees? You the jury.

Speaking with a cracked nose and an alarming medical condition which the boxer himself described as 'numb teeth', the defeated Billy Hardy was nevertheless able to look on the bright side: 'He never knocked me out like he said he would.' Scant consolation, one felt. Yet one had to marvel at the mental agility involved in being able to find a positive spin for an event while still physically spinning from its outcome.

Hardy also had the good grace to apologize to the people who subscribed, a little piece of etiquette which, by rights, ought to have fallen to someone from Sky, but never seemed likely to.

At the opposite end of the financial spectrum – at the opposite end of almost any spectrum you care to mention, actually – sits L!ve TV, Britain's cheapest cable station. We may have to concede that the golden age for resourcefulness at L!ve has passed. Recent efforts to capture the nation's

* Barry Davies's carefully researched pronunciation of 'Solksjaer', the Manchester United striker, which involved the use of an impossibly precise and utterly invisible to the naked eye final syllable, went on to win awards at the very highest level. See also page 255.

heart and mind (the trampolining dwarf who reads the weather, for instance) have smacked of, shall we say, desperation. That said, if it's coverage of ten-pin bowling you want, featuring members of the public in a brightly lit alley in Essex, then there is simply no other station to fulfil your needs.

Some might claim that ten-pin bowling does not easily make for a televisual experience. But this is to overlook the potential for human complexity just beneath the game's surface. I tuned in just as our commentator Richard Bacon was maintaining that Andy Lowe – one of three players competing for the £50 jackpot – was 'using the game to forget his recent troubles. He's split from his girlfriend and didn't want to talk about it.'

Bacon, however, had no such qualms. As Andy stepped up to bowl, he whispered: 'Let's hope thoughts of his girlfriend don't enter his mind.' A few minutes later, he returned to the theme. 'She may have been an aerobics instructor but there's no need to be disheartened.'

Andy, disheartened or not, held out and took the cash. 'Says he's going to spend it on a meal,' said Bacon. 'Sadly, that's going to have to be on his own.'

There is, in the end, no substitute for research.

FOOTBALL DOES ITS OWN THING

12 MAY 1997

OVER the last ten days, no one has fought harder to secure the Premiership title than Sky Sports. They cut up the final parts of the fixture list like a jigsaw and then went about resorting the pieces. They travelled to Leicester in the morning;

they travelled to Liverpool in the evening; they went to Manchester a couple of days later. And still the results would not come and the trophy eluded them.

Until, that is, the games at West Ham and Wimbledon. And so the championship was decided, not in the twin-screen, simulcast drama of recent years, but mundanely, while Manchester United and their manager were at home with their feet up/out with a Spice Girl (delete as applicable).*

And were we upset when the pot failed to boil? I have to confess to taking a small pleasure in it, even as the hours of inconclusive viewing racked up. At a time when the gap between football and television has narrowed to the point of invisibility, this refusal to rise to the occasion felt hearteningly like a small victory for the independent life of the game, coming to its own conclusions in its own time, resisting the tidy narrative frame which television wants to force down upon it.

Beyond the Premiership, other issues moved more swiftly to conclusion. 'It's more than a football match: it's an occasion, it's a meeting of cultures, it's a war,' said Sky's Rob Palmer. No, not Cardiff v. Northampton in the Third Division play-offs, but Barcelona v. Real Madrid in the Spanish League, a rich treat for which anticipation was high. 'The Bernabeu Stadium,' breathed Palmer in his opening remarks. 'Most imposing.' Indeed it is. And so is the Nou Camp in Barcelona, where we actually were.

Of course, there are cold-hearted observers who will tell you that the commentators are not really anywhere near

* In a small ceremony in Dublin, the Manchester United midfielder David Beckham married Victoria Adams, a singer with a pop group called the Spice Girls. They have lived quietly together ever since.

these European games: they are in a cosy studio somewhere closer to home, watching them on telly. Away with such cynicism. How could Rob's comments through the ninety minutes have been so colourful and informed if he had not been right at the heart of the action where, as he informed us, '115 fans are on the edge of their seats'?

This may be the first time in the history of Sky Sports that the viewer has been required to multiply by a thousand to get an accurate sense of scale, rather than divide by a hundred.

The realm of the truly ticketless is, of course, Channel 5, our newest terrestrial, yet their sports magazine programme, *Turnstyle*, is a gutsy little performer, even though it has almost no sport to call its own and even though it cannot spell 'turnstile'. Channel 5 will not have exclusive access to a major sports event until England visit Poland in the World Cup qualifiers later this month. Until then, their flagship sports programme must operate in the margins. But it does so with all the energy and resourcefulness of a swot annotating a library book.

Typically, there was a report on how awful it was for Manchester City fans that Manchester United had won the title again. And in the studio to discuss relegation battles was David Busst, the Coventry player who suffered that horrific leg injury last season.

One fears the programme's good work is always going to be threatened with obscurity by the sheer glamour of the other available options. Take, for instance, the moment when *Turnstyle* partially coincided with ITV's live coverage of the qualifying session for the Monaco Grand Prix. For a while there, the viewer was presented with a stark choice: it was Monte Carlo or Busst.

Tag Heuer timings reveal that I hesitated 0.142 seconds

before switching over, a nippy performance, but one which did not even put me halfway up the grid when the national average was worked out. That is not intended to reflect unkindly on *Turnstyle* or on Busst, who is a brave man. But, quite simply, how often does television grant you the opportunity to watch Jim Rosenthal bobbing up and down?

For out in Monaco, ITV were playing it cool on a hired yacht in the harbour. The sun shone, the hotels and casinos behind them gently rose and fell, the leisurewear was crisply ironed, and only Rosenthal's verdict – 'It's a bit of all right, isn't it?' – let the side down, like someone entering one of Monte Carlo's most salubrious cocktail bars and asking for a pickled onion.

On dry land, watching Michael Schumacher, Martin Brundle came over all Harry Enfield: 'You don't want to be going sideways, you want to be going forwards.' Fair comment, though Schumacher might have found it a bit rich, coming from someone who, only last year while still competing as a driver, managed to flip his car and go upside down.*

Qualifying has its moments of dead air and downtime. 'As we watch Nakano trying to improve on twenty-first place . . .' said Murray Walker at one point, and it was beyond even his capacity for unnecessary excitement to make

* On the opening lap of the opening race of the 1996 season, Martin Brundle was involved in a collision which caused his vehicle to turn over and fly through the air. Formula One cars aren't really designed for flight and pretty much all that was left of the car after it landed was a seat and a seatbelt – out of which Brundle casually stepped before sprinting back to the pits to rejoin the race in the spare car. The incident did his television career no harm; he was given his own series on near-death experiences.

that sentence ring with delight. But with Monte Carlo for a backdrop, you notice them less than anywhere.

For the opening moments of the programme, Rosenthal was too overawed even to get a sentence out. 'Glamour,' he said. 'Money. Success. Colour. Speed.' This could have gone on and on ('Cars. Pits. Spanners. Tyres . . .') but finally he turned a corner and found a verb. 'Welcome to the millionaires' playground of Monaco!'

Inadvertently, Rosenthal may have happened here on a radical new style for sports presentation, one with potentially time-saving wider applications: 'Hello. Football. Leeds. Goalless. Goodbye.'

ENTER CHANNEL 5; EXIT VIEWERS

2 JUNE 1997

England's World Cup qualifier in Poland was Channel 5's first major sports purchase. I think we should organize a national whip-round right now to ensure that we can outbid them if they ever come anywhere near another.

Has coverage of a football international ever been this bad? For a while one could at least marvel at its crassness, but eventually even the appeal of that wore off. It was tawdry television; crude, trivial and distorting. It formed also an utterly depressing essay on the state the mad market in sports broadcasting rights has reached.

Never, even in these days of Sky Sports, has a sporting event been so nakedly subjugated to the ambition of a television channel. Without a regular presentation team of its own, Channel 5 adopted the Bryan Robson managerial approach at Middlesbrough: buy up some old, far-flung talents and just pray they muck along. It worked for Channel 5 almost as well as it has worked for trophy-free Middlesbrough.

I felt sorry for Brough Scott – an intelligent and informed man adrift here in a sea of ego and incompetence. 'Broff', as Gail McKenna referred to him, was charged with anchoring this shambles. But how do you anchor a gas leak?

The set was a nightmare in which the *Top of the Pops* studio has opened for business as a themed sports bar, but there has been no publicity, so only the owner's friends are in. Presenters circled the tables, offering a big hello to, for instance, some bloke from *Family Affairs*, the Channel 5 soap. It seems to me that when a sports programme reaches the point where it is canvassing for an opinion someone who 'used to be Scorpio in *Gladiators*' (used to be) then it is no longer merely scraping the bottom of the barrel; it is lying on it, flat on its back with its tongue hanging out. In another corner sat Dominick Diamond, in his usual role as professional irritant. Personally, I've always preferred his brother, Neil, but that's just a question of taste. Of more consequence was Diamond's preparedness to mislead us about the status of the match we were about to see. 'If England lose,' he told us, 'they'll be taking holidays in Bognor next summer rather than France.'

Let's leave aside the foolhardy ambition of attempting a Bognor gag in 1997, when the life was widely agreed to have gone out of the last of them in about 1874. The fact is, the result on Saturday night – win, lose, or draw – was set to have no absolute consequences for England's appearance, or otherwise, in the World Cup finals in 1998, an issue which will be settled elsewhere. But, hey, why not iron the story out a little and make it easier to wear? And what's a little dull reality between friends when you're hyping?

Elsewhere in the build-up, Phil Thompson, apparently oblivious to the last decade in history, was referring to 'the eastern bloc'; Brough Scott was anticipating the potential effect on the players of '70,000 Poles baying for your blood' – this just moments after Jonathan Pearce had estimated the crowd at 32,000; and Jeremy Nicholas was interviewing Tom Watt, who used to be in *EastEnders*, and someone dressed as a moose.

What grated hardest was the notion, doubtless bandied around in production meetings, that this patronizing carnival of mindlessness was pitched at the level of the fan. In an ideal world, fans across the nation would now rise up as one and sue for libel. When Gail McKenna says, several hours before kick-off, 'It's going to be a great match,' one does not sense the enthusiasm of the fanatic; one senses only money and advertisers and viewing figures. There is no advance guarantee that any football match is going to be great. Football fans know this. Only desperate people in television pretend that it is not so.

It should have been a relief to get out to Poland for the game, but the commentator Jonathan Pearce got in the way. Here was an experiment which failed. Pearce had done his homework: we know this because he had brought it with him and kept reading bits of it out.

But stats alone do not a Motson make. Relentlessly puffing the players, referring to Gascoigne as 'Gazza' and Ince as 'the Guv'nor', Pearce only made you long for authority, objectivity and a clear-eyed view. Pearce on the radio can be urgent and funny. But television is not an urgent medium.

One had hoped to mark the arrival of a new voice in televised football commentary, but one had overlooked the degree to which Pearce would play the part of a pawn in the bigger broadcasting game. 'Live on Five!' he kept saying, like a baby patting a mobile. Shortly after Alan Shearer struck for England, he went further: 'Channel 5 live – the channel that brings you England goals.' Of all the things which sucked that night, that sentence sucked hardest.

NOEL ENTERS LE MANS FOR FREE

16 JUNE 1996

Noel Edmonds first had the idea of taking a team to race in the fabled 24-hour event at Le Mans as he strolled along the pit-lane there last year with his pal Jeremy Clarkson. And in one of those startling coincidences which make television the revelatory medium it is, a camera and sound-crew just happened to be on hand to record the thought as it hatched. 'Well, you'd better go and buy a Porsche, then,' said Clarkson.

These extraordinary scenes opened *Noel's Le Mans Dream* (BBC1), a two-part documentary following Noel as he attempted to turn his vision into a reality and, simultaneously, into a television programme. 'This is not the most stupid idea I've had,' said the man who gave us Crinkley Bottom, the Gunge Tank and Mr Blobby, and a scalded nation nodded slowly in agreement.

(Incidentally, for devotees of *Noel's House Party* with a cable or satellite hook-up, I heartily recommend the syndicated German version. It's got all the excitement of the original, plus that extra little twist of humour which German television does so well.)

Anyway, someone told Noel early on that a car for Le Mans would cost him $1 million, and he'd need two of them.

'It's an astonishing amount of money,' said Noel, and you had to hand it to the man for doing his best to make that line ring with conviction. As one of British television's highest-paid performers, a high-profile helicopter-owner and the holder of the world rights in Mr Blobby, Noel can surely be no stranger to the idea of loose change in seven figures.

Nevertheless, Noel's wife was pictured out riding across some of the many square miles of Devon which the Edmonds own, and she then dismounted to give her views on her husband's latest scheme. And despite everything, you could understand that anxious expression she wore: if this project got out of hand financially speaking, she was going to be down to her last herd of horses.

As it turned out, we could all breathe again, along with Noel's bank manager, because a useful meeting at Lotus acquainted Noel with the method of acquiring cars without writing cheques. It's called 'sponsorship' and my tip would be – on this briefest of exposures to the concept – that it could well be an idea which catches on.

In the end, the cars and engines came from another of Noel's pals in America and the mechanics to bolt them together were supplied by David Price, who happened to have a ready-made team knocking about. 'It's a two-valve, push-rod, aluminium, six-litre Ford V8,' said Price, who was, I think, talking about the car's engine, rather than Noel's chequebook.

The idea that Noel might drive one of the cars hit a wall of tyres early on. Noel, of course, has some form as a racing driver. But that was back in the 1970s and here, when he emerged from the cockpit after a couple of test laps and collapsed, enervated, on to the tarmac, it was fairly clear that some of the old touch had deserted him. So two younger drivers were imported instead.

I have to confess to experiencing a slight confusion from this point as to what Noel's role now was. If he wasn't stumping up the money and he wasn't driving and he wasn't managing the team . . . well, what exactly was he doing? Maybe this will be cleared up in the concluding episode.

But already, even at this halfway stage, the programme has formed a powerful reminder of the democratic spirit which continues at that famous 24-hour event – a spirit unique to motor sport. Formula One, Noel pointed out with a slight sniff, was 'a closed shop'; whereas, by contrast, on the level playing field of Le Mans, any old multimillionaire with his own television show can scrape a team together and be given a fighting chance. Fair brings a tear to your eye, doesn't it?

FOOTBALL: THE INSIDE STORY

23 JUNE 1997

Channel 4 sentenced us to a complete evening of programmes about prison – one of that channel's reliably ambitious pitches for ratings and a project which lent a whole new dimension to the idea of being in for the night. A documentary called *Rules of the Game* was worth doing some time for. It took us to Barlinnie Prison in Glasgow, where the prisoners were preparing for their annual football match with the prison officers. The prisoners' XI included an armed robber, a drug dealer and at least two people convicted of wounding with a knife: one of those rare squads, then, with more – or at least worse – criminal records than Arsenal. 'It won't be a friendly,' one of the wardens informed us.

The continuity announcer gave notice before the programme started of 'strong and explicit language and fierce competition', the first time, I think, that a television channel has thought to warn sensitive viewers of imminent competitiveness. As a spokesperson for any viewers' watchdog would certainly tell you, the argument that sport, like nudity, is likely to cause offence or distress has been at best infrequently addressed. Maybe now, at last, it will be: the makers of *Ski Sunday*, take note.

Barlinnie's big fixture bred weeks of anticipation and an entire textbook of niggly banter between screws and lags: 'I've seen six-month sentences move faster than you,' and so forth. The prisoners reckoned they had fitness on their side and also enthusiasm. 'What would I do without football?' one of them pondered. 'I would invent it.'

That said, the prison-issue grey slacks and pink shirts (someone's idea of a joke, surely, to dress Glasgow's hardest offenders in pastel) would have to count as one of the less ritzy team suits worn by a football club to a big occasion. Still, they were more tasteful than Liverpool's for the 1995–96 FA Cup final.

In the event, the match was not beautiful – but then, eagerly awaited, showpiece games so rarely are. The pitch didn't help. I thought I caught a hint of grass in one of the corners, but I could be wrong. The rest was impacted sand.

We were in one of the last football stadiums in Britain in which a persuasive argument can still be made for perimeter fencing. It was there to contain the players, of course, rather than the crowd which, in any case, did not require much in the way of containing: it was made up entirely of the substitutes and coaches, though supplemented overhead by a small collection of prisoners in balaclavas, staging a rooftop protest. It was not made entirely clear what this protest related to, but given the prison's dominant concern, as we understood it from this programme, it was probably over team selection.

Doubtless the protesters were as sick as anyone to see the staff stick three away: another victory for the system. The prisoners were guilty of what Alan Hansen would call 'sloppy defending'. Or rather, 'slop-out defending'. They seemed surprisingly slow on the breakaway, too. But then what could they do? They were up against wardens who, inevitably, were thoroughly adept at locking up the game.

Understandably, in the circumstances, the referee – brought in from outside – was more twitchy than one of FIFA's finest. This was not a game one would have wished to lose control of – which perhaps better explains the three sendings-off than any theory involving outright malice. In fact, at the end, as prisoner and officer shook hands and embraced, the programme took on a strangely old-fashioned glow and, despite those troubling warnings, appeared to have become a tribute to football's ability to contain and suspend more hostilities than it induces.

In a different kind of film, the wardens would have been strangely uninquisitive about the presence of a wooden horse in the prisoners' penalty area and about the prisoners' habit of retiring to the touchline during breaks in play and shaking displaced earth from the legs of their shorts. But this was no Stalag. This was Barlinnie; they were too concerned with football to be thinking about flight. Tunnel out? You must be kidding. Not with twenty minutes to go and everything to play for.

Last week, we left Noel Edmonds in a garage at Le Mans, chewing on his nails and wondering if the cars in his team would make it through qualifying for the 24-hour race. And for many of us, the ensuing days have passed more agonizingly than a six-month sentence at Barlinnie.

Hallelujah, they made it. And let's face it, the second part of *Noel's Le Mans Dream* would have been in the market for padding if they hadn't. After it, some of the mysteries raised in Part One were still hanging in the air: for instance, what the television chef Gary Rhodes was contributing to the team effort by hanging around in the background. But Noel's own role was finally clear: the team director gave him a job as a petrol-pump attendant.

Neither Panos car completed the race but Noel's pal Jeremy Clarkson popped up to put in perspective what it was, exactly, Noel had pulled off. 'Astonishing,' he said. 'It's like saying: "I know, let's walk to the sun."'

Over a shot of Noel and his wife at home, leafing through Noel's Le Mans scrapbooks together, as they doubtless do on many a long winter's evening, Noel said: 'I've followed the Le Mans story since the Sixties and now can't believe that I'm part of it.' Neither can we, Noel, neither can we.

TYSON BITES OFF MORE THAN HE CAN CHEW

30 JUNE 1997

'We wanted to see Tyson as a hungry fighter again,' said Sky Sport's Ian Darke, speaking to us from Las Vegas in the early hours of Sunday morning, 'but not like that.'

Perhaps not. Tyson had just brought the evening to a premature close by snacking on the ears of Evander Holyfield. The rules of boxing are quite clear on this: fighters are not allowed to eat each other. Not even featherweights, who often look like a decent meal wouldn't go amiss.

Naturally, when a boxer ignores this rule, amazing scenes are apt to break out – though only for people with satellite or cable and £14.95 in pay-per-view fees to spare. They are, of course, the kinds of scenes which appal one to the marrow. Which, for £14.95, strikes me as a total bargain.

On Sunday, the ring immediately filled with uniformed security guards, throwing themselves recklessly in the way of a flailing Tyson, who was at this point trying to get over to Holyfield's corner in order, presumably, to finish what he started.

The quantity of people who had suddenly materialized in the ring, and the fact that everyone seemed to be jostling at least one other person, made developments over the next few minutes a little hard to follow. But it was pretty clear that the prospects for finding that missing piece of the defending champion's right ear were now fairly remote.

We next saw Holyfield leave the ring and enjoy an unencumbered retreat through the arena and into the wings. For someone who had recently been cannibalized, he retained a remarkable air of dignity. Unlike Tyson, who seemed to be having to crawl out under the combined weight of half the Las Vegas police force, his own posse and perhaps up to twenty-five other people involved in fights of their own.

One of these side-brawls seemed to claim our unfortunate cameraman, who was doing a brave job of tracking this carnival until brought down well short of the exit – but not before clinching one of the night's most memorable images: a shot of his own legs, lying in a shower of popcorn.

We then cut back to the throng in the ring where Mills Lane, the referee, was telling an interviewer that one bite was probably, in all honesty, enough, but that he absolutely drew the line at a second. If he ever decides to turn his back on the fight game, Mills could walk straight into a job advertising Fun-Size Milky Ways.

Then it was out to the corridor where Holyfield – still preternaturally calm and gracious – confirmed that his plastic surgeon was keen to operate that night, said that he would enjoy a small period of reflection before considering a rematch, and added that he simply wanted to praise the Lord that his injury wasn't any worse than it was. What a guy.

Then back into the ring we went, for further developments in the Security Guards v. Aggrieved Members of the Public Free-For-All (rules on biting and headbutting yet to be set in stone); and then out into the corridor we came again, but this time to meet Tyson's manager, who was as mad as hell. He claimed that a Holyfield headbutt had opened up 'a three-inch cut' above his client's eye and he seemed to be saying that, in those circumstances, it stood to reason that you would want to try to bite someone's ear off, twice.

That was pretty much the promoter Don King's verdict, too, when he stepped up to the microphone – although Don could see how one might feel differently. In fact, in a classic of equivocation, which any budding politician would do well to study, Don made it clear that he felt there was no excuse for that kind of behaviour while at the same time smoothly excusing it. You would never have known that millions of dollars with Don's name on them might rest on a rematch.

When Tyson himself came out of the dressing room, perhaps as a result of some particularly ingenious cosmetic surgery, the cut above the eye seemed to have shrunk by about two-thirds. But that didn't mean he was any less angry and confused. 'I'm ready to fight him right now,' said Iron Mike, bristling terrifyingly and clearly not committed as yet to a PR makeover.

Sky, whose capacity for both having and eating cake is unrivalled in sports broadcasting, had called the event Judgement Night 2, which seemed to be stretching the Biblical analogy. Whatever next: Four Further Horsemen of the Apocalypse?

Everyone in the studio agreed that the original Judgement Night – Tyson v. Holyfield, back in November 1996 – had been a classic. Barry McGuigan called it 'the biggest fight I have ever remembered in my entire life'. This kept open the possibility that there were some pretty enormous ones which McGuigan had forgotten, but it was hardly faint praise, even so.

It was generally agreed, though, both in Las Vegas and in the studio back in London, that the second fight had, as an example of sporting brilliance, fallen short of the calibre of the first. Nevertheless, rallying slightly, Darke managed to conclude that it was 'a fight that will go down in history – in its own way'.

Don's own title, for the American market, was The Sound and the Fury. Snappy, but with a familiar ring to it. Rumours that he wishes to call the re-match Tyson v. Holyfield: the Second Course, or even Tyson v. Holyfield: This Time They're Staying for Coffee, could not be confirmed.

BIKE RIDE TO THE MOON

7 JULY 1997

The opening stages of the Tour de France had a little competition for our enthusiasm and amazement this weekend, from an event in the far reaches of space. Given that the United States could land a probe on Mars, just how impressed were we meant to be at the prospect of a bunch of blokes taking three weeks to get from Rouen to Paris by bike?

Nevertheless, Channel 4 were out there as usual, ready to play Ground Control and assemble the first of their nightly half-hour bulletins on the state of the mission. And good for them. Mars may have its fascination, but so, too, does France, where the landscape is altogether more interesting, the climate a touch more hospitable and the food a definite improvement.

Our location for lift-off was the city centre in Rouen where the Prologue Time Trial took place to establish the race order for the first leg. This business had apparently been going on all day but, through a piece of interdepartmental planning of which NASA would have been proud, we arrived bang on time to catch the British interest, Chris Boardman, as he levered himself out of the starter's hut and, without so much as a hand signal, set off on his 8.5-minute sprint.

It was clear immediately, even to those of us who would claim no expertise as professional cyclists, that Boardman was about to log a time to be reckoned with. After all, he was successfully holding in his wake two motorbikes, dangerously overloaded with cameramen, a police car with flashing lights and several other bicycles attached to the roof of a bright red Fiat.

But what, exactly, was he riding? A black, tubular construction, with a pair of garden shears where the handlebars ought to have been, it looked like a spare prop from Batman and Robin. It also condemned Boardman to a riding position in which his backside was at least four feet above the level of his head. Our commentator, Phil Liggett, who also excitedly alerted us to the bike's electric gear-shift, gave us an intelligent paraphrase of the ergonomic benefits accruing to Boardman from riding with his nose just above the front mudguard. It gave him 'great penetration from the air', apparently, which sounded a lot more enjoyable than it looked.

That Boardman's machine actually qualified as a bicycle we only had Liggett's word for. That and the fact that the judges had not moved to disqualify it in advance, which, we were told, had happened to one of the other riders. Frustratingly, we were not given the reasons for the ban. In a world in which electric gear-shifts get the nod it was hard to imagine what, exactly, would tip a bike over the limits. Perhaps the jet engines had infringed Rouen's regulations on noise pollution.

Anyway, Boardman stormed through to take the yellow jersey despite a late challenge from the police car, which seemed to be finishing strongly but, sadly, had to brake sharply to avoid the various officials and spectators in the road beyond the finish line. In a touching closing ceremony, our man waved aloft a gold trophy in the shape of a Coca-Cola bottle; and just in case those of us at home weren't getting the sponsor's message loudly enough, an aide hustled a red plastic Coca-Cola bottle into his other hand so that he could wave that, too.

This was, of course, just the beginning and, as Virginia Wade said, referring to Jana Novotna's frustrated comeback efforts during the third set of the women's final at Wimbledon recently, there is 'still a long mountain to climb'. Still, if Virginia's grasp of the geographical features had become – understandably, after a hectic fortnight at the Championships – a little slippery, her understanding of the broadcasting technology held firm. 'How quickly Hingis scoops the ball off the court,' she said. 'It doesn't look quite as quick, obviously, in slow motion.'

Those shots of Mars, incidentally, will have looked instantly familiar to viewers of *Turnstyle*, Channel 5's boldly sport-free sports magazine programme where the studio set has a similar thematic feel: cold, reddish and disappointingly bereft of intelligent life.

Always an interesting study in pointlessness, on Saturday morning *Turnstyle* promised to keep us up to date with the Test score – which may have deterred some people from turning to BBC2, where the match was unfolding live – and offered an extended feature on the Wimbledon finals without being able to show us any tennis.

'Now, on the line is Roger Taylor,' said the host Dominick Diamond. There followed a long silence. A sobering moment, this, for civilization. The United States might be able to get to the red planet, but Channel 5 can't reach Roger Taylor by phone in south-west London.

LENNOX LEWIS GETS A BIG HUG

14 JULY 1997

Since the Mike Tyson affair ('pay-per-chew' as one American reporter definitively described it), those directly and indirectly involved in the business of brain concussion have found themselves somewhat on the defensive about their sport. Many would have been hoping the heavyweight title bout between Lennox Lewis and Henry Akinwande was going to come good and speak on their behalf.

And what happened? Another disqualification, another stroppy Nevada crowd chucking drinks around in disapproval, and further controversy, albeit of a quite different kind. For this was a fight in which not only did no one get bitten, but neither did anyone get hit.

Sky Sports had the action – or rather, the lack of it. At some point between arranging the fight and the bell going, Akinwande had decided that his best route lay in putting his arms round Lewis and holding him close so that no one would get hurt. Several times, the referee Mills Lane (the same official who so resourcefully improvised the 'two bites and you're off' rule in the Tyson match) warned Akinwande and his trainer against this. But still Akinwande clung on until, after four whole rounds of clumsy smooching, Lane, described by Glenn McCrory as 'a very convicted referee' (Glenn omitted to say what the exact offences were) called it off.

McCrory took a firm moral line on this: 'He wasn't prepared to get beaten up!' he complained. Beside him, a muted Ian Darke could only conclude that it was 'another night when boxing did itself no favours'.

But not for the want of trying, surely. Seen from an armchair, Akinwande seemed to be involved in a one-man mission to redeem boxing, post-Tyson, by bringing it more into line with say, country dancing, or with one of those obscure but hallowed medieval games practised in small English towns on August Bank Holidays in which two men smeared in locally-made butter attempt to push each other into a rosemary bush. Maybe the man deserves more praise than he has received.

Instead, all the sympathy has gone to Lennox Lewis. Lennox was wearing those huge, white, Daz commercial shorts which served him so effectively in his battle not long ago with Oliver McCall. That was the occasion when McCall, in some terrible psychic distress, burst into tears almost before any blows had been exchanged, causing the fight to be stopped, and Lewis maintained that his shorts, functioning in some unexplained way as symbols of purity, had put the guy off.

So naturally, one was excited to hear what Lewis would make of Akinwande's supposed failure of will. Would he deem the shorts to have worked their magic once again, or would he maintain that the lacing on his boots had immediately identified him as an angel of vengeance?

Even though Lewis gamely managed a couple of sentences interpreting Akinwande's flakiness as a tribute to his own awesome power, you could tell his heart wasn't really in it. He wore the unhappy expression of a man who had not specifically come into the fight game to have people blub all over him or ride around all evening holding on to his shoulder blades, and his deflated comment may well go down in history as one of the most unlikely ever to fall from the lips of a champion pugilist. He said: 'Either a guy starts crying, or a guy starts hugging me up all night. What can you do?' What indeed, apart from give up on boxing.*

Back in Britain for the Grand Prix (ITV), the commentator Murray Walker excitedly reported a sighting of the Schumacher brothers in a curry house in Daventry – 'which,' Murray added, 'with all due respect to the people who live there, is not generally regarded as the centre of the universe.' What struck one here was the boyish assumption (the more touching for coming from a man in his mid-seventies) that you would only expect to see racing drivers at the universe's heart.

Less impressed, Martin Brundle promptly offered his

* Lewis persisted. But he still had two more major farces to get through before he was heavyweight champion. See pages 272 and 303.

opinion that the Schumachers would still be arguing over the bill, Michael in particular being, apparently, tricky about such things – 'First out of the taxi, last to the bar,' according to Brundle. Walker's wide-eyed keenness, Brundle's narrow-eyed shrewdness: truly they are sports broadcasting's good cop/bad cop routine.

ALLISS WEATHERS INTEMPERATE FANS

21 JULY 1997

Peter Alliss has many, frequently noted virtues as a commentator on golf, but it became apparent over the weekend that a supplementary role is unlikely ever to open for him as a weather man. 'There was a stiff breeze here on Thursday,' he told us at the weekend, speaking to us from Royal Troon. 'But today it's . . . oooh.'

Not specific enough, really, for Michael Fish. ('The outlook, then, for Tuesday and Wednesday: oooh.') Then again, in the context, 'oooh' seemed richly descriptive. Coming from Alliss, it often does. As, for instance, when Fred Couples acted a little dangerously on the green: 'Oh, Fre . . . oooh, he got away with it.' Or when Ernie Els bunkered at the fifth: 'Oooh, Ernie.'

Any television commentator will tell you that the skill of their job lies in letting the pictures speak for themselves sometimes. But few pursue this art as dangerously far as Alliss. His speciality is the sentence which lacks many of the grammatical parts for which sentences are famous. As when a ball was seen rolling into the rough. 'And that could be . . . well, I don't know.' And when the camera caught Tiger Woods at a rather unfortunate moment, inspecting his right arm-pit through the neck of his shirt, Alliss simply said: 'Oops. Well, I . . .' And he left it at that.

You may or may not be familiar with the work of the early 1980s pop combo and flash-in-the-pan teen sensation, Kajagoogoo, who were all coifed like parrots and had a hit with a song called 'Ooh To Be Ah'. I think Alliss may have written it.

But this isn't to suggest that Alliss never gets down to the nitty-gritty. As Couples came up the fairway, our commentator saw fit to draw our attention to 'his jaunty walk and his well-fitting trousers'. The image will stay with those who witnessed it for a long time to come.

You have to credit Alliss for sounding as relaxed as he does. He has to contend not only with the slew of images, tossed randomly in front of him from anywhere on the course's many acres, but also with the noises picked up by seemingly hundreds of outdoor microphones positioned around the place. For one ear-punishingly shrill moment, three Scottish seagulls seemed to have chosen one of these as the location for a fight to the death. Hard, surely, to remain at ease in these circumstances.

Still, the rewards for Alliss's labours include the gratitude of his public. 'You dah man!' people bellow as he makes his way towards the commentary box. Unless that's Tiger Woods they're talking about.

At one point, the camera abruptly found a line of five people in the crowd. They had each stuck a life-size photo of Alliss's grinning head on a stick and were holding these in front of their own faces, as if they were guests at some kind of eighteenth-century ball sponsored by *Golf Digest*. 'Now, now,' said Alliss quietly. 'What's this, you naughty lads?' One brief criticism of the appearance of his own teeth

('Cost me thousands, those choppers. They don't look so good there!') and he was silent again.

Meanwhile, the voyage of the Tour de France from Rouen to Paris has reached the Alps. I don't know what kind of map the person planning this trip is using, but surely there has to be a more direct route. Anyway, Channel 4 are still clinging on for dear life and their nightly bulletins from the roadside continue to offer more colour, action and downright weirdness than one has any right to expect from a half-hour sports broadcast.

The reporter Paul Sherwin, who was crouched in some kind of outside broadcast caravan, briefed us with the tactical low-down on hill-climbing, just in case any of us were thinking of trying it at home. One came out of this lecture clear that the inside line on the corners is often the best bet. But what Sherwin didn't offer any tips on was how to cope with people in fancy dress. Because, while stance and pedal-position are obviously important, the key to a successful hill-climb is surely not minding when the cast of a pantomime turns out to crowd your path.

It cannot be easy maintaining your sense of the seriousness and dignity of your sport while someone dressed as a cow is running alongside you. Yet, out there on the Tour, this is by no means an unlikely outcome. People in daft outfits are everywhere. What's more, with a devotion to self-publicity of which even the horse-racing tipster John McCririck would be in awe, the same ones keep cropping up during every stage.

Thus, each night, we see the riders routinely menaced by an elderly man with a white beard, wearing a red jumpsuit (Peter Alliss, one feels, would have something to say) and touting a trident. This leads to unlikely moments of resignation in the commentary. 'There's the devil keeping pace with Cedric,' someone said, with a slightly bored tone.

'Here's our Indian friend,' came the call later, as someone with an enormous plume of chief's feathers danced out of a side road and set off on foot after the leader. 'Pantani doesn't really want him that close,' said the commentator. Indeed. Pantani had just indicated as much by elbowing the Indian in the kidneys. Where else could one turn for this kind of entertainment, outside American wrestling on Sky Sports?*

COLEMAN SWALLOWS FROG

4 AUGUST 1997

The BBC were out in Athens for the World Athletics Championships – and a good job too, because very few other people seemed to have turned up. Des Lynam was in the studio with David Moorcroft and Linford Christie and the scene through the window behind them (a serene, sunlit vista of empty white plastic) revealed that they constituted, by a rough calculation, a quarter of the crowd. Still, as people kept pointing out, the crowd might have been sparse, but at least they were keen. (Funnily enough, that's always the way with sparse crowds at televised events. The thought

* There's a widely held theory that the people who unhelpfully run alongside the cyclists in the Tour de France are the same people who, in the winter, menace downhill skiers by shaking cowbells in their ears and shouting 'oi-oi-oi-oi'. When the weather warms up, they come down from the mountains. When it gets cold again, they go back.

that a crowd might be both sparse and indifferent is not one that television is prepared to entertain.)

And none keener than David Coleman. During the heats for the men's 100 metres, Donovan Bailey seemed to pull up early with a hamstring problem, but not before Coleman, up in the commentary box, had seemed to pull up with a frog problem.

As Bailey clocked a time under ten seconds, Coleman shouted, 'Nine eight eight is unbelievable.' Or that's what he was revealed to have shouted after a sophisticated, FBI-endorsed voice-decoder had been run over the tapes which, until that moment, seemed only to contain the obscure information, 'Nigh aid aid iz unburgle.' Even by Coleman's unimpeachable standards of excitability, peaking as early as round two would have to stand as a PB.

PB, by the way, was the phrase everyone was using – Des, David, Linford, everyone. It stands for 'personal best' – hence the expression 'I'm just hoping to get out there and run a PB' – though everyone was using it so easily, no one had to stop and explain that.

An edition of *In the Chair* gave the psychiatrist Oliver James twenty-five minutes to grill some explanations out of George Graham – an arresting prospect, though the programme turned out merely to be a PB for Graham's PR. James sought to connect the Leeds manager with what he claimed was a long line of 'outstanding achievers' who had lost their fathers before the age of fourteen, including the current president of the United States. This was lofty company indeed. Peace in the Middle East and a goalless draw at Middlesbrough – one struggle.

James is unique to television in being the only person prepared to ask someone like George Graham the question:

'When did you come into puberty?' He is also unique in believing this might be a worthwhile question to put to him if you only had twenty-five minutes of the manager's time. James was also brave enough (or shameless enough, depending on how you see it) to encourage Graham to recall his first sexual experience – an opportunity which Graham politely declined.

Graham also succesfully stalled James on the issue of whether he slept with football groupies in the sixties, a line of questioning which might not have dissuaded you from the suspicion that what you were witnessing was basic, tabloid prurience under a very thin academic veneer.

'It's interesting that you can't remember,' said James at one point, as Graham failed to retrieve a memory from his childhood. Interesting if you can, interesting if you can't: a theory if you speak and a theory if you don't. It's a nice little earner, psychiatry, and a wonder more of us don't go into business with it.

For all James's firmness of voice and his willingness to knock briskly at the bedroom door, it was revealing that when we got to the nub – Graham's uncharacteristically naive behaviour in the matter of a £285,000 'unsolicited gift' from a player's agent, which led to his sacking by Arsenal – our analyst was more compliant than Terry Wogan in his chat-show heyday. With what sounded like embarrassed haste, James asked Graham to 'summarize, as briefly as you can' his version of that pivotal event – when all logic, surely, demanded that he go into it at some length.

This was the event, after all, which earned Graham not just his P45 but also such notoriety that he would figure in the plans for a series like *In the Chair.* But, thus released, Graham merely ran through his usual lines (silly him, thought it was a present, didn't think Arsenal should have got rid of him) while James let him run. Still, we don't want to get into anything too messy, do we? *Off the Hook* would have been a better title for this programme.

If you wanted to see minds genuinely on the rack, you had to turn to Sky Sports and the World Matchplay Championship darts tournament, snatched by Phil 'The Power' Taylor. 'It's the nearest thing to public execution this side of Saudi Arabia,' bawled our commentator Sid Waddell.

Saturday night's scenes were jubilant, as you would expect given the combination of Sky Sports and several hundred families on holiday in Blackpool. ('The family that darts together shares its hearts together,' Sid reckoned.) When Taylor flung the winning arrow, a dustbin full of glitter exploded beside the stage, filling the screen so thickly that you wondered briefly whether the aerial might have dropped out of the back. 'Don't adjust your sets, folks,' said Waddell reassuringly. 'That's Blackpool dazzle greeting the greatest darts player of all time.'

A week with Sid gave us, among other joys, a phrase to set alongside PB in our personal lexicons of sporting jargon: namely, 'the feed-hand', used to describe the hand which holds the darts and 'feeds' them to the throwing hand. Let no one say darts isn't a physically complex sport. Like athletics, really, only it draws a bigger crowd.

CILLA CHUCKS PHIL DE GLANVILLE

25 AUGUST 1997

Life, as the theme song from Cilla Black's *Surprise, Surprise* (ITV) usefully points out, is 'full of surprises'. How true that is. For example, could you have foreseen that Phil de Glanville, captain of the England rugby team, would pop up alongside Cilla in an edition of the show? If you hadn't read the television listings, that is; and if history hadn't informed you that England's rugby players know little embarrassment when it comes to publicizing themselves.

Not primarily renowned for its sports coverage, *Surprise, Surprise* is an adult version of *Jim'll Fix It* in which the fearlessly Liverpudlian Cilla – who wears less jewellery than Jimmy Savile but is otherwise no more introverted – gets to play dream-maker by, say, springing a long-lost relative on someone or rebuilding a couple's patio while they are out. It's an occasion for naked emotions, tears and profound gratitude, so long as you don't mind Cilla Black picking out your garden furniture for you.

The show had already taken a turn for the surreal (the ex-Manchester City player Mike Summerbee had awarded a turf-obsessed City fan a day out with the groundsman at Wembley Stadium) when Cilla, roaming in the audience, said, 'Budge up, chuck,' and sat down next to a rugby fan called James. 'What is it about rugby that you like?' Cilla asked. 'Er, anything,' replied James, perhaps not wishing to limit in any way the scope of the fantasy which Cilla was about to realize for him.

And lo, down the stairs came Phil de Glanville. 'Did you ever think in your wildest dreams you would meet the captain of the England team?' Cilla asked James, as Phil handed over a signed shirt. And James looked as if he didn't. Needless to say, it wasn't James's attentions which embarrassed Phil, but Cilla's. 'God, he's gorgeous,' said Cilla to the audience, briefly palpating Phil's upper arm. All credit to the captain. No one has smiled so bravely through a prime-time television appearance since . . . well, since members of the England rugby team appeared on *The Generation Game*.*

What happened next, though, was, in televisual terms, quite extraordinary. Just as Phil was preparing to leave, Cilla steadied his arm and, with a conspiratorial wink into the camera, said: 'Hang on a sec, chuck.' At which point the England coach, Jack Rowell, bounced down the stairs and informed Phil that he was resigning and that, though it was not yet clear who would succeed him, it was fairly likely that the new man would want to strip Phil of the captaincy and give it to Lawrence Dallaglio instead. 'Surprise, surprise, Phil!' said Jack and Cilla, together. (All right, I made that bit up.)

* In December 1995, under the supervision of the coach Les Cusworth and in the presence of a studio audience and Jim Davidson, Mike Catt, Dean Richards and others ran through a short training routine, involving ball-handling and punting. And then a couple called Baz and Jan had a go. Far from screwing things up, in the traditional *Generation Game* manner, Baz and Jan were deemed by some observes to be slightly more comfortable on the ball than the England squad members.

RYDER IS LONG-DISTANCE RUNNER

29 SEPTEMBER 1997

As we moved into the third day of the Ryder Cup golf, the fatigue was beginning to tell. Was that Justin Leonard out there on the course? Or was it Prince Andrew? They appear to have been separated at birth. And was that Prince Andrew in the Sky Sports studio? Or was it Justin Leonard?

How could exhaustion not get to one in the end? Sky had announced their coverage in advance as the 'most televised' golf event ever – sixty-five hours of it in total (including highlights and review packages) and thirty-one hours of live broadcasting over the weekend. Basically, if it moved at Valderrama, Sky chased after it in a van. When the club secretary pasted the order of play on to a sheet of paper, Sky's cameraman was looking over his shoulder and all but squeezing his Uhu tube.

The channel's patient attention to detail included dutiful attendance at the opening ceremony on Thursday afternoon. 'Very colourful. Very Spanish,' was Richard Keys' heartfelt verdict, and who were we to quibble?

Like all opening ceremonies, it offered those of us at home the irresistible drama which arises when sport meets international protocol and when sports commentators are forced to come over all hush-voiced and worldly and attempt to do a Dimbleby. There was much standing and cheering for the arrival of Spanish royalty. 'This is one popular family,' Ewen Murray informed us quietly from the commentary box. 'They live as normally as they can,' he added, without elaborating.

'Please be upstanding for the blessing,' said the master of ceremonies. At which point, with the sensitivity and timing which have brought it recognition among broadcasters around the world, Sky cut to a commercial break.

When we got back, the captains were all set to stand up and introduce their teams. Here was our first proper opportunity to assess what shape the sides were in, and what was immediately clear was that, under Tom Kite's careful stewardship, many of the American players seemed to have grown some additional vowels: 'Braad Faaxon . . . Tiiger Wooods.'

But it was nothing to worry about, for in the bracing charge of Seve Ballesteros, the European team were virtually unrecognizable as the men they used to be: 'Coleeng Mong Gomuree . . . Derren Clek . . . Neek Fuldo.'

At the other extreme, the BBC were left trying to compress the action into nightly, hour-long bulletins, which must, at times, have felt like trying to push a sofa inside a Mini. They must have been about the only people out there in Spain actually hoping the action would slow down or thin out; the shows were almost too dense to make sense of.

Absurdly brilliant chip shots seemed to be falling on to the greens like rain, and all Peter Alliss could do was put up his umbrella and try not to lose his breath. 'At my old age,' he said at one point, 'I don't know whether I can stand this excitement.' But this was disingenuous of him. Time and again this weekend, Alliss proved himself more than capable of keeping up with the pace, while still finding time to comment invaluably on things at the edge of the picture – for instance, the dribbling of a nearby police horse.

As Tiger Woods knocked one into the water, the camera cut to a familiar couple in the crowd, the woman wearing a grim expression. 'Doesn't amuse Mrs Bush,' Alliss said. 'Or the old man, for that matter.' I am not sure what *Debrett*'s has to say on the proper manner for addressing ex-leaders of the free world, but I'm fairly sure 'the old man' is not among the recommended formulations. It's a mark of the unique social position Alliss occupies that he can float free of such formalities and that nobody winces to hear him do so.

In many ways the most arresting pictures from the coverage on Sky came from the driving range, deserted in the morning dew but for the figure of one man. It was Neek Fuldo. There he stood, club in hand, patiently depleting a vast pyramid of golf balls in the manner in which someone with a chocolate problem might work their way through a mound of Ferrero Rochers. No fatigue for Neek. You glimpsed what it might take.

FANCY FOREIGNERS CLEAR NORWEGIAN SNOW

27 OCTOBER 1997

'Only the brave and trolls turn out on nights like this,' said the commentator Jonathon Pearce as Dennis Wise emerged from the dressing room in a short-sleeved shirt. We were in Norway with Channel 5, the temperature was descending to a parky minus five, the pitch looked like a tramp's trousers and snow was about to start dropping out of the sky in quantities unwitnessed since *The Shining*. Ideal conditions, then, for Tromso v. Chelsea, perhaps the most remarkable game of football ever captured live on television.

Much has been said about the state of the playing surface, post-snowfall. But let's not forget the state of the pitch before the blizzard, when sixty tons of snow and a plastic sheet had been removed from it, leaving what was, in effect, a rectangular fen.

'It's disgraceful – and I'm being generously polite,' said Paul Elliot, who was sitting alongside Pearce. 'Be honest,' said Pearce. 'You'd be off and back to the rub-a-dub, wouldn't you?' ('Rub-a dub': pub. Subtitles were on Teletext for people outside the Bow Bells catchment area.)

Pearce also noted that the texture of the pitch at the start was 'like Shredded Wheat that's been left in the bowl too long'. Of course, following Glenn Hoddle's recent announcement about the dissolution of his marriage, there's a vacancy for someone to advertise Shredded Wheat. But Pearce might be making his move too soon. It was suggested to me recently that, even though now unable to endorse things with his handsome family, a solo Hoddle may well retain his job at Nabisco by advertising those individual-serving boxes you get in hotels. Or he could always stay on in some capacity on the Mini-Wheats campaign.

Anyway, the fen was about to become a rink. And the air was about to grow so thick with snowflakes that soon even the special radioactive orange ball would be off-radar. It seems that UEFA had developed a non-cancellation policy specifically for the evening. Their officials were out there getting cold with everyone else and they didn't want to go back and do it all over again. The regulations which relate to calling a game off would seem to be clear enough and there was certainly room to apply them here. The referee, Pearce told us, has to be able to see both his assistants at all times. At the height of the storm, I don't think he would have been able to see both his own shoulders.

But it's clear that another set of criteria had been drawn up for the night, and for as long as both of the diminutive Gianfranco Zola's elbows were still visible above the playing surface, the game was to go ahead. The snow only ever drifted up to his thighs – hence no replay.

It was hell for players out there, but it was tough for viewers, too. The temperature in the sitting room seemed to tumble in sympathy. What's more, we had to endure the sound of Pearce dipping into his Bumper Book of Cold Weather Gags. Pearce often sounds like someone commissioned to predict the following day's tabloid headlines, and these conditions really played into his hands. 'This is snow joke for Chelsea,' he said, as Tromso's second goal went in. 'They're being frozen out. The big chill for Chelsea.'

In the studio ahead of the game, some time had been spent discussing whether Chelsea's pricey Italians would be 'up for it'. This hoary old debate gets dusted down almost every time a team with some foreign players in it plays away from home. It rests on the tenuous logic that the more you are paid, and the more foreign you are, the less likely it is that you have ever experienced a cold wind, or would know what to do in the event of one. The sight of Gianluca Vialli, deep in injury time, ploughing determinedly through snow and Norwegian defenders alike and burying the ball in the ice in the back of the net, was thus doubly sweet: firstly for keeping Chelsea's chances alive and healthy in the second leg, and secondly for giving the lie to this nastily insular argument about 'commitment'. Whatever Chelsea pay him, it is not enough.

Elsewhere, the only person whose commitment reached anything like Vialli-levels was the motor racing commentator Murray Walker. The Formula One season had gone right down to the wire in Portugal, leaving what Murray referred to as 'a faaaabulous battle for the woooorld championship'.

Jim Rosenthal asked Murray how tense it was getting and Murray replied: 'It's a bit like me waiting for my maths results at school, Jim.'

Which brought an image to mind: a crowd around a noticeboard; Murray leaping above it, screaming, 'There! Is! My! O Level!'

AWARD 'CANNOT BE WITH US' SHOCK

3 NOVEMBER 1997

Anyone who has seen a few televised awards shows will be familiar with that warming and traditional moment when, after the nominations have been announced, the clips shown, the envelope opened and the winner called, the compere steps smoothly in front of the guest presenter, leans into the microphone and says: 'Well, unfortunately, [insert name of global megastar] could not be with us tonight . . .'

Inevitably, the ITV Barclaycard Champions of Sport Awards had its share of this kind of action (insert the name Tiger Woods in the box above), but it had more. In fact, in a tremendous genre-busting variant on the established theme, and in a moment which will go down for ever in the annals of televised gong-presentation, Greg Rusedski could be with us – but his award could not.

This was the evening's very climax. Everyone up to now (Jeremy Guscott, Linford Christie, Jeremy Guscott again) had left the stage holding the usual wood-mounted glass briquette. But as Greg climbed the steps and shook hands with Tony Banks, the Minister of Sport, our compere, Ulrika Jonsson, just out of shot, was heard to say with some urgency: 'Where's the award?'

Perhaps we will never know what became of Greg's briquette. Had Lennox Lewis decided to attach it to his lapel as the finishing touch for his outfit? (Lennox, bless him, came gift-wrapped for Christmas.) Had Tony Banks put his foot in it?

Doubtless panicked production staff were backstage ransacking the Wembley Conference Centre's cupboards in search of something which could be given away on behalf of the real trophy. But nothing was forthcoming. 'Well, I'm sure they'll be able to knock you up an award,' Ulrika said, brightly, like the true professional she is. Anyway, it's the thought that counts, and Greg was Best British Sportsperson, as voted for, apparently, by viewers of ITV.

'No wonder so many thousands of you voted,' said co-compere Dermot Murnaghan, without specifying exactly how many thousands of us, or how our votes broke down. Nor did he explain what policy, if any, was adopted by the returning officers to compensate for the weighting given by fans of the Spice Girls entering multiple votes for David Beckham, nor what measures were taken to counter the effect of wilful spoilers, energetically e-mailing votes during bored moments at work in the hope of swinging the whole evening Melinda Messenger's way.

It is clear that ITV's Champion of Sport award – though less established than the BBC's Sports Personality of the Year award – shares with it an election procedure which would not be acceptable even in militia-run South American states. The ballot papers are taken into a closed room somewhere, guarded by people with machine guns, and, though only a bitter cynic would claim that scandalous acts of shredding then take place, no one is ever admitted as an independent witness and the release of official figures is notoriously patchy, so rumours are bound to linger.*

However, Rusedski looked happy enough. He said he was so sure he would not win, he told his girlfriend he would streak in the King's Road in the event. 'Get 'em off,' shouted the Minister of Sport. Which is not a sentence I was ever expecting to be able to write.

However, Greg appeared to lose his smile when Ulrika (who took very seriously her role as the evening's comic interlude) said: 'It's only thanks to his girlfriend that he's here, because he was being quite stubborn about turning up.' Greg looked very chilly to hear this tittle-tattle made public and suddenly you wondered if it wasn't uniquely to Ulrika's advantage that he didn't have a glass briquette in his hand.

'After the break,' said Murnaghan, 'music from Robbie Williams. And who's the best young sportsperson in the world?' That was the kind of evening it was: bright and brassy, but unsure of its priorities and its tone. David Beckham didn't get an award, but deserved one for agreeing to sit all evening in a remote studio in Manchester in front of a photograph of the city's skyline, just so we could see him smile faintly during his two nominations. Even under Alex Ferguson's famously restrictive managerial regime, you can bet Becks has had more exciting Saturday nights than this.

Still, for anyone who had imagined a Barclaycard Champion was someone who was very good at buying things

* It may well be an urban myth that the winner every year of the BBC's Sports Personality Award is, in terms of actual viewer votes, Bob Nudd, the champion angler; and that the BBC doesn't think he's glamorous enough, so they give it to, say, Lennox Lewis instead. But until the BBC allows impartial observers to witness the election procedure, this story will continue to circulate and continue to feel perfectly plausible.

on the never-never, the evening served a certain corrective purpose. Most of all it was an advertisement for ITV Sport, whose cameras had brought us almost none of the exciting moments relived here – apart from those in Formula One, a sport which seemed to bulk larger in the evening's review of the year than it might have done on other channels. Otherwise, during the action sequences, a rather forlorn label blinked in the corner of the screen, revealing the provenance of the images: 'Pictures from Sky Sports', 'Pictures from the BBC' and even – unimaginable as recently as six months ago – 'Pictures from Channel 5'.

A collection of archive clips was shown, designed to impress upon us how ITV had been 'at the heart of sport for years' – if not this year. Which may be true but it would take a little more than a shot of Dickie Davies in a cravat and some footage of the late Brian Glover rolling around a wrestling ring to make the point really sing. Now, if they had could have produced Glover in the cravat and Dickie Davies rolling around in the wrestling ring, then we might have been talking.

MAJOR INQUIRY INTO STEWARDS' INQUIRIES

1 DECEMBER 1997

What the *Cutting Edge* documentary taught us about the internal workings of the Jockey Club could be written on the back of a jockey. The club, who are responsible for the upkeep of horse racing's rules and regulations, admit cameras into their inner sanctum about as readily as Michael Jackson and they made only a partial exception when Channel 4 came to call.

Confronted by reluctant subjects such as these, makers of television documentaries have two choices: they can pack up their cameras and go and find a story which can be told properly; or they can stitch their painfully thin material together to make a post-modern programme in which the failure to get to the story becomes the story itself.

The Englishman and his Horse took the second of those two paths, and, unusually, got away with it. Such was the quality of the material it managed to assemble at one remove – backstage at the races, where the officials were doing business on the Jockey Club's behalf – its failure to get the bigger picture seemed negligible.

Clearly being a racing steward calls for many qualities, too many for the programme to list in detail. But having a highly polished accent and a seat on the board of a major retailing business, such as Marks & Spencer, seems to help. Also, possessing a broad-brimmed hat and the nerve to wear it will never be a disadvantage. The stewards' deliberations did not put you in mind of Twelve Angry Men; they put you in mind of a handful of comfortably off ones.

We watched these men (and two women) scrutinizing races, firstly through their binoculars and later on videotape, with a sharp eye for bits of naughtiness, such as an apprentice jockey over-flogging his horse or Frankie Dettori cutting into the fast lane without indicating. One of the stewards would finally turn to the others and say: 'I think we ought to have an inquiry.' With repetition, this became the documentary's catchphrase; a bit like the spoof chat-show hostess Mrs Merton's great rallying cry: 'Let's have a heated debate.'

Modern technology assists them in their task – and might assist them still further if a few more of them learned how to operate it. Stewards still don't work fast enough as far as the bookies are concerned, but things have definitely got better. One of the stewards recalled the days when the races were shot on black and white film which had to be developed before they could study it for improprieties. Apparently, this process could take about twenty minutes. It's a good job they weren't using my local chemist, who only offers an overnight service.

An interesting development, meanwhile, at the beginning of *On Side*, BBC's sports-themed chat show. John Inverdale, our host, has always walked on to applause from the studio audience, but now he has to wait quite a while for that applause to subside, while giving little nods and smiles of pleasure and amazement as perfected by, among many others, Bob Monkhouse and David Letterman. This is star treatment indeed. Is the programme becoming a one-man show?

Note for *Match of the Day* viewers: this may be a different kind of one-man show from the one the commentator John Motson mentioned at a moment of excitement involving, among others, John Hartson during West Ham's match against Aston Villa. 'It looks like a one-man show here,' said Motson. 'Except there are two people involved. And a third one, in the sense of the goalkeeper.'

Actually, *On Side* will never be a one-man show while its guest list keeps up to current standards. Last week the ex-Wimbledon player John Fashanu spoke about his innocence with regard to match-fixing charges, while the camera locked tight on his face, as if it had its own doubts. And the Minister of Sport Tony Banks came on to try to tell us exactly what he does all day.

The hounding of Banks is one of our time's less lovely episodes. He has made a couple of slips and now it seems the crowd is shouting 'dodgy keeper' wherever he goes. He was booed at Wembley after newspapers reported his opinion that the English football team wasn't necessarily the most stylish side he had ever seen and might not win the World Cup next year (a comment of enormous reasonableness and which was, incidentally, dragged screaming from its innocent context towards the end of an interview in a low-circulation men's magazine).*

The assumption here was that it was the function of the Sports Minister to be a tireless and unreflective propagandist – a view which would have terrifying consequences if applied right across a government. Banks claims to be a passionate man, which need not be bad thing in his job, even if one of his greatest passions is clearly for publicity. You can tell this about anyone who, without irony, sits on the television, blaming the media for their lot. Banks claimed he was quite regularly the victim of 'some sports journalist with the intellectual span of a Polo mint', which was almost a good line but not quite. The sports journalist John Inverdale, sitting opposite him, raised a knowing smile. But he got the last laugh. Just after Banks had spoken grandly of his ambition to bring the World Cup to England in 2006, Inverdale asked him if expected to be still in his job in twelve months' time. Timing: the secret of great comedy.

* England did not win the World Cup in 1998. But did Tony Banks get his job back? No, he did not.

PANORAMA NOTICES LINK BETWEEN FOOTBALL AND MONEY

15 DECEMBER 1997

First to the big stories as ever, *Panorama* (BBC1) put the question: is money changing the face of football? Our smartly suited presenter Steve Bradshaw took up a position in the streets around Old Trafford and, as Manchester United fans brushed past him in millions of pounds worth of replica shirts and accessories, asked: 'Has the glory game become the money game?'

Interesting notion. Meanwhile, tonight on *Panorama*: 'Santa Claus – fact or fiction?' And next week, a searing investigation into shock government plans to introduce decimal currency.

What kept them? *Panorama* arrived at the scene of this crime perhaps as much as five years too late, and Bradshaw came across like the man emerging from the jungle to find that the war is over and that Newcastle United have changed their strip again. He watched the crowds flow into St James' Park and observed: 'The days when Geordie kids could turn up with a quid and a rattle and walk through the turnstiles are over.'

A quid, you say? A quid? In the old days, a quid would have bought you a top-of-the-range rattle, a ticket for the football and a fish-and-chip supper afterwards, and you would still have had enough over to pay Stanley Matthews his weekly wages.

Those other stunning *Panorama* revelations in full: that fans are now required to sit down at football grounds, rather than stand on terracing; that players cost more and more money; that Lincoln City from the lower divisions have not done very well out of all this.

It's not that there isn't an investigative programme to be made about money in football. One, perhaps, which takes a hard look at those giant paper fortunes that the game seems to be sitting on, discovers what they really amount to and asks itself: 'What happens when the wind blows?' There, surely, is a subject for patient exploration by a current affairs team. (*Panorama* just quoted the figures and left it at that.)

What we got here was a bunch of old truths bound up with much sentimental and unreflecting use of the term 'the people's game'. It was like being a teenager and watching a programme on your favourite pop group made by your parents. You know a documentary on football is in trouble when, inside two minutes, it refers to the sport as 'a religion'. Quite apart from being potentially offensive to those football fans who have, as their religion, a religion, this hackneyed formula has become the hallmark of the baffled observer. 'Some fans say that [money] is changing the culture of the game,' said Bradshaw. Blimey.

Lost in some peculiar past of rattles and £1 tickets, the programme had little to say about the good side of some of those changes: like the fact that football fans are now less likely to get their heads kicked in at a game or die in a crush. But perhaps it was a wonder it had anything to say at all. Near the end, Bradshaw produced an impressive list of people who had not spoken to him during the making of the programme.

They included the chairmen of all the major Premier League clubs, every representative of the Football Association, Minister for Sport Tony Banks and David Mellor from the Football Task Force. In a familiar gimmick of current-affairs television, the silence became evidence of some dark purpose. Bradshaw, now getting jostled outside another ground, said: 'The people's game may be changing, but the representatives of the people, it seems, just don't want to talk about it.'

The arrogance of this, on *Panorama*'s part, stopped one dead. It is both smug and tricksy of a television programme to imply that, if someone refuses their offer of an appearance, it can only be because they have something to hide. Whereas the truth may be that the person simply has something better or more pressing to do: some work, for instance, or a hair-wash. In any case, if Bradshaw genuinely has found a way to stop David Mellor talking about 'the people's game', he shouldn't moan about it: he should market it.

1998

WHITHER SHEEPDOG TRIALLING?

5 JANUARY 1998

Hats off this week to *One Man And His Dog*, simply without peer among television programmes dedicated to the sport of sheepdog trialling and which yesterday commenced its twenty-first series. Just think of it: twenty-one years. If the sheep aren't knackered by now, they never will be.

At the top of the programme, Robin Page, our presenter, had a little semi-rehearsed exchange with Gus Dermody, the Alan Hansen of sheepdog trialling, in order to bring into focus some of the changes witnessed by the sport and the world around it in those two decades. And who better to fill us in than these two men of the country, as signalled immediately by their garb? Robin was wearing a leather jerkin which could probably have stopped bullets, while Gus stood before us in a thick tweed suit which seemed to have been woven from a selection of pickles and chutneys.

Gus mentioned 'the improvement in the dogs' in the lifetime of the programme and congratulated the series for 'bringing sheepdog trialling right into everybody's home'. Not literally, of course, which would play havoc with the carpets. Gus also happily noted how the sport had been largely unaffected by the increasing sophistication of rough-terrain vehicles, a development which some feared would limit the work for dogs, not to mention bringing sheep house prices down to new lows.

To no small extent, the programme itself embodies a sterling resistance to the advance of technology. Traditional crafts inform it through and through. This is not just because it invites us to take pleasure in watching a dog cause seven sheep to pass through a gate, though, as on-screen spectacles go, this is bound to look ambitiously understated in the age of the computer game.

Consider in addition its method for showing us the intended course – which this week was a small green slice of Wildboarclough in Cheshire. Not for *One Man and His Dog* one of those computer-generated simulations, offering us a sheep's eye view of three-dimensional fetch gates and shedding rings. Gus just points with a pen at a drawing on an easel. The drawing, you may notice, has a rather nice, bevelled wooden frame.

But the world is out there, and Gus and Robin know it. Word is the sport has been all but obliterated in highly litigious America because of the increasing likelihood that a sheep will sue the dog for harassment. Also, Robin and Gus were tastefully silent on the whole controversial topic of sheep-cloning, whose repercussions for *One Man and His Dog* are potentially myriad. And if the scientists ever move on to sheepdog-cloning, then it is clear that both the sport and the programme are going to be in big trouble.

Robin asked a question behind which one sensed in advance a slight tinge of despair. 'So when people say sheepdog trialling is dead on its feet, they're wrong?' 'Yes,' Gus replied, as somehow one knew he would. 'Most definitely.'

These days the sport does not exist which isn't worried for its profile, its public image, its share of the marketplace. Big, unwieldy – and perhaps, finally, unhelpful – questions about 'the state of the game' hang over sheepdog trialling in the same way that they hang over darts. These two sports have more in common than you might think, in fact, with their television-inspired boom years receding into the past and no sign of another explosion. Darts and sheepdogs both once tweaked the nation's curiosity, but then the nation moved on to other things. 'Darts has become so popular in Holland,' observed Tony Green at the Embassy at Frimley Green on Saturday. There was just the hint of a sigh in his voice.*

WINTER OLYMPICS OPEN; HATS STAY ON

9 FEBRUARY 1998

An Olympic first during the opening ceremony of the Winter Games in Nagano: artificial doves. 'For reasons of ecology, the Nagano committee felt that the doves should be in plastic,' the BBC's Barry Davies told us as the screen filled with a cloud of white balloons in the shape, approximately, of birds.

Some viewers may have been left wondering exactly what environmental disasters had been precipitated by Olympic-generated dove-clouds in the past. But it is a little-reported fact that, following the release of several hundred doves at Lillehammer four years ago, feathers fell on the Scottish Highlands for months afterwards, causing many sheep to die sneezing.

* Astonishingly, in 1999, the BBC tried to pull the plug on *One Man and His Dog* for good, on the grounds, it appeared, that the programme was antiquated. Only an intense campaign of protest, featuring in no small measure the readers of the *Daily Telegraph*, saved the programme's bacon.

So, bogus doves it had to be. Their presence seemed all of a piece with this strangely wingless opening ceremony. Before things got going, Sue Barker had been confident that the Japanese hosts would stamp the occasion with 'their own brand of magic'. Back in the studio afterwards, Barker was bravely containing her disappointment. 'It may have lacked the razzmatazz of previous opening ceremonies,' she said, 'but it did have peace and harmony.' Sure. But where's the fun in that?

Things started ordinarily enough with the erection of some giant tree-trunks, accompanied by singing. 'The more plaintive part of the Chi-ari log-chant is the prelude to much hard work,' said Barry Davies. You can see why he enjoys these opportunities to broaden his commentating portfolio. How often would he get to say that kind of thing while doing Bolton v. Coventry for *Match Of The Day*?

When the trees were up, on came the wrestlers. Sumo, as Davies illuminated us, means literally 'mutual bruising' and the biggest bruiser in the pack right now is Akebono, who was granted special ceremonial duties. Or maybe he just took them: no one was likely to argue with him.

Clearly no relation to the late Sonny Bono, Akebono was thirty stone of forcemeat in a towel. His preparatory ring-ritual involved some stamping – a big hit with the local crowd – and some pointing, during which, rather sweetly, he resembled an extremely large air hostess indicating the position of the emergency exits.

As a result, during the next item one might have found oneself reaching instinctively for the lifejacket stowed under one's seat. This was the singing of the Nagano Games Peace Appeal Song which, as Davies warned us during the introduction, was 'based on Andrew Lloyd-Webber's "When The

Children Rule The World".' Talk about founding a building on sand.

Anyway, one of Japan's biggest pop singers, whose name I omitted to write down, and several hundred Nagano schoolchildren, whose names I also omitted to write down, gave it their best shot, instructing us to 'whistle down the wind', to 'try to burn a torch' and to 'try to build a bonfire' – though perhaps not all at the same time.

We were now as ready as we would ever be for the entry of the teams. It's at this moment one realizes that a Winter Games is actually, as much as anything, an international festival of the hat. So a special mention to plucky Belarus, each of whose team members wore titfers which made them look like Sherlock Holmes being attacked by a ferret.

The lighting of the flame, when it happened, was a major let-down. Recent Olympic ceremonies have sought eagerly to make the arrival of the torch and the ignition of the flame unnecessarily perilous, just for thrills. We have seen a rocket launched up a wire to explode in the bowl. We have seen a blind archer fire a flaming arrow into the cauldron from a distance of many yards. There were rumours that this quest to subject the torch to the greatest possible risk of non-arrival would this year lead inevitably to the flame turning up in a train supplied by Virgin West Coast.*

But it didn't happen. Someone simply trotted the torch up the staircase and handed it over to Midori Ito, an ice skater, who then rose up to bowl level on a hydraulic

* For the 2000 Olympics in Sydney, scientists developed a special Olympic torch which could be carried underwater, without peril to the life of the eternal flame. Even Virgin West Coast would now stand a chance of getting the thing through.

platform. It was a stunt you could have pulled off at home, had you access to a forklift truck and a big bucket.

There followed the singing of Beethoven's 'Ode to Joy' by choirs around the world, hooked to Nagano by digital link. Even this fell short of wondrous – a clinical victory for wires and screens. And it could have been so different. Listeners to the radio show *I'm Sorry I Haven't A Clue* will be familiar with a game in which a team member must sing along with a record which is faded out underneath them. The team member must then continue singing and try to hold their place until the record comes back in again – at which point they are found to be either heroically on the money or hilariously adrift. On Saturday morning, a unique opportunity for a truly global and astonishingly expensive version of this game went begging.

COMMENTATORS 'NOT ALL THERE' CLAIM

9 MARCH 1998

The shocking revelations made by Murray Walker concerning his past have sent extraordinary reverberations through the house of commentary. Cracks have appeared everywhere and some now wonder whether the whole edifice is about to fall.

The storm struck during the sustained publicity jamboree which accompanied the opening of Walker's fiftieth year as the peerless voice of Formula One. Walker let slip that there had been occasions when those commentaries of his, which always seemed to us to be soaked like an oily rag in the essence of the pit lane, were actually coming from a small room in Shepherd's Bush, where he was watching the pictures and faking it. What a cruel medium television can be. You think you know exactly where you are with it (at the Japanese Grand Prix at Suzuka, for instance) when reality comes crashing in, with all the disillusioning impact of a pet death on Blue Peter.

It was some consolation to learn the number of Murray's deceptions was not great in proportion to the times when he really was at the race. As the BBC made clear, after losing the Formula One television rights to ITV, their commitment to the sport had always been total, even if it did not run to finding their chief motor racing commentator an airfare and a hotel bill every now and again. We can be confident that the do-it-from-London-and-pretend procedure was a long-haul measure only. There would have been no question of Murray not actually being at Brands Hatch just because the traffic looked iffy.

But even having satisfied ourselves to this extent, we cannot prevent our minds from worrying about the broader implications of Walker's confession. He mentioned having seen Peter O'Sullevan commentating on a horse race from the warmth of the studio. How far does this rot go? The problem is, once suspicions such as these are unleashed, they run riot. Take last week's European football coverage, for instance. I am sure I was not alone in being unable to shake off, post-Murray, the thought that Brian Moore was not actually out in Monaco with Manchester United, but was watching the game at home on the portable in his bedroom.

One can see how suspicions such as these threaten to diminish the great work done by so many skilled commentators – people who know that the freshness of the first-hand report is everything, who are dedicated to getting themselves out there to the front line on our behalf, and who work for broadcasting corporations who are prepared to shell out for their expenses.

It would be disappointing if Walker's revelations adversely affected the public standing of these heroes. I'm thinking of people such as Archie Macpherson, whose commentaries on European football for the cable channel Eurosport take him to the sport's great continental theatres – sometimes to more than one of them in the same evening – and yet who tirelessly makes vivid for us the atmosphere, the setting and those thousand little background details which the cameras cannot get to, but which are essential to the recreation of an experience for the viewer at home.

If Walker's confession were to cause so much as one person to wonder whether Macpherson was, in reality, in front of a monitor in Eurosport's operations centre in Paris, and making all the other stuff up, then how unjust that would be.

The *Murray Walker Story* (ITV) steered clear entirely of the controversy surrounding absentee commentary. Despite that appetizing title, it also steered fairly clear of Murray Walker's story, being rather more substantially a piece of surrogate tub-thumping for ITV's new season of Formula One coverage.

The setting was the final race of last year at Jerez. We watched Murray walk the course with Martin Brundle, stick lots of pieces of paper up in his commentary box and attend a pre-race briefing for the ITV crew. With slightly more rapt attention, perhaps, we also watched him perform his exercises, while below him the cars revved on the grid. Walker's commentary style is part carnival barker, part livestock auctioneer, but he is all athlete when he is in the middle of it.

BARNES SHOWN DOOR AT NOEL'S HOUSE

23 MARCH 1998

So there we are at Crinkley Bottom with Noel Edmonds for *Noel's House Party* (BBC1) when suddenly the doorbell goes. Edmonds turns to answer it and a tall figure in a crash helmet bumps up against him in the doorway. 'Wooo!' says the studio audience.

Who could this mystery guest be? At this point, all the smart money is on Nigel Mansell. He's got every qualification: famous, popular and in that strange sporting champion's twilight zone where there's not a lot else to do other than be famous and popular and go on Saturday evening entertainment programmes to provide a link with a section of the show in which a motorized seagull passes above the audience on a wire and dumps a milky liquid on them. So Mansell it has to be. But go on, Noel, surprise us.

'It's Nigel Mansell!' says Noel. And off comes the helmet to reveal Britain's favourite Brummie. Mansell, however, in an unusual development for this kind of moment, has an important announcement to make. He's in a position to confirm the stories that he's returning to racing, this time at saloon-car level. 'Weee!' says the studio audience. Cue a little set-up joke with Noel about air bags. And then cue the incontinent seagull.

As our hero waves and smiles on his way out, a question hovers awfully in the mind. Would you rather be allowed to remember Nigel Mansell as a) a brilliant and fearless Formula One champion; b) a saloon car driver; or c) a man who provided a link with the incontinent seagull portion of *Noel's House Party*?

One was still mulling this over when John Barnes appeared. Two sportspeople in one House Party: truly we are spoiled to within an inch of our lives. Barnes was the victim of this week's 'Gotcha' slot. For those who are not frequent visitors to Crinkley Bottom, this is where Edmonds traps celebrities into making fools of themselves on camera.

Like Jeremy Beadle, Noel Edmonds has built a career on the back of a talent for making people the heart-warming victims of practical jokes, but without ever entirely persuading one that the transaction would be quite so heart-warming if he himself were in the position of the victim. With Barnes, the idea was to send up his fondness for ambitiously constructed clothing. It's true that Barnes is one of the few people in Britain who wears shirts so furiously fashionable that they button up at the back. Many of the jackets he wore as an ITV pundit during Euro 96 are said to have played a key experimental role in the development of the material for the shell of the Millennium Dome.

Here Barnes was tricked into dressing up and presenting what he thought would be a short educational film on football in the nineteenth century. Except 'tricked' is too strong a word. Footballers like Barnes are requested to do ridiculous things in front of cameras all the time. In a world in which Ruud Gullit gets asked to pretend that he actually eats at Pizza Hut, why wouldn't John Barnes be asked to dress up as a Victorian schoolboy? It would just be another day's work. And as a consequence of this, what actually is the humorous content of a set-up which reveals no gullibility whatsoever on the part of its victim?

Who had delivered Barnes into Edmonds's merry hands? His wife, Susie. 'I think it was about time,' she explained, on the couch in the studio. 'He's always moaning about me doing too much shopping, and then he just sits around watching his kung fu movies.'

There was little time to ponder this infinitely fascinating glimpse of domestic life chez Barnes, because we were straight away off to the scene of the Gotcha, where Barnes, in fluffy sideburns and tight trousers, was talking about kicking vegetables around in the days before affordable leather. Again, you've seen footballers do more barking things in advertisements for Adidas.*

By the end of this scenario, Barnes was wearing a jester's outfit and locked in some stocks (our Victorian theme had come a little unknotted by now) and we had reached the point Edmonds – stealing shamelessly from the language of magicians – refers to as 'the reveal'. This is where Edmonds comes out of hiding and everyone laughs and hugs. Edmonds then handed Barnes, as is traditional, a shiny statuette to remember his humiliation by. It was a touching moment. The truly remarkable thing, of course, is that no one ever tells Edmonds to shove it up his Crinkley Bottom.

On the subject of trophies, congratulations to Brian Moore and Kevin Keegan who, during ITV's coverage from Old Trafford last Wednesday, were shown receiving an award for commentary team of the year from the readers of *Football Monthly*, and who promptly celebrated in style.

'United's best effort so far,' said Moore, as a shot from David Beckham whistled over.

* In 2000, an Adidas commercial called upon Jonah Lomu, the New Zealand rugby giant, to snatch up from the middle of a road a large, gasping fish, tuck it under his arm and run with it to the nearest harbour. By then, *Noel's House Party* had been cancelled. And little wonder.

'Well, it's their only effort, Brian,' said Keegan. 'It certainly was their best.'

Later, the always reflective Keegan would offer us his view that 'there's always time in football,' which was certainly an odd thing to say while the first half was ticking away, but would have been odd at any other point, too. He also said, of another Beckham shot: 'It probably would have gone in, had he put it exactly where he wanted it, which was just inside that post.' Long may his trophy cabinet overflow.

BRENDAN FOSTER GA-GA OVER LA-LA

27 APRIL 1998

How the term 'fun run' ever made it into common currency is one of the great linguistic mysteries of our time, the implications of 'fun' and 'running' being so self-evidently contradictory. But doubtless the London Marathon (BBC1) has had a lot to do with it.

'I've found a bunny here,' said Sue Barker, pointing her microphone at a giant mound of fake fur, allegedly containing a taxi driver and possibly also his taxi. It was Sue's task to mingle with the starters at Blackheath yesterday and pick out the runners who were fun. And this at 8.45 on a Sunday morning.

Many of the costumes with which Sue rubbed shoulders (not to mention antlers) were astonishingly lifelike. The rhinos, for instance, would have alarmed the hell out of you, had you noticed one coming up on your inside. And hats off, I thought, to the person who had gone to all that trouble to come dressed as Steve Rider from BBC's *Grandstand*. But it was Steve Rider from BBC's *Grandstand*.

Here was a turn-up: Rider a runner. He said he was hoping to be back in time for *Blue Peter* on Monday. Since he had never run further than fifteen miles, it seemed more likely that *Crackerjack* would be back on our screens before he made it home.*

This year, David Coleman informed us, the organizers were supplying pacemakers for the race. One's initial thought was that this represented an extraordinary commitment to health and safety on their part. In past years, the runners have simply relied on a sensible provision of ambulances along the route.

But in fact the pacemakers turned out to be runners who would lead off the elite racers, tow them along, then pull over halfway round. The point of this was never adequately explained. And it became no clearer when, in the women's race, the pacemakers left the field standing.

Roadside stalls offered the runners water – and for the rhinos, presumably, a selection of reeds and grasses. Liz McColgan, we were informed, had dropped her drink and gone back for another. But how did she know – while running past a table crowded with plastic bottles – which drink was hers in the first place? And if the drinks were personalized, what would be the consequences of accidentally snatching up someone else's and discovering they took four sugars?

London passed before us. 'Docklands, a major feature of the London landscape now,' said Paul Dickenson. 'A combination of the old and the new.' Discuss. Later, Dickenson pointed out '*Cutty Sark* – this famous landmark of British

* Appearing in the London Marathon became something of an annual ritual for Steve Rider, who deserved a break. He may have been contractually prevented from joining ITV's glamorous Formula One team, but at least he gets to run twenty-six miles in the rain each year.

history'. And Brendan Foster spotted another piece of our national heritage. 'There's the Wombles,' he said.

Before long, Foster was in soft-toy overdrive. 'I just saw a Teletubby go through there,' he said excitedly. 'Looking to be the first Teletubby home.' But in an extremely unusual moment of amateurism, Foster could only confirm that it was 'a yellow Teletubby'. A commentator who had really done their research prior to the race would have been able to inform us instantly that the yellow Teletubby is called La-La. Black mark, Foster.

Clearly the event's organizers deserved the high praise they received from Foster, and from Coleman. Anyone who can arrange a party for 30,000 people over twenty-six miles of road in central London without noticeably irritating the neighbours is obviously some kind of genius. That said, some of us think the organizers don't work hard enough to purge the Marathon of elitism. Presently, the top runners set off in advance of the 30,000 others and thus enjoy the privilege of a course free of fund-raising animals and Steve Rider. How much fairer the competition would be if the athletes were obliged to mix it with the chickens and the rhinos. Abel Anton, of Spain, the men's winner, ran a tremendous race, but our admiration for him would have increased tenfold had he been obliged to work his way past two Snoopys and a man with a step-ladder.

CELEBS TELL WRIGHT ABOUT IT

11 MAY 1998

When Arsenal's Ian Wright was carried off on a stretcher at Anfield last Wednesday, the first question television viewers asked was: 'Will this render him doubtful for *Friday Night's All Wright*?' As any viewer will tell you, the last thing you need when you've got a crucial chat show pending, is for your host to be carrying a niggle.

But the worries proved needless. We knew this from the moment Wrighty came on stage pretending to limp. Wrighty is the first Arsenal player to be given his own show since Bob Wilson got *Football Focus*, but his style is a little noisier. 'Wotchew fink?' he said, giving the pin-stripe suit an injury-defying twirl.

Television needs another chat show like it needs another series about vets. Still, you get something a little different from Wrighty, even if only in terms of chaos and competence. And despite the fact that the show has only appeared once before, stars are apparently falling over themselves to get near it. 'None of them are here plugging anything,' Wrighty said, referring to his guests. 'They're here because they want to be on.'

Stars such as the pop group Cleopatra, for instance. As their number gave way to deafening applause, Wrighty advised us to 'look out for that record. Top Five by Sunday.' But he didn't mean it in a plugging sense, obviously.

The boxer Chris Eubank, too, was here first and foremost for the company – even if he did take time out during his interview to announce the date of his next fight. 'I'm a conscious and gentle human being and I'm in a barbaric sport,' said Eubank, the only thesaurus to have boxed. Later he would earn our congratulations by becoming the first person since 1754 to use the term 'besmirch'. (Wrighty gave him a puzzled look. 'Slandered,' explained Eubank. 'Thanks Chris,' said Wrighty.)

The grim battering which Eubank received last time he stepped into the ring seems to have completed a remarkable transition in the public perception of him from posturing dandy to have-a-go heart throb. 'It's fantastic to be loved,' he said. News of the rematch caused the audience to whoop wildly – though surely this was akin to someone agreeing to get run over by a truck again, simply because they got a lot of sympathy the first time.

When Wrighty introduced the actress Rosanna Arquette, he told us she was 'all the way from Hollywood with nothing to plug', and we were impressed to think the magnetism of the Arsenal and England striker could exert itself at that distance. Our admiration faltered only temporarily when Arquette sat down and explained she was in London to start work on a film, but it had fallen apart, leaving her at a loose end until Sunday.

Whatever, she chose good company in Wrighty. True, he has a tendency to say 'What can I say?' a lot, where some might argue that, as the show's presenter, it is his job not to be confused about this. But when he gets round to it, he has a crisp way with a question. ('You and Naseem Hamed,' he said to Eubank, referring to a dust-up the two boxers were alleged to have had at Heathrow Airport. 'What's going on?')

That said, an exchange took place during the Arquette interview which pointed up at least one of the problems faced by a chat show in which the host is himself a celebrity. Arquette mentioned that the British press could be cruel.

'Tell me about it,' said Wrighty. 'Tell me about it,' replied Arquette. 'Tell me about it,' insisted Wrighty.

This threatened to go on all night. And for as long as the celebs were telling each other about it, no one was going to be telling us at home very much about anything.

START THE BUS: NEWCASTLE UNITED WANT TO GET ON

18 MAY 1998

Gloomy times: Sinatra dead and no Des Lynam in the Wembley FA Cup Final build-up. ITV took over from BBC, so it was Brian Moore in for John Motson and Bob Wilson sitting where Lynam normally sits. Poor Bob, to be constantly measured against Des. As Crosby said of Sinatra: 'A voice like Frank's comes just once in a lifetime. But why did it have to be in my lifetime?'

You'd say this in Wilson's defence: he's the first Cup Final presenter to be an employee of one of the finalists (Bob coaches David Seaman at Arsenal, and there he was in a tracksuit in the report on Arsenal's final training sessions). And unlike Des, he's won the Double (there he was again in the interviews with the squad of 1971). Which makes him, at the very least, versatile.

Aside from the personnel changes, the build-up was in pretty much its usual shape. But then this is a slice of immutable televisual heritage we are talking about. 'Well, it's all rather quiet here at Arsenal's team hotel in Chelsea Harbour,' said Gary Newbon. With blanks where the team and hotel names go, these words are engraved on a stone tablet and handed down across the generations.

Newbon was at least able to bring us up to date with the contents of Arsenal's lunch: 'A choice of boiled food, mashed potatoes, rice and pasta.' But he should have been at the Newcastle United hotel in Hendon where, unbelievably, a story was unfolding. Newcastle team coach in flat battery mayhem! Amazing live pictures showed the coach sitting in the hotel car park and most definitely not moving.

On ITV, Bob Wilson was tempted to speculate on the possibility of a delay to the game – even though the Newcastle players were not due to leave the hotel for a while. Bob also wanted to know what, for the players, would be the psychological repercussions of this major disruption to routine, on a day planned right down to the last plate of mashed potato. And luckily Ruud Gullit was on hand to fill several valuable minutes of airtime with a lengthy peroration on transport anxiety from the perspective of a former World Player of the Year.

'I think they will be stressed,' said Ruud. 'If you want to enter in the bus and the bus is not there, you are annoyed. The thing is, is difficult to get focused again. It will take them at least forty-five minutes to get back in that.'

'OK, thanks, Rick,' said Bob.

Sky Sports' programming had begun at 8.00 a.m. – a new world record for the generation of Cup Final-related hot air. Somewhere in the middle, the reporter George Gavin went to Newcastle to interview Stevie Charlton, on the grounds that Charlton was a) a Newcastle United fan and b) 77 years old. Adopting a strange, sing-song voice, such as one might use in conversation with a three-year-old, Gavin asked Charlton: 'Did you get the bug inside you when you were seven years old?' To which Charlton replied: 'What?'

Meanwhile, ITV went to the garden at No 10 Downing Street to interview Tony Blair, on the grounds that he was a) a Newcastle United fan and b) the Prime Minister. Many of us were still rigid with embarrassment following the Prime Minister's appearance an hour earlier on the lunchtime news bulletin, where he was heard to refer to the world leaders assembled for the weekend's economic summit as 'guys'. 'Come on, guys,' he said, leading them back inside after the morning walkabout (which had presumably followed their choice of boiled food, mashed potatoes, rice or pasta). I wonder what the guys made of that.

Anyway, asked by Bob Wilson to name his all-time great Newcastle XI, Blair did a superb impression of someone who had no idea the question was going to be asked. And then he did another one of someone who had not had a team of advisers and focus-group co-ordinators working feverishly on his answer for many days beforehand.

Eventually, there was a game of football. ITV's production team should be commended on their decision to stay with Ian Wright during the singing of the National Anthem. Wright could be seen – though sadly not heard – closing out with a magnificent final 'Queeeeeeee-nah!', the last syllable accompanied by a violent jerk upwards of the chin. It's good to note that even in the age of Tony Blair, some people still value the essential dignity of ceremony.

FRANCE 98; HODDLE QUESTIONS REALITY

18 JUNE 1998

Our special Glenn Hoddle Award for Party-Pooper of the 1998 World Cup seems destined to end up on the mantelpiece of David Pleat. Pleat, in his role as co-commentator for the BBC, has rocketed into a seemingly unassailable position by accusing the Cameroonians of 'trying to impress individually', a remark so dour and dispiriting that it put one in mind of the grim football panel days of Don Howe and Denis Law.

It seems to be Pleat's opinion that football is a team game. I suppose he's right, but somehow it's not the kind of thing you want to hear during a World Cup. Sitting at home, you would trade as many hours as were available of Austria playing 'as a team' for a single flash of Cameroonian brilliance.

And the same applies to commentary and presentation. 'I was reading a profile of the Brazilian team in one of the French papers today . . .' said ITV's Clive Tyldesley, casually dropping his shoulder and revealing to us his fluency in a foreign language. Doubtless Pleat would mark this down as a needless attempt to impress individually, but here we welcome it as one of those gratuitous displays of skill which make the World Cup the compelling television spectacle it is.

The big story was the dumping of David Beckham from the England side to face Tunisia, not long after Becks was pictured out and about wearing a highly fashionable wrap and just days after he had told the BBC's Ray Stubbs that he wasn't thinking of filling the role vacated by Geri Halliwell in the Spice Girls. Now he may have to think again.* Clearly, in the mind of the England manager Glenn Hoddle, two sarongs do not make a right.

Still, this decision meant that for the first time one was able to use the words 'clearly', 'mind' and 'Hoddle' in the same sentence. 'What you see with your cameras sometimes isn't the real thing,' England's media-savvy coach mysteriously told the BBC last week, during one of its many fruitless visits to the English camp in Nantes. So confusing was Hoddle's furtiveness that Barry Davies went into the game with Tunisia believing that Tony Adams, rather than Alan Shearer, was England captain. I don't blame him: I went in believing it was Geri Halliwell.

Meanwhile Hoddle, subject to a sudden attack of realism, was telling anyone who pointed a microphone at him that 1–0 would do him just fine. The team went one better than that, of course. Or they certainly seemed to. But if Glenn is right about cameras, how can any of us really be sure?

'Those of you with your World Cup wallcharts will doubtless have worked out . . .' began the commentator John Motson – a man for a wallchart if ever there was one – before referring to the likelihood of England and Germany meeting in the quarter-finals. Moments of individual brilliance seem to be coming from Motty in unusual quantities. 'And we just caught a shot of Bert Millichip there,' he informed us during the Germany v. United States game, effortlessly rising above the clamour to pinpoint a suit from

* Beckham was eventually restored to the side. Then he got sent off against Argentina (see page 261). And then effigies of him were strung from gibbets outside London pubs and it looked as if he would have to spend the rest of his life wearing a sarong – over his head. But he clung on and, armed only with his footballing skills and a very canny publicist, returned to glory.

the Football Association. 'Dangerous play has been decreed and a booking ensued,' said Motty, apparently translating, as so often, from his own Latin. So much for Tyldesley's French.

But everyone's at it, seeking their opportunity to shine and, if necessary, inventing the language to do so. Referring to a fall which deceived the referee into awarding a free kick, Ron Atkinson coined the phrase 'a stumble-job', which one hopes to see taken up widely next season. And Brian Moore has spoken of his fear that 'the dice might go the other way'. He should get those dice inspected.

FRANCE 98; TIME RUNNING OUT FOR GULLIT

22 JUNE 1998

Sometimes the World Cup is Holland v. South Korea – lively and goal-filled – and everything in the living room is dandy. But just occasionally the World Cup is Spain v. Paraguay and one maintains consciousness only by regularly dunking one's head in a bucket of cold water.

Television's own fast-cut hype and all those overheated advertisements for sports equipment in which footballs noisily girdle the globe or burst into flames do not necessarily prepare the viewer for the meeting of two barely functioning sides in a goalless deadlock. Yet this, more than any amount of samba-led romping by Brazilians on beaches, is the story of football, and it can only be good for us to be reminded now and again.

In broadcasting, it is the bad games, rather than the good ones, which separate the sheep from the goats. The tough get going, not when the going gets tough, but when the dullness settles in. 'There must be some temptation to bring on the drummer,' said Barry Davies as the camera panned across the Spanish fans on Friday evening. Having commentated on the opening ceremony – a sort of fertility rite in which men dressed as bees caromed around the stadium on wires and with balloons bursting out of their backsides – Davies knows all about gently counterpointing the meaningless. Luckily most of the people on his team are the same.

The tournament dealt the BBC an uninteresting card early on with Austria v. Cameroon in Toulouse when, as John Motson memorably put it, 'the pink city provided a pale first half'. Back in the exclusive, roof-top apartment in which the BBC has based its analysts, Lynam and Hansen properly put those forty-five minutes down, yet without seeming unduly concerned: there would be other games, they seemed to be saying. Much the same happened with Spain v. Paraguay. This is the BBC's strength: they do a poor game well.

Incidentally, quite aside from the man's calmness under an absence of pressure, Barry Davies is also a commentator who is unusually sensitive to foreign languages, and it is as well to have one of those around when, as on Friday, there are players on the pitch called things like Arce.*

Moreover, top linguists agree that standards of pronunciation in general during this tournament have been higher than at any World Cup in living memory – something we can presumably put down to the presence in the Premier League of so many continental players. When Aljosa Asanovic is a pundit's weekly bread and butter, the odd random 'Arce' need hold no fear. Nevertheless, do listen out

* See footnote on page 185.

for Trevor Brooking's 'Raul' which sounds like a fire engine going past extremely quickly. And Chris Waddle's Geordie take on the Frenchman 'Lizarazu' ought really to be released as a single.

Over on ITV, where the tone is ratcheted that much higher, there can only be a kind of embarrassment, a sense of personal failure, when the football doesn't deliver. If only Bob Wilson had an apartment with a roof garden to chill out on. Even the presence of the famously icy Ruud Gullit cannot stop those pitch-side studios where ITV are based from looking sticky.

ITV clearly regard Gullit as a major magnet but I'm not sure how well it's working out. Occasionally the take-as-you-find circumstances of live outside broadcasting dictate that Bob and Ruud appear before us perched uncomfortably on stools and clutching unfashionably fat white microphones in a rather unfortunate visual echo of the great singing duo Peters and Lee.

Gullit has many strengths as a pundit but concision is not one of them. Or as Ruud might put it himself, in his best Dutch English, 'You 'ave also to think to yourself all the time – you 'ave the strength of what it take. At this level. You know? [Pause, serious expression.] Same thing in life also. [Toss of dreadlocks, thrust outwards of lower lip.] But maybe what I don't *'ave* [abrupt emphasis, sudden backwards movement of upper body, outspread gesture with open palms] is – I don't know – quickness of getting to the point maybe [shrug, toss of dreadlocks again, confusingly sourceless smile] and you need to 'ave this also, perhaps, I don't know also [weird giggle].'

During Euro 96, the BBC's set-up gave Gullit, like Eric Cantona in that advertisement for Eurostar, room to work, to breathe.* There's simply less time for him on ITV. Commercial breaks come and go while Ruud is still casually fashioning a path in the direction of his first verb.

It doesn't help ITV's quest to create a distinctive service that BBC figures keep popping up in the opposition's half. There, during the commercials, is David Ginola shaking his beautifully illuminated hair on behalf of L'Oreal shampoos. And Des Lynam is the voice of Sainsbury's. Still more cheekily, in an advertisement for the video release of the Arthur Smith television play *My Summer With Des*, which featured clips of Des's Euro 96 performances, Des speaks directly to us from the other side, as it were. This advertisement popped up first of all during half-time in the match between Italy and Chile, right before we cut back to Bob Wilson, and it has naughtily subverted ITV's coverage on at least one other occasion since.

Would it be merely fanciful to see in this bald evidence of a dirty tricks campaign? After all, how often do you see videos of plays advertised on television? Movies, yes; but plays? We demand to know who paid for this advertisement, whether they currently enjoy employee status in the sports department at the BBC, and exactly what their motives were and are.

* In the best and most far-reaching analysis of Cantona's Eurostar advertisement, the author Julian Barnes pertinently wondered what kind of work, exactly, a footballer did on a train.

FRANCE 98; BIG RON PUSHES UP

29 JUNE 1998

The Golden Boot (awarded to the player who scores the most goals during a World Cup) is still up for grabs, but the Golden Throat award seems certain to go home with Ivan Zamorano, following his devastating rendition of the Chilean national anthem. Microphones and cameras, provided by our host broadcaster, are bringing us closer than ever to the heart of the anthem ceremony, and this weekend, as Zamorano's wired eyes and throbbing tonsils filled our screens, we saw the policy come good.

These images were so forceful that the BBC's panel returned to them at half-time. 'He's a great singer,' said Alan Hansen, moving smoothly from football pundit to music critic, and leaving one wondering whether there might be a future role for him alongside Richard Baker at the Proms. ('He'll be disappointed wi' that. You go'tae get tight in behind the woodwind or you go'nae get punished.')

The necessity for a pre-match commercial break means that ITV often bypass the anthems altogether, which is a great loss. Otherwise, though, the channel are putting together a worthy performance in France. The nightmare of USA 94 has not been revisited upon us.

The BBC's apartment-led approach aims to cultivate an easy-going atmosphere in which, say, Jimmy Hill will feel free to maintain that the decision of the Romanian team to bleach their hair was in some measure a tactical one – and to look rather hurt at the scoffing response of his teammates. On ITV, meanwhile, the talk might be crisper, but it is hard-edged and authoritative. And thus far the one genuine broadcasting innovation of the tournament is taking place on that channel, in the performances as match analyst of Ron Atkinson.

Like Brazil's Roberto Carlos, Atkinson looks to come forward at every opportunity. Subverting the traditional commentator/analyst relationship, Ron speaks whenever, and for however long, he likes and the commentator jumps in only when there is a gap. At the peak of his form, Ron is even more dominant than that. On Saturday, during Italy v. Norway, with Ron still mid-anecdote, the action swept dangerously goalwards. And Ron, without drawing a breath, took up the commentary. He has blurred the boundaries between attack and defence like no other analyst before him. It's exciting for the fans, I guess, though some traditionalists will doubtless be anxious about seeing the game go this way.

Kevin Keegan plays, by and large, a straighter game for ITV – though he too spoiled a nicely judged dramatic pause left by the commentator Brian Moore, in the wake of England's goal against Romania, by shouting 'Michael Owen'. All in all, that match was not Keegan's happiest ninety minutes as a pundit, but it was his fault for adopting the persona of Gypsy Rose Kev and trying to read the future.

Gypsy Rose Kev told us many times that Romania would tire in the last twenty minutes. Apparently they had done so in a game a week earlier. Keegan did not seem distracted by the thought that they might have got some rest between then and now. When England equalized, Keegan said: 'There's only one side that's going to win this game now.' The Romanians would be 'happy with a draw', he said. We could tell this, he reckoned, just by looking at them. Romania promptly poured forward in numbers and scored their winner.

With analysts staging takeovers, these are anxious times for commentators. Even the great Brian Moore sounded nervous at one point. 'FIFA have declared there shall be seven spare balls around the ground so that there's no time-wasting,' he said. Then, apologetically, he added: 'There's a piece of useless information for you.' Not at all. We'll take useless information over useless astrology every time.

And in the case of reports from the England team camp, we'll take any kind of information that's going. At half-time during Italy v. Austria, in the run-up to England's game against Colombia, ITV's Gary Newbon reported solemnly that the England team had passed a night of only 'fitful sleep'. Worrying news. But how reassuring to think that the players had, at this troubled time, in the form of Newbon, a Florence Nightingale figure padding quietly along the hotel corridors, casting gentle shadows with his candle and watching angelically over their slumbering forms.

FRANCE 98; KEEGAN BLOWS IT FOR ENGLAND

2 JULY 1998

So that's it; England out on penalties to Argentina. This was not a night for blame. But, personally, I blame Kevin Keegan. David Batty was stepping up to take his penalty and Brian Moore said: 'Do you back him to score? Quickly. Yes or no?' 'Yes,' said Keegan. And we all know what happened next. But you didn't need to be Eileen Drewery to see it coming. This, after all, was Kevin Keegan.

Kevin Keegan: the man who had confidently told us, after England had equalized in their match against Romania:

'There's only one team who's going to win this now, Brian.' And he meant England.

Kevin Keegan: the man who assured us that Romania would be 'happy with a draw'.

Kevin Keegan: the man who said that Romania would tire in the last twenty minutes of that game.

Kevin Keegan: the man who, directly after David Beckham received a red card for a petulant kick at Diego Simeone, dug deep into his managerial experience to tell us: 'I had a player sent off in the play-offs against Grimsby.' (Which has nothing to do with predictions going wrong, but was just really annoying of him.)

Let's face it, the minute Keegan backed Batty, it was all over. The curse of Gypsy Rose Kev had struck again.

Of course, some will say that Keegan should never have been put on the spot like that by Brian Moore. Not with a place in the quarter-finals of the World Cup at stake. You would think a man of Moore's experience would know better than to expose one of his young charges in that way.

And, what's more, as the incident gets examined and re-examined in the coming months, conspiracy theorists are bound to emerge who will want to argue that Moore did it deliberately to make Keegan look a berk. But, as I said originally, this was not a night for blame.

And so, after the defeat, the recriminations. Disappointment, accompanied by a refusal to blame anyone, seeped out into the schedules – from Ian Wright at the end of the game ('gutted for'em, gutted for'em') through Trevor McDonald on *News At Ten* ('The Queen missed it – but she said she thought it was going to be difficult') and over on to BBC1.

'It's a bitterly disappointing dressing room,' said Glenn Hoddle afterwards in the BBC's highlights programme, as if there was something wrong with the lockers or the hot water didn't work. It wouldn't have been a surprise to hear Glenn blaming the facilities. He had blamed almost everything else by this point, including the David Beckham incident, the unseen Argentinian handball, the referee and (that old Hoddle favourite) 'destiny'.

'But this is not a night for blame,' Glenn added, when he had finished blaming things.

Alan Shearer also thought it wasn't a night for blame. 'There's no blame attached to anyone,' he said, shortly after describing the referee as 'horrible', accusing him of creating for England 'a mountain to climb' and chastising him for disallowing what Shearer thought was a perfectly good goal by Sol Campbell. Then again, it's no wonder Shearer didn't see what the referee whistled for on that occasion: replays revealed him to have been busy sticking his elbow in the goalkeeper's face at the time.

Ian Wright really didn't blame anyone. Not Batty, not Beckham, not Paul Ince, who also missed a penalty. He was only sorry because he had been hoping Gareth Southgate would get to take a penalty. Southgate famously missed one against Germany in Euro 96 and Wrighty said he thought a second chance might have helped Southgate to 'exercise his demons'. Now, along with everyone else, Southgate will have to settle for taking his demons for a crisp walk round the park.

EUBANK BEATEN INTO POPULARITY

20 JULY 1998

When the fight was finished, the people from Sky Sports trooped backstage into Chris Eubank's dressing room and asked the defeated and panting challenger whether his career was now over. And with the modesty and absence of unnecessary drama for which the world knows and loves him, Eubank was silent for a full ten seconds (which is a long time in television) before looking up and saying: 'Let the public decide.'

Well, we, the public, say: don't leave us, Chris. Stick around. Come back. If not as a boxer, then at least as a politician, or a philosopher, or a chat-show host. Something. Anything. Britain needs you. Television needs you. Sky Sports definitely needs you. Eubank v. Carl Thompson was the only half-decent event they've had for weeks. You can't desert Sky now, Chris; this is their season of need.

'Ask the *Sun* newspaper to do a little survey,' Eubank said, referring to whether he should quit. Chris is smart enough to see that if you're on one of Murdoch's television channels, you might as well mention one of Murdoch's newspapers and keep the whole thing tidily in-house. You don't sustain yourself at the top in boxing for as long as Chris has without understanding the business; and not for nothing did we see him arrive at the Sheffield Arena for this fight carrying not a sports hold-all but a briefcase.

Given his perfectionism, it was something of a surprise that, twenty-four hours earlier, Eubank had nearly failed to make the required weight for the fight. He had just two hours to lose the surplus. How, we all wanted to know afterwards, had he managed it? Chris said he had soaked himself in a hot bath, where he 'read a little Shakespeare, a little Oscar Wilde'. A hot tip, that: use literature as part of a calorie-controlled diet and watch those pounds simply melt away.

Even then, only by bravely ridding himself of his underwear at the second public weigh-in could he get the scales to dip to where he needed them. Sky Sports shot this great sporting moment very decorously, I thought: from behind and to one side. Nevertheless, we were in Sheffield and Eubank was doing a Full Monty. You don't suppose anyone had thought of that link beforehand, do you?

Some queried the wisdom of the rematch for Eubank. 'Should he quit before he gets hurt?' Paul Dempsey wondered during the build-up. A little late for that, surely. At the end of the first bout with Thompson, Eubank's head appeared to have grown a Victoria plum where his left eye used to be. It made you wince to look at it. Yet that grim injury and Eubank's willingness to fight on with it were the beginning of his reinvention in the public's mind. People began using words like 'grit', 'determination' and 'heroism', where lately they had only used words like 'gold-topped cane', 'monocle', 'drives a huge American lorry instead of a car' and 'nerk'.

It must have been an odd kind of triumph for Thompson. He had defeated Eubank in some style, only to watch the loser vacuum up all the post-fight glory. But that's British boxing for you. We love a loser and can't abide a winner. It took Eubank four consecutive defeats to make him what twenty-three knock-outs had failed to: popular.

Despite the Roman-style tunic he wore on his way to the ring, it was clear that Thompson did not have the gods of showbusiness on his side. Ian Darke, Sky's commentator, scrambled hard for ways to describe him and finally came up with the line 'the family man from Bolton'. In today's strobe-battered, laser-lit, disco-slamming world of boxing, this seemed unlikely to cut it: Chris 'Simply the Best' Eubank v. Carl 'Family Man From Bolton' Thompson. It wasn't hard to see who the crowd were going to come out for.

Indeed, as Johnny Nelson, the likely next opponent of the winner, told Sky beforehand, he was hoping for a Eubank triumph because 'no disrespect to Carl, but he doesn't fill a house very well.' Eubank had another way of putting it: 'I've probably seen more charisma in a bag of Brussels sprouts, to be honest.'

Still, charisma doesn't get you everywhere and it was Thompson who got to dance with delight as once again Eubank's left eye tried to take cover behind his ear. Thompson's post-fight speech, which echoed as if around a quickly emptying arena, was strictly School of Hamed: lots of boasting, lots of prophecy-fulfilment and about as charming as a blow to the kneecap.

Meanwhile, Eubank was backstage maintaining 'I would have fought him with both eyes closed.' Absurdly game to the last then – assuming that was the last. 'He's thrilled us, he's entertained us, sometimes he's bored us silly,' was Darke's necessarily Churchillian summing up. But it may not yet be over.*

* It was. Eubank's post-retirement job as a Sky Sports boxing analyst did not always run smoothly. See page 339.

SKY PLAY THE GIDDY GOAT

27 JULY 1998

It HAS been a quiet summer for Sky Sports. While the terrestrial channels have smilingly shuttled audiences in their millions from one golden sporting event to another (the World Cup, Wimbledon, the British Grand Prix, the Open golf), Britain's richest sports broadcasters have been left in the unusually precarious position of trying to drum up an audience for county cricket and wondering whether Rodney Marsh was available for a phone-in. (He was.) It has felt a lot like old times.

But you underestimate Sky at your peril. It's when they've been wounded that they're most likely to strike. Create three dedicated sports channels and then have them ignored for months on end? That's just not Sky's style. Hence last Wednesday night's amazing scoop: exclusive footage of Brian Kilcline, who used to play for Coventry City, in a race against a goat.

The event was the Sky 'Soccer Sevens' – a title which did no justice to the tournament's full range and glory. The sevens were held in Trinidad and Tobago, for no clear reason that was given, other than that the weather there really is very nice at this time of year. There were several, short, floodlit games of seven-a-side football, before a crowd whose exact size would remain a mystery, and between loosely affiliated teams made up of players who may have performed professionally at any time in the last thirty years. Thus the Chelsea-themed side featured Dennis Wise, Tommy Langley (1974–80) and Alan Birchenall (1967–70). And between the matches there was goat-racing: football stars of the 1970s and 1980s running up and down with Caribbean goats. Jimmy Quinn won his heat. What a pleasure it would be to report a similar triumph for Kilcline. But, alas, the goat beat him.

The next night, the goat racing had been concluded. It was all over, bar the bleating. But there was bright consolation in the form of limbo-dancing with goalkeeper Dave Beasant and (the eventual winner) Danny Cadamarteri, of Everton. You would have to say, the quality of the football was not excellent. In fact, it was pretty much as you would expect from people in their forties and fifties who were on holiday. There would be a flurry of running in the opening minutes, and then a lot of walking. The phrase 'sudden-death', applied to the shoot-out stage, threatened briefly to assume a literal meaning in the case of Frank Worthington. The London All-Stars (featuring Paul Allen and Martin Chivers) managed to lose one of their matches 9–1 – remarkable in a game that lasted only twelve minutes.

Yet Sky, realizing they had on their hands a viewer-winner as powerful as anything else on their summer schedule, pulled no punches. The goals were replayed from two angles, each replay separated by that sparkly graphic of Sky's which says 'Goal'. The commentary, by Ian Crocker, with expert analysis from Brian Marwood, was detailed and studious and threw out all sorts of sentences which one was not expecting to hear again on television, such as 'Brian Talbot is racing away', 'A chance for David Speedie', and 'Mick Harford's no slouch'.

Sky are often attacked by critics for being arriviste, brash and money-centred. But programmes in which former Coventry players race goats surely display an entirely level-headed commitment to quality broadcasting.

Meanwhile, ITV were trying their hand with boxing again, after several years away from the sport. They were in Widnes on Tuesday to watch Liverpool's Shea Neary retain his World Boxing Union light-welterweight title against South Africa's Naas Scheepers. Jeepers creepers: how do you pronounce 'Naas Scheepers'? (Answer: 'Skippers', 'Skoypers' or 'Shippers', depending on whether you are the MC, the analyst Steve Collins or the commentator Reg Gutteridge.)

The coverage was presented, with a smile and an unusual amount of make-up, by Jim Rosenthal, whose portfolio continues to grow and whom ITV clearly see as the only man with the versatility and cool to go up against Des Lynam on the BBC. Unfortunately, Lynam raised the bar another notch at the end of the recent World Cup in France by reciting Kipling's 'If' against a video montage of big moments from the tournament. So until Jim does Wordsworth's 'She dwelt among the untrodden ways', we won't really be able to assess his challenge in full.

COME OFF IT, EILEEN

7 SEPTEMBER 1998

The thoughts of Eileen Drewery, as bestowed upon Sky, were not the feast of mind-expansion for which one had craved, the closeness of her controversial psychic bond with the England coach Glenn Hoddle revealing itself only in her tendency to start sentences with 'at the end of the day'. Was it too much to hope that Britain's most famous faith healer would turn to the camera at one point and loudly invite us all to touch the screen, in the manner made popular by American evangelists? Apparently so.

Instead, in what appeared to be, above all, an act of damage limitation (albeit a rather late one, and perhaps a strangely damaging one), Eileen did her best to come across as an ordinary woman, leading an ordinary life, who just happens to think she can heal people by touching them. We briefly saw her at work, holding a woman's shin. Later we saw her holding another woman's head. Otherwise, the piece was low on specifics but high on denials. A bit like Glenn Hoddle after England's recent game against Sweden.

(Hoddle, as ever, put England's loss down to misfortune: should have had a penalty; shouldn't have had a player sent off; team was in full control of the game until the moment at which they lost control of it, and so on. On ITV, Ron Atkinson's view seemed to bear a closer relation to the game we had just seen. 'We've just gone completely brain dead in the team,' Ron said.)

With regard to her importance to international football, Drewery denied she had any involvement in the selection of the England side, a rumour which not even the most gleeful of Hoddle's ill-wishers had taken seriously. She denied also that her £25 per hour fee (covered by the Football Association in the case of England squad members) was anything other than a fair remuneration for her services. After all, she said, vicars get paid for their work, so why not faith healers? If vicars were in the business of taking umbrage, they might well have done so at this point. You need qualifications to become a vicar.

Debating the interview on *Sport Saturday* (Sky Sports), the ex-pros Rodney Marsh, Alan Brazil and Phil Thompson were attacked by the giggles. 'Marshy's laughing his head off,' Brazil said. 'Don't bring me into it,' Marsh said. And fair enough, really. Looked at from most angles, the Drewery affair is risible. At the same time, coming from footballers, the most superstitious men on earth – men who like to leave the dressing room in a certain order and put on their left sock before their shorts, and so on – the laughter seems a bit rich.

Back on earth, in the week's most eagerly awaited contest, Vinnie Jones was up against Sharron Davies on *Ready Steady Cook!* (BBC1). Who would create, in the studio audience's eyes, the tastier dish over the allotted twenty minutes?

From a nutritional point of view, it was interesting to contrast the swimmer's bag of food with the footballer's. Davies came bearing free-range chicken breasts, oranges, pasta, French beans and yoghurt. Vinnie, who may well have felt he had a reputation to live up to, brought in a tin of baked beans, a packet of Mighty White, a black pudding, a clump of what he described as 'the best sausages in Watford' courtesy of his butcher, 'Gibbo', and, in what appeared to be a token concession to the natural world, some mushrooms. 'Picked from the farm,' Vinnie said. 'Next door's farm.'

While Davies, along with the television chef Ainsley Harriot (whose name, rather suitably in this context, makes him easily confused with an athletics club) began to construct something life-enhancing, protein-rich and nigh-on fatless, Vinnie and a chef called Phil set about assembling what was clearly going to be the mother and father of all breakfasts, assuming it didn't get burned.

Things went promisingly for them at first. 'Gibbo's sausages are looking well,' Vinnie commented. But a slide commenced when he insisted on preparing one of his special omelettes. For anyone wishing to try it, Vinnie's way with an omelette includes controversial use of the grill in the later stages of the cooking. 'Have the grill full blast,' he advised, 'get it in there – comes out nice and fluffy.'

Except on this occasion (put it down to the pressures of early-evening television) it didn't. It looked like a baby's changing mat. The audience, apparently in a state of some shock, had no choice, really, but to go with Davies's pasta number.

Still, this had been by no means a wasted half-hour for Vinnie. Not satisfied with beating eggs, removing the zest from an orange and whipping a bowl-full of cream with a hand-whisk, he had also found time to hold up a sliver of the skin from the black pudding and attempt a joke about practising safe cooking which, given the programme's time-slot (7.00–7.30 p.m.) was abnormally risky. Now, there's mind-expanding.

LENNOX LEWIS: NEW RESERVATIONS

28 SEPTEMBER 1998

The career of Lennox Lewis, who retained his WBC heavy-weight title in America, makes for one of television's more unusual soap operas. Recent plot-twists have included the fight in which the challenger, Oliver McCall, broke down crying and had to be escorted from the ring before the encounter really got going; and the bout where Henry Akin-wande simply clung on to Lewis's waist and was eventually disqualified for being a sissy.

Lewis, of course, would rather prove himself against more solid opposition – for instance, someone who stayed in the ring and hit him a bit. But somehow he can't convince the American promoters to give him a shot at the big boys, and this weekend's fight took place not in Las Vegas or New York but on an Indian reservation.

It's not the case, however, that Lennox only gets to fight against pushovers. Indeed, in the cases of both the weeper and the clinger, he didn't even have to push them over. But those two freak bouts aside, the fights that Lewis gets are in some respects more dangerous than the fights he would face were he more generously acknowledged. If you go up against Evander Holyfield (which is the fight Lennox so badly wants and which the promoters and the television people are keen to deny him), then to some extent you know what to expect. Whereas Lennox's weird position as a champion in the sidings seems only to increase the chances of his being put in the ring with, say, some random Colombian only recently released into the community.

Lewis fought Zeljko Mavrovic, a Croatian who has yet to set fire to the world stage, but a man who, with a Mohican hair-do and a face like a housebrick, looked as though he might well set fire to it as a last resort. The American MC pronounced it 'Choco Marvoree' which made him sound like an ice cream, but did nothing to diminish the terrifying aspect of his demeanour.

Yet the statistics were all in Lewis's favour. As Paul Dempsey and his team in the Sky Sports studio explained, Lewis was taller than the challenger, heavier than him and had a longer reach. He probably would have whipped him at Trivial Pursuit as well, had there been time. Even to the inexpert eye, Lewis seemed the more athletic figure. For instance, he didn't have, as Mavrovic did, breasts which went up and down when he jogged on the spot.

Except Mavrovic turned out to be solid. He fought to the end when the fight was turned over to the judges, who scored in Lewis's favour. So there it was: a points victory against an unknown Croatian. If you were looking to bang the drum for your talent, could you have asked for a worse result?

Sky's Ian Darke informed Lewis that his next fight would, in all likelihood, be against . . . and then I didn't quite catch the name. Or if I did, I've forgotten it. Anyway – some German underling or other. Lewis gamely said he would accept the fight, but added sadly that he would regard it as 'just a snack' on his way to a bout with Holyfield.

One's heart went out to Lewis though he should be aware that, after the Tyson ear-chewing incident, food metaphors in connection with fights involving Holyfield are not to be indulged in, except with extreme caution.

Meanwhile, it's our duty to draw attention to some shoddy behaviour by ITV's Formula One crew this weekend, out at the Luxembourg Grand Prix. One of their number managed to secure footage of Michael Schumacher emerging from a ladies' lavatory. The attendance of cameras at what must have been a very personal moment, was surely not in accord with recent moves within the media to respect the privacy of celebrities.

The sequence, though clear and explicit, was also under-explained: we simply saw Schumacher come out from behind the door and dash off in the direction of the pits. Maybe he simply got taken short. In any case, what's the world coming to when a man can't go to the ladies in peace?

KEEGAN BOUNCES BACK;
EVEL KNIEVEL BOUNCES OFF

5 OCTOBER 1998

It's always good to see a sportsperson spring up again after a potentially career-ending incident. And when that person manages to re-attain the levels of performance we were seeing from them before the incident hit them, then one's pleasure is doubled. Thus it was a happy thing indeed to listen to Kevin Keegan on ITV.

After last summer's World Cup finals in France, many wondered whether Keegan would ever work again as a summarizer. A miserable month for the Fulham manager was compounded during England v. Argentina when he actively contributed to David Batty's penalty miss by reassuring viewers that Batty would score. Many assumed afterwards that Keegan's life on the gantry was over.

We reckoned without the man's immense resourcefulness and character. There he was, watching Arsenal v Panathinaikos in the Champions League as if nothing terrible had ever happened to him. We knew we were witnessing a rebirth right from the moment Keegan commended Arsenal's Nicolas Anelka on 'a fair turn of foot'. Sure enough, Keegan was back to his baffling best, maybe better. 'He's about as tall as they get for a goalkeeper of six foot five,' he said triumphantly at one point.

Fabulously, his pronunciation skills promptly deserted him all over again. (Panathinaikos coach Vassilis Danill, was referred to as 'Mr Vassilius'.) The strange pieces of geographical wisdom were back, too. On Greece: 'It's not an easy place to play football at the best of times.' And so were the moments of insight into individual players which, on closer inspection, seemed to beg more questions than they answered. 'He's got that extra ability which not a lot of tall people have.'

And time and again he would make an instant judgement on a refereeing decision (an offside, perhaps, or a foul), only for the replay to prove the opposite, at which point Keegan would have to say something like: 'Well, there might be something in that.' All in all, it was a performance chock-full of the flair which in the past made Keegan a mustn't-miss item for viewers in their millions up and down the land. It's good to have him back on song.

A theme-night tribute to Keegan cannot be far off, but, in the meantime, BBC2 spent many hours paying homage to Evel Knievel on his sixtieth birthday. It's been a while now since Evel entertained us by leaping strings of double-decker buses while astride a motorbike – and quite often by spectacularly spatch-cocking himself on the tarmac on landing – and many of us have long since been forced to seek substitute thrills elsewhere; in *Gladiators*, for instance, or in the driving of Damon Hill.

But the programming brought the memories flooding back, not least the portion of the evening given over to rescreening David Frost's coverage of the fabled Snake River Canyon Jump of 1974. While President Gerald Ford was publicly forgiving Richard Nixon (Ford wisely chose a time for this act when he figured the fewest people would be paying attention), Evel, live on television, was lowering his spangly catsuit into the cockpit of X2, otherwise known as the 'Sky-Cycle'.

To be literal about it, X2 bore little relation to a conventional bike, appearing rather to be a missile with a seat. Yet, up to a point, one looked at this rocket-led project and thought: 'Big woo.' After all, America had succeeded, not long before this, in putting a man on the moon; where lay the challenge in putting a man on the other side of a canyon?

Still, Frost, granted exclusive access to the proceedings, certainly seemed to find it all very serious, not to mention interesting from a scientific point of view. 'Evel has control of roll,' explained Frost in one of several moments in the programme at which he seemed to be talking in crossword clues.

The possibility that Evel would die or, at least, do himself a mischief in front of a national audience was not ignored by Frost's programme. Indeed, the programme acknowledged that this prospect might be part of the event's appeal for many tuning in. It did so not least of all by playing, during a lull in the action, a moving composition entitled 'The Ballad of Evel Knievel', which was mostly a list of Evel's extraordinary qualities but which also included the line (part threat, part promise): 'Yet he knows one day he's gonna have to face that canyon in the sky.'

That day almost arrived on this occasion. Even as it trembled on the laughably steep launch chute, X2 was showing signs of developing a life of its own. At blast-off, it mockingly deployed its landing parachute and twisted wildly in the wind. Poor old Evel had to be fished off a ledge down by the water.

Was this, strictly speaking, a sporting event? Well, it was certainly an athletic endeavour of a kind, especially for the people who set off in the rowing boat to collect Evel. What's more, it would have satisfied all contemporary Olympic criteria. And it seemed as rational as anything witnessed at White Hart Lane, the home of Tottenham Hotspur, in the last decade or so.

NEARY FIGHTS; EARTH MOVES

26 OCTOBER 1998

Can any other sport match boxing, pound-for-pound, for sheer, unbridled televisual entertainment? Recent memories alone provide a peerless showreel of golden occasions: Tyson's assault on Holyfield; the open-air heavyweight bout in Las Vegas which was interrupted by the arrival of a free-lance self-publicist on a parachute; the night Oliver McCall burst into tears and wouldn't fight; the night Naseem Hamed's big entrance went wrong and he was stuck behind a screen for five minutes, dancing with diminishing enthusiasm . . . Even viewers who have their doubts about the suitability of boxing as a pastime for civilized people would have to admit: when it comes to top-class, glad-you-made-it-into-your-armchair, small-screen moments, boxing spoils us.

And the tradition continues. Consider ITV's *The Big Fight Live*. There we were in Liverpool, several rounds into the fight between Shea 'the Shamrock Express' Neary and his Argentinian challenger, Juan-Carlos 'no one liked him enough or knew enough about him to give him a nickname' Villarreal. Thus far, no weeping, no parachutes, no illegal eating. It was looking like we were going to have to consign this one to the file marked 'Perfectly Conventional Boxing Encounters' and take our disappointment off to bed with us.

And then, bingo: the ring began to fall apart.

Villarreal had already slipped over on the canvas several times and early indications were that he had a problem with his footwear. 'They don't wear the leather boots any more,' said our commentator Reg Gutteridge with a sigh, sadly evoking a more noble and generally more upright age, pre-rubber.

But as the fight wore on, an area of the flooring, inconveniently close to the centre of the ring, began uniquely to take on some of the characteristics of a trampoline. 'Something to do with the ringboards, we suspect,' said Gutteridge. Not even leather boots would have spared a man here, though a surfboard might have helped. What with the hostility of the local crowd and the pasting he was taking from Neary, Villarreal might well have hoped, from time to time, that the ring would open up and swallow him. Suddenly it looked like it might.

Twice the referee was obliged to call a halt while panicked builders with torches crawled around under the ring. As is often the way with builders in a hurry, they solved one problem and left a new one behind them. 'It was a dip,' remarked Gutteridge. 'Now we've got a bump.' So back in went the builders. We knew they were down there because an inspired ITV cameraman dropped to his knees and followed them in. 'We've got a shot underneath the ring,' said Gutteridge. In a long career in boxing commentary, this cannot have been a sentence he had ever imagined himself saying.

There wasn't much to see – rafters and dust, mostly – but one was still boundlessly grateful for that cameraman's work. These were unique pictures from boxing's dark underbelly. 'They're trying to put a staunch under there,' said Gutteridge, using, I assume, a technical term. Gutteridge would also maintain that it wouldn't be a bad idea for someone to prop up the faulty board 'with a heavy stool'. I'm not sure this would have complied with local building regulations, nor necessarily with the stringent sanitary laws affecting places with public access. Suffice it to say, if Reg Gutteridge ever offers to help you with an extension to your kitchen or a loft conversion, just quietly shake your head.

It fell to ITV's Gary Newbon (as it so often does) to go into the throng with a microphone to play the part of the punter who wants a decent explanation or his money back. Newbon collared Danny Gill, the fight supervisor – literally collared him, if, as I think I am right in saying, that was Newbon's hand we could see holding Gill steady in the direction of the camera. 'Very embarrassing,' admitted Gill, before passing the buck with superb slipperiness. 'I wouldn't want to be the ring-man who put the ring up,' he said.

Taking a more objective view, the analyst Steve Collins reckoned the floor had been unsettled by a tumbling heavyweight earlier in the evening. Collins also unsentimentally pointed out that if the challenger had been thinking a bit more clearly, he could have claimed a twisted ankle and got the contest declared void. But he didn't: he soldiered on and lost on points. By miles. So, at the very last, a nickname: Juan-Carlos 'None Too Smart' Villarreal.

Upstairs in the studio, alongside our host Jim Rosenthal, Chris Eubank considered this unusual situation and said, with positively Santa-like beneficence: 'It's no fault of anyone's.' Though wrong, this remark was emblematic of the admirably comprehensive makeover Eubank has undergone in recent months, from monocled poseur to cuddly charmer and amiable dispenser of wisdom and largesse.

The general point to be made, of course, is that all this was available, without additional charge, on terrestrial television. For too long now, satellite television has been allowed to monopolize boxing and we should be grateful to ITV for their gritty efforts to woo the sport back. This kind of showbusiness warrants the widest audience possible.

SCHUMACHER FINISHED BEFORE HE STARTS

2 NOVEMBER 1998

'And it's go, go, go!' shouted Murray Walker at the Formula One Grand Prix at Suzuka, but the cars didn't go anywhere. 'Aborted start,' pointed out Martin Brundle, with that way he has of correcting Walker in his minor errors of judgement.

With everything riding on the final grand prix of the season, we were ready for mistakes. But we suspected they would come from the commentator Murray Walker rather than the Ferrari driver Michael Schumacher. Walker simply has the better record at that kind of thing. In the event, of course, it was Schumacher who stalled on the grid and had to start from the back, denying us a head-to-head finish and sending, perhaps, a sizeable portion of ITV's early-morning audience straight up to bed.

A shame if so. 'There are ways and possibilities,' Schumacher had said, chillingly, after qualifying. That was before he knew he would have to carve his way through the entire field to get a look in. When he did so, all the way up to third, only the camera on board the helicopter could make sense of what we were witnessing. 'You are seeing a meaty-yorick drive!' shouted Walker, with characteristic understatement.

It wasn't enough. Doubtless Mika Hakkinen's championship-winning drive was faultless, but the cameras were on Schumacher. Which has been the story of the season, really. Still, Schumacher will be back. And so will Walker, who has pledged to return, despite the efforts of other teams to retire him.

Will the ex-cricketer Geoffrey Boycott be joining them on our screens? Boycott will soon learn whether a French judge believed him when he said he did not hit Margaret Moore twenty times while she was throwing items of his clothing from a hotel window.* After the recent hearing, Boycott seemed rousingly dismayed that a French court should have the temerity to conduct its business in French. But they do things differently on ITV, so Boycott got to rehearse the matter in English last week, agreeing to an interview with Trevor McDonald for the fetchingly titled programme *The Life and Loves of Geoffrey Boycott.*

Archive footage revealed how Moore v. Boycott was a case which had already been played out exhaustively in the cushioned debating chambers of morning television, probed and prodded by Anne and Nick and Eamonn and the rest. But here was the word from Boycott, pointing out, among other things, that he would find it impossible to hold a woman down with one hand and hit her with the other because his hands were too small.

Around these arresting details, the programme built a picture of Boycott's career in cricket. Let's say that, as a player, he divided people – chiefly between those who didn't like him and those who really didn't like him. But Boycott had some people on his side when he needed them. Surveying that huge team of character witnesses with whom Boycott entered the French court recently, Trevor McDonald's voice-over noted the presence of 'even the publicist, Max Clifford'. But no more was made of Clifford's presence. This

* Boycott lost the case and a subsequent appeal.

programme, one felt – granting Boycott a chunk of national airtime to express his side of the story with the authoritative and respected figure of a newsreader nodding away on the other side of the room – was exactly the kind of image-redressing exposure Clifford would have recommended for one of his clients, had it been available. Not that one is suggesting for a minute that it was Clifford who brokered ITV's exclusive access to Boycott.

The programme took its most extraordinary turn with the entrance of Tony Greig. Greig these days resembles an unlikely mix of former President Gerald Ford and the once-popular computer generated television presenter, Max Headroom. With the gravitas of the one and the twinkling eyes of the other, he was able to offer us detailed evidence direct from the communal shower. 'I've seen him stripped,' Greig said, 'and I can tell you that he's pretty well built.' It was clear from the height of Greig's eyebrows as he said this that he was referring to one area of Boycott's build in particular. Greig then added: 'I suppose there's just the chance that he might be a magnificent lover.'

We weren't told when this interview with Greig had been conducted, but in its blazing openness and its attention to personal detail, it felt distinctly post-Kenneth Starr report. It was certainly hard to imagine it being considered suitable for broadcast in times before the Clinton intern scandal. What we were witnessing here was nothing less than the cold, or otherwise, hand of Monica Lewinsky, reaching into the realm of the sports documentary – a shocking development.

WRIGHTY GETS BREAK; MOTTY GETS SHEEPISH

16 NOVEMBER 1998

After a couple of trial run-outs last season, Ian Wright now gets an extended spell in the ITV first team. Which will surprise many analysts who, on the evidence of those early performances, questioned whether Wrighty could genuinely compete in the pressure-cooker atmosphere of the television chat show. *Friday Night's All Wright* is back, though, and this time it's a series.

Sensitive as ever to contemporary sporting issues, Wrighty described the first programme as 'the show with more kick than John Hartson'. And accordingly the show gave us at home more reasons to wince than Eyal Berkovic.* As, for instance, when, in a low-point in chat-show history, Ulrika Jonsson came on to advertise her availability for a film role (preferably, she said, with the specificity of someone who has thought long and hard about this matter, in 'a romantic-comedy type of thing').

But part of the wonder of Wrighty's abundant, restless and leather-trousered enthusiasm for the job, is that it places him, personally, somewhere where wincing cannot occur to him. Guests get fog-horned on to the stage ('Ulrika Jons-ooorn . . . Tony Ad-oorms', etc.), spend a few moments trying to unpack Wrighty's peculiar, portfolio questions, and

* The rather large John Hartson, then a West Ham player, had been photographed in a training ground incident, kicking the head of the rather frail Eyal Berkovic. Hartson later joined Wimbledon. Wimbledon later got relegated.

then get fog-horned off again. You might not learn much, but it sure goes by quickly.

And meanwhile Wrighty's own contacts enable the programme to surprise us with the kind of notable, cameo events which you are unlikely to see on, say, Des O'Connor's show. 'This,' said Wrighty at one point, 'is Frank Sinclair of Leicester City Football Club making some noise on the drums.' It was. And he did.*

In a quieter mode, the documentary series *Match of Their Day* (BBC2) led us eventually to the study of the football commentator, John Motson. There are, of course, universities in Britain these days where the study of John Motson can secure you an honours degree, but here was meant, straightforwardly, the actual room in his house.

It seemed only fitting that we should confront Motty in his lair after he has spent so many years confronting us in ours. As our vigilant presenter Garth Crooks said: 'There is a corner in every British home that is for ever Motty.' Indeed. Or even a little room in some cases.

Sadly, the fascinating tale of how Motty had put his study together ('I got an office furniture company to give me a quote') occupied only the first few minutes of last week's programme. For the rest, we listened as Motty faithfully and with great scruple retraced the arc of his broadcasting career ('It started in radio, really, Garth, to be honest') and revisited the sites of his greatest glories (Ronnie Radford's muddy goal for Hereford among them) and his most baffling misdemeanours ('Anyone watching in black and white, Spurs are playing in all-yellow today').

* In a subsequent series, the Aston Villa boss John Gregory sang – very well – a plangent, country-rock ballad, accompanying himself on the guitar.

This was cosy viewing for afternoon audiences, but let no one claim that the programme shied away from the harsher issues. It got Motty to agree that, at the conclusion of Portugal v. France in the European Championships of 1984, when a last-minute goal by Michel Platini stole the game for the French, our commentator had gone to a land beyond the grasp of reason. 'I was hysterical,' Motty said, in the touching tone of someone apologising for a major public indiscretion. 'I was over the top there.'

And it got Motty to discuss, in full and on camera, that critically important sheepskin coat matter. Some might think it trivial to be concerned in detail with the history of Motty's greatest contribution to fashionable winter wear for the discerning outside broadcaster. But they should note that Motty's earliest sheepskin was some time ago gifted to the curators of a football memorabilia exhibition, whence it is surely en route to permanent sanctuary in the Victoria and Albert Museum. The question of how Motty came to swathe himself in almost a hundred yards of baked animal is, therefore, of interest to the social historian as much as to the football trainspotter.

'When I started in television,' Motty explained, 'the other commentators had sheepskin jackets – half-length. I just happened to tumble across a chap in Essex who made full-length sheepskin coats. He had the skins in his garage and he came and measured you up, and you had a proper coat made to fit you.'

Even as Motty solemnly told this story, one sensed something untoward hovering in the details. It was a lot to do with that image of an Essex lock-up, hung with hides. And as it turned out, Motty's coat supplier later 'totally disappeared', leaving Motty to wonder poignantly 'whether his sheepskin coats were a cover for something else'.

Quite apart from the potentially police-arousing implications of all this, the case of the vanishing coat-dealer had left Motty with a practical problem. 'The one I have now is on its last legs,' Motty confided. I thought they removed the legs before they put those coats together, but I've never bought one from a garage in Essex, so what do I know? The point is, anyone who understands where a tailor-made full-length sheepskin can be had at a reasonable price had better contact Motty at the BBC as a matter of some urgency.*

EILEEN MOVES TO THE CENTRE

23 NOVEMBER 1998

Ian Wright had a fairly typically busy week: at Wembley with England on Wednesday; on stage briefly with Lionel Richie the night afterwards; and then on the telly on Friday to tell us all about it on his chat show. With perspective, the significant crosses Wright delivered against the Czech Republic seemed to have the edge, in terms of accuracy and penetration, over the top note he delivered during Lionel's 'All Night Long'. The expression 'don't give up the day job' came to mind, though these days, with Wrighty, the question of what exactly constitutes the day job is a complex one.

Similarly, what constitutes the day job of Eileen Drewery, one of Wrighty's guests this week? Britain's most famous layer-on of hands may not have dreamed she would one day

* The mother of a leather-retailer read these words in the *Daily Telegraph* and passed them on to her son. Soon after, Motson was measured for, and took delivery of, a new, full-length sheepskin. It's heartening to think that journalism can be a force for good in this way.

figure on the same chat-show bill as Sheryl Crow and All Saints. 'This show is so rockin',' said Wrighty's DJ sidekick as we approached a commercial break. 'Still to come, Eileen Drewery.' If a pair of less likely sentences was ever spoken on television, I didn't hear it.

Rockin' Eileen was with us after the break, introduced by Wrighty as 'healer Eileen'. Wrighty would later say that he didn't care what other people said about Drewery's job description, but that he certainly believed in her powers, and there was a warm burst of applause from the audience at this endorsement.

'I think people have a misconception that you just do pure footballers,' said Wrighty. Drewery confirmed that this was, indeed, a misconception: she does pure footballers, impure footballers and lots of other kinds of footballers besides.

Drewery also set out the extraordinary theories behind her work with people who have taken recreational drugs. 'People are going to find this hard to take on board,' Drewery said. Apparently, when someone takes drugs ('even marijuana,' she said, meaningfully) something Drewery referred to, without further explanation, as 'their aura' opens up, as do certain 'centres' within the person. At this moment, the tormented spirits of the unhappily deceased, at large within the world, step into those centres. 'Then the aura closes,' Drewery went on, 'and you take on the personalities of these earthbound people. This is where a lot of your suicides come in,' she added.

Drewery, by methods she did not elaborate upon, reckoned she could reopen the aura, reopen the centres and have those spirits out of there 'within fifteen minutes'. 'Well, we wish you all the best with that, Eileen,' said Wrighty.

The conversation had, inevitably and without irony,

turned to the topic of Drewery's treatment by the press. I say 'inevitably', because this is something Wrighty seems to ask all his guests about. Wrighty could have his local butcher on there and he would still want to know how he felt about getting grief from the papers.

Drewery, equally inevitably, said she thought the press had been 'very unkind'. Perhaps a historical perspective might help her feel luckier. In the past, people who claimed unusual powers for themselves were not routinely offered warm welcomes on chat shows. In the seventeenth century, Eileen Drewery would have been tossed into a pond. Preferable, probably, to be teased in the papers. This is, surely, a golden age in which to be a healer.

Anyway, directly after this astonishing stuff from Drewery, someone from *The Bill* came on and did a Spanish dance. It's hard to know where *Friday Night's All Wright* can go from here.

COUCH SURRENDERS TO ANALYSIS

30 NOVEMBER 1998

It would have taken a lot of effort to miss Britain's first official women's boxing match. No other sports event penetrated television so deeply. The film of Jane Couch doing her stuff was seen not just on the sports channels, but on national and local news reports and on the quiz show *Have I Got News For You*. The fight was even on Channel 4's Saturday morning sports magazine, *No Balls Allowed*, a programme which is very pleased with itself for having got the word 'balls' into its title and which normally centres its excitable attention on what young people like to refer to as 'extreme sports' – that is, blokes in dull-coloured fatigues finding ever more complicated ways to fall over in the snow.

'Our cameras were where it really mattered,' said *No Balls*' presenter, Margherita Taylor, who was, I think, being ironic, though the exact weight of a presenter's remarks can be a little tricky to measure when that presenter is speaking to you from the comfort of a brightly coloured inflatable plastic chair, parked in the middle of the pitch at Upton Park.

At Caesar's in Streatham, where the Couch contest took place, the ring wasn't lit for television, so, everywhere they appeared, the clips brought to mind precisely the shadowy underworld from which the bout was intended to signal an emergence. What one saw through the gloaming did not exactly quicken the pulse. One particularly affronted commentator remarked later that it was 'a freak show', but the truth is it wasn't nearly as exciting as that. The fight was only a handful of seconds long when the referee stopped it, inadvertently producing the evening's most committed piece of athleticism by leaping through the air like an overdressed Superman to clutch Couch's newly dizzied German opponent to his bosom.

Afterwards, Couch told *No Balls Allowed* she was 'a nice normal girl that likes to go out to a disco and have a dance'. The fact this even needed saying is an indication of the mountain she senses up ahead – a mountain so steep it would scare the goatee off the most intrepid snowboarder *No Balls* could supply. In the end, Couch's prosperity, and that of her sport, will boil down to something much blunter than sexual politics and her own bravery. It will depend entirely on whether television companies regard women hitting each other as a powerful enough magnet for viewers.

In this matter, the stakes are higher than ever. BSkyB, who

are not known for modesty and restraint when it comes to the acquisition of sporting events, did not, apparently, even bid for the rights to Mike Tyson's comeback fight in January 1998. Those rights, along with Tyson's following bout, went exclusively to the digital television supplier OnDigital, who will doubtless use the purchase mercilessly in their campaign to get us to fork out for one of their set-top devices – boxers for boxes. But if BSkyB won't think about purchasing Mike Tyson fights until there's a title at stake in them, then what hope for the next Jane Couch bout?

Later in the week, Gary Lineker took time out in *Football Focus* to show us some kind of *Match of the Day* calendar for next year. It was open at February and it had a big colour picture of Garth Crooks on it. Lineker said warmly that another page featured Mark Lawrenson.

What a week. Women are boxers. And Mark Lawrenson is Mr August. The sexual revolution is complete.

ARGENTINA RECALLED; A GENERATION MOANS

7 DECEMBER 1998

England's World Cup meeting with Argentina in France was the subject of two competing documentaries. Imagine the number of programmes which would have been dedicated to the game had it been a final. Or a semi-final. Or a quarter-final. But it wasn't. It was a game for a place in the quarter-finals – the equivalent of the fifth round of the FA Cup, or the second Monday at Wimbledon. That's how close England were to glory last summer.

One of the programmes was much better than the other, but both bore sturdy witness to the nation's magnificent ability to dramatize itself in defeat. You want trophies? Forget it. You want tears and whining? Now we're talking.

ITV's programme, *When England Met Argentina*, was the more wildly tangential and should really have had the title of the BBC's programme, *Where Were You?* It proceeded on the basis that it might enrich our appreciation of the game and its context to learn that Richard Madeley's daughter was appearing in a school production of *The Tempest* on that night in June.

But people who don't regularly appear on television were included too. We heard from the bridge school who found the game so compelling that they put their cards down for a while. We met a vicar who set his video. We heard from a man whose shed caught fire near the end of the first half, and from the firemen who came to put it out. A woman who gave birth during the game spoke about her waters. And also her catheter and her kidney infection.

But between the hopeful jollity of these coincidences (fancy that – a kidney infection! And England losing to Argentina!), something more sour began to creep through. 'I really felt as if I'd been robbed,' a fan said, and here was something as recognizably English as stoicism in the face of a charred shed; the overarching sense, in defeat, of having been cheated.

It was there in the BBC's programme, too, along with a number of the same interviewees. Incredible to relate, Darren Anderton made two consecutive appearances last week without sustaining an injury. 'It was stick your chest out time,' Sol Campbell told ITV. 'It was stick your chest out time,' Sol Campbell told the BBC.

But the BBC's programme was better looking and better

centred. Ignoring the claims of people who had amusingly spilt crisps on their sofas, it stayed closer to the football and took its testimony from eyewitnesses. Mick Jagger, who was in the stands, spoke enlighteningly about the surges of unified emotion in the crowd, but without explaining his own, strangely contrapuntal clapping. (Picked up in close-up during the game, Jagger appeared to be creating a rhythm entirely his own.)

Not everyone who was there had a clear view. David Ginola preposterously suggested that the referee gave the English a penalty because he was still feeling guilty about having awarded one to the Argentinians and he was looking for the opportunity to restore justice – as if a referee's job amounted to the distribution among children of a bag of sweets. Or, as Gary Neville told ITV, 'we got nothing off him'.

But the BBC's programme had the courage to use the word 'hype', even if it did not dwell on the ways in which the game had been hyped, nor consider the contribution to football hype in general of a programme which accompanies match footage with a soundtrack of amplified booms and thuds. (If it was once the aspiration of computer games to resemble real football, it is now the aspiration of television to make real football look like computer games.) And it included, from the football writer Patrick Barclay, a pungent and entirely proper analysis of the incident in which Michael Owen gained England a penalty. 'Owen's a diver of world-class proportions, but, of course, at the time it was politically incorrect to say so,' Barclay said.

These words were all the more refreshing for appearing in close proximity to a Glenn Hoddle quotation on the topic of defensive tackling: 'South American players will turn that situation to their advantage.' This was just a polite way of referring to cheating foreigners and it betrayed the insularity and suspicion which may, in part, explain why England so badly underperformed in the World Cup. Though, of course, given the posthumous clamour, few now rate it an underperformance, least of all the players. Shearer said he looked down the pitch at the dancing Argentinians and thought 'that should be us'. But no coherent argument had been produced to suggest why. Only Englishness could account for that feeling.

In the week's biggest technological advance, Sky Sports 2, in conjunction with the Auction Channel, took us live to central London for an auction of Formula One memorabilia. At home, we could bid by pressing the buttons on our phones. On the screen was the auctioneer, working the room but also – occasionally and alarmingly – looking directly into the camera and saying 'the bid is against you, Hemel Hempstead'. One trusts the system is secure. But a worrying scenario presented itself: of trying to phone out for a pizza and suddenly finding oneself the owner of a Mika Hakkinen nose cone at £12,500. These are terrifying times.

1999

HODDLE PUSHED INTO ANOTHER LIFE

8 FEBRUARY 1999

What did television news make of Glenn Hoddle's sacking? As much as it possibly could. Hoddle, a reincarnationist, had tendered his belief, in a newspaper interview, that the disabled are paying for their sins in an earlier life. It was clear that he would pay for this with his job in the present one. On Monday, Channel 4's Kirsty Lang told us: 'The word on the street was that the England manager would be dead by lunchtime.' Dead?

But that's the new, punchy, zippy Channel 4 News for you – a deskless, restless zone in which no one will say 'out of work' if they can say 'dead'. Also symptomatic of its new energy (or its latest ratings panic) is a taste for 'the word on the street'. Which street?

More importantly, the word from the Football Association's acting chief executive was that no decision was expected until the middle of Tuesday at the earliest, which left a lot of space to be filled. But there was no shortage of fillers. There never is. David Mellor, who had surrendered to the cameras without, one suspects, too much coercion, wanted from Hoddle 'nothing less than a fundamental retraction', which sounded like a particularly nasty dental operation.

On Sky News, in this limbo period, talking for his job, Hoddle said he had the backing of his players. 'I've had messages,' he said. 'Via the phone,' he added, carefully. We already knew he was safe until morning, but at 7.53 p.m. Sky decided anyway to look at the odds on his successors. Gazza was at a disappointing 10,000 to 1, along with Eileen Drewery. If I was Eileen, I'd be offended by that.

Over on *News at Ten*, it was Trevor McDonald's turn. Hoddle proposed that his beliefs were too complicated to explain in 'two or three minutes on a TV show'. I liked Hoddle's idea that *News At Ten* is 'a TV show'. He's completely right. Less than a year ago, one might have said 'a news programme'. Now one would say 'a TV show'.

At 10.45, still hard at it, Sky News turned for guidance to Father Lionel, a leather-jacketed man of God and 'an investigator of the paranormal'. The topic was what Glenn might have meant when he talked about the karma from another life affecting disabled people. Father Lionel embarked on a lengthy sculpture analogy: 'It's not a question of punishing the marble, it's a question of giving the marble a different experience.'

Search me: I had lost his marbles. But several minutes later, Lionel wound up: 'That, in a nutshell, is what I think Glenn was trying to express.' It was one of the biggest nutshells ever seen on television. An entire colony of squirrels could have lived a lifetime on that nutshell.

On BBC2, going for greater economy, *Newsnight* showed us a picture of Hoddle captioned 'Professor Eileen Barker, London School of Economics'. In another life, perhaps. *Newsnight* brought to the story its usual challenging mix: adult analysis in the studio, preceded by a film report with the sophistication of a children's point-and-speak book. Imagine having to make this stuff. There was a metaphor in the script concerning Hoddle's 'off-the-shelf' religion, so some poor bloke had to trudge off to a bookshop and film some shelves.

On Tuesday, David Davies from the Football Association announced the termination of Hoddle's contract and then we spent the early evening awaiting Hoddle. You knew it was a significant moment because people were saying 'awaiting' instead of 'waiting'. 'The world awaits to hear his explanation,' said Sky's anchor. 'Er, that was brief but poignant,' he said after Hoddle had issued a statement which didn't explain anything.

And then we went live to Eileen Drewery's house, as you do. 'That's all I have to say on that subject,' she kept saying, but it was always plenty. 'The public, unfortunately, are very gullible,' said Eileen, incautious about causing offence on the widest possible scale.

By 8.48 p.m., Sky News had an American 'branding' consultant on board. 'If I was Mr Hoddle at this point, I would probably get myself involved in some charity works, maybe be seen and photographed with a mainstream music band . . .' Not to be cynical about it, or anything. 'Lose the faith healer?' asked Sky's anchor. 'I think so,' said the consultant.

On *News at Ten*, they were discussing the successor. 'There's already talk of a Howard Wilkinson–David Platt dream ticket,' said the reporter Graham Miller. Good to see, in the midst of all this confusion and oddness, that someone still had the presence of mind to crack a genuinely funny joke.

'The media frenzy pursued him to the end,' said a reporter on the *Nine O'Clock News*, over pictures of Hoddle trying to shove his way through the cameras at his press conference. 'Later in the programme,' said Michael Buerk, 'we'll be examining the media's treatment of Glenn Hoddle and how it contributed to his downfall.' Sky News had referred to a 'media feeding frenzy'; 'They have contributed to his downfall,' said their reporter on the scene.

They? Of course, some of the people we were seeing, clonking each other on the head with their arc lights and booms, were employees of Sky News and the BBC. But it's always breathtaking to witness the loftiness which television adopts on these occasions, pretending to peer down into the pot as if it weren't itself a meaty part of the stew. In any analysis of the impact of 'the media' on somebody's fortune, television begins speaking as if, at will, it can shrug off its media uniform and stand before us as . . . well, what? A mirror held up to nature? In a pig's arse, my friend.

ARSENAL IN GAME OF FOUR HALVES

5 FEBRUARY 1999

'Unfortunately, we scored a second goal.' Thus, unimaginably, Arsene Wenger, the manager of Arsenal. *Match of the Day* had not, I think, been intending to devote much time to Arsenal v. Sheffield United, but the agenda shifted. It's bound to, really, on a day when two players nick a game by ignoring football's only remaining gentlemanly procedure and then their manager, in a fit of remorse, offers to start again from the top.

So at the beginning of the programme, a brief reel of highlights was shown, during which we all did our solemn best to pretend that Gerald Sinstadt had actually been at Highbury, commentating on the game, rather than sitting in a studio in Shepherd's Bush and dubbing on his voice in an emergency afterwards.

'The tall Brazilian has put Sheffield United back in touch,' said Sinstadt, 'and we've only had three minutes of the first half.' Classic post-synched commentary: too much information. It's the sporting equivalent of those overburdened lines in bad television dramas: 'Have you met my brother, the property tycoon who is married to the shipping magnate's sister?'

And then we saw Ray Parlour throw the ball back towards the opposition's goalkeeper (commonly believed to be the thing to do if the ball has been put out to allow an injured player treatment) only for his teammate Nwankwo Kanu to gallop after it and square it to Marc Overmars for 2–1. Shocked Sheffield defenders appeared to be saying: 'But . . . but . . .' And other things.

Everyone in the studio agreed with the Football Association's decision to stage a rematch. In his excitement Des Lynam referred to Steve Bruce, the Sheffield United manager, as Ken Bruce, the Radio Two DJ. And in his excitement, Trevor Brooking had an idea: Why not donate the gate fees from the replay to children's charities in Sheffield and north London? There's nothing like a generous gesture – particularly one made with other people's money.*

It had already been quite a week for games which didn't count: three days before Kanu passed to Overmars, Sky Sports had the live rights to England's 2–0 defeat against the world champions France – an international friendly and therefore, to most people's minds, a meaningless and irritating intrusion upon the club season.

'This match stands in its own right,' insisted the commentator, Martin Tyler, without expanding. Later, Tyler would try bravely to give the game added value by mentioning the

* Honesty paid. Arsenal won the replay

millennium. This is always worth a shot these days if it falls to you to make something unpromisingly mundane seem to have a thrilling historical resonance: 'This week, as the year 2000 hoves into view, we examine the state of vegetable canning,' or whatever.

Tyler went millennial as follows: 'For France this is the last chance to win at Wembley this century.' Good point, yet it was hard to imagine it forming the framework for the manager Roger Lemerre's pre-match team-talk: 'Gentlemen: the millennium is upon us.' He would have been too busy telling Zinedine Zidane: 'Paul Ince has had it. You'll cruise.'

Both the myths traditionally produced to bolster England on these occasions were satisfyingly present in Sky's coverage. The first is the enormously patronizing 'You'll never beat David Seaman from there' myth. Both Stuart Pearce and Andy Gray greeted a mis-hit long-range volley with remarks to the effect that the player had to be mad even to attempt such a shot against a keeper of Seaman's calibre. This despite the famous fact that Seaman was once beaten from the halfway line.

The second myth is that the team everyone wants to beat is England, and the place they want to do it is Wembley. Andy Gray pointed out that this was 'the first French side that's won at Wembley', adding 'that really is impressive'. This, surely, gets the current world order slightly askew. It is not Zinedine Zidane's privilege to play at Wembley; it is our privilege to be allowed to watch him.

But old habits die hard. In the studio, Pearce said: 'I can't see the French beating us.' You waited for him to finish the sentence ('because I've got to leave now for a prior engagement at a dinner near Peterborough'). But, astonishingly, the second half of the sentence never came. That said, it's Pearce's televisual duty on these occasions to be unyieldingly patriotic and very, very wrong.

The national anthem of France was buried in an avalanche of whistling from the home fans and Richard Keys grew solemn. 'What a pity we couldn't have been more respectful. I thought we'd got away from all that. What a shame.' Do we need to get that upset about the booing of national anthems at football matches? It's rarely done in anything more venomous than the spirit of pantomime. But then, who knows? Maybe Keys takes the same admirably firm moral stand at performances of *Cinderella*. The ugly sisters enter and the place erupts. Keys leans over to the person sitting next to him and says: 'What a pity we couldn't have been more respectful. I thought we'd got away from all that.'

LEWIS ROBBED; KING AMUSED

15 MARCH 1999

Lennox Lewis v. Evander Holyfield offered twelve rounds of intermittently entertaining boxing, one brief glimpse of Bo Derek in the crowd, and then the collapse of an entire sport into shoddy farce and dark insinuation. Great value, all in all.

And hats off, in the middle of it, to Sky's commentator Ian Darke, who saw the end coming as early as round nine when he chose to remind us that, even though Lewis was seemingly heading for victory on points, his opponent was 'a Don King fighter in a Don King promotion in America, and we've seen strange things happen before'.

Sure enough, the American judge said Holyfield, the South

African judge said Lewis and the English judge – who used to be indecisive, but now isn't so sure – couldn't make his mind up. Result: a tie. On one side of a split screen, Lewis's jaw dropped to roughly where it would have been if Holyfield had managed to hit it. On the other side, Holyfield seemed to be saying another one of his prayers. 'I'm going to go out on a limb here,' said Darke. 'I think he's been robbed.' I'm not sure that really qualified as a limb. Even Bo Derek had marked Lewis ahead.

Lewis wasn't hanging around. He was off before you could say: 'What happened to the English judge?' Incidentally, Lewis found it a lot easier getting out of the arena than getting in, when he was badly impeded and turned aside to have words with a security guard. A ridiculous moment into which a full inquiry should be launched: the last thing you want on the night of a heavyweight title bout is for a boxer to get into a fight.

Lewis's eventual arrival in the ring prompted our presenter, Paul Dempsey, to speak of 'the moment we have waited so long to see . . . a moment we thought would never come'. Dempsey was alluding to the frustrating path of Lewis's career, but he could equally well have meant the length of Sky's coverage, which had been running for a punishing five hours by now.

For much of that time, inevitably, people had been attempting to make sensible predictions about a fight which, even without so much hype, would have been uniquely tough to call. It was broadly agreed that all of Lewis's strengths could be accounted weaknesses under a different analysis. Either he was so big that he would crush Holyfield simply by falling on him; or he was so big that he wouldn't last ten minutes without melting.

This was great fun for all fans of equivocation, but it

played merry hell with the studio punditry. In London, Sky had assembled Julius Francis, Gary Mason and Earnie Shavers – or what Dempsey justly referred to as 'a line-up of threatening heavyweights with no hair'. All of these men were, without question, as informed as they were bald, but because there was nothing any of them could say about the fight which couldn't be contradicted immediately afterwards, their conversation was slow to move forward.

To help jolly things along, Sky fed a pile of statistics about the fighters into a computer ('conditioning', 'aggression', 'technical skill', 'friendliness with Don King', etc.) and instructed the machine to call the fight. In what would turn out to be the evening's only impartial judgement, the computer predicted a Holyfield win on points.

The members of the studio panel – perhaps niggled by the assumption that a machine could do the job they were getting paid for – were less than impressed. 'To me, that's all jargon,' said Francis. 'A lot of that is codswallop,' said Barry McGuigan. 'Perhaps I should emphasize, it's just a bit of fun,' said Dempsey, sounding a little hurt.

Darke said the event was 'a real Anglo-American confrontation', and never was this more so than during the singing of the national anthems. The American anthem was sung by 'R & B recording artist, D'Angelo'; 'God Save the Queen' was sung by 'Henry Brown'. Say what you like about Henry, he gave it everything and was sometimes even in key. 'England! England!' he shouted at the end. 'Thank you very much, Henry Brown,' said the MC, bravely.

After the fight came the recriminations. These were carefully worded. 'It worried me because it was a Don King promotion,' said Lewis, without being any more specific. The message, though, didn't take much decoding. We had tuned in hoping to witness what Darke called 'a sporting moment for the millennium'. What these people seemed to be suggesting was that we had just watched an episode of 'Don Takes All'.

You don't need to be Sky's computer to figure the likelihood of a rematch. And the hype-rocket will go up once more and the whole ludicrous farrago will begin again. Can't wait.*

CARS ONE JUMP AHEAD

10 MAY 1999

Heavy weather at the Badminton Horse Trials – or rather, to give them their arrestingly cross-cultural full name, the Mitsubishi Motors Badminton Horse Trials. Occasionally, during Saturday's cross-country section, the BBC would throw us a long-shot in which a rain-lashed rider was dimly discernible forging a lonely path across the Somme. Frankly, these were conditions which you wouldn't have braved in a Mitsubishi Motor, let alone on the back of a Badminton horse.

Yet out they went, regardless. And, this being Badminton, what they faced, apart from raindrops the size of soup cans, was a succession of jumps and obstacles named to evoke both good old country charm and good old multinational corporate sponsorship. Riders were obliged not only to jump the Churn Stand and the Sheep-Feeder, but also to make their way through the Shogun Hollow – named after the Mitsubishi Motor, I take it, rather than the movie – and the first fence wasn't a fence at all, but rather a pair of

* Honesty paid again. Lennox Lewis won the rematch.

Mitsubishi flat-bed trucks which had been backed together and planted with flowers.

What with the incredible names of the jumps, the even more incredible names of the horses, and the still more incredible names of some of the riders, the event offered viewers at home the chance to savour an array of the most intriguingly poetic sentences spoken in sports commentary. 'Broadcast News very positive leaving the Beer Barrels', for instance; or 'Pippa Funnell away from the Picnic Tables'. What with everything, it took me a while before I was entirely confident that Pippa Funnell was a rider, rather than an especially devious fence. 'Leaves on her hat – she won't know about that,' said Mark, our commentator, and there was, one felt, a song in there somewhere.

How unsentimentally this event brings hope into contact with absurdity. You would set off, go encouragingly well for a while, jump a few Japanese cars, and perhaps even a random Portaloo for good measure, then lose it in the Carisma Pond and end up astride your horse's nose with your boots full of water.

There can be no other sport in which people go to such extraordinary lengths to entertain us; 6,840 metres, to be exact. Some of the riders were complaining politely that this year's course design featured too many turns. To the uninitiated eye, that looked like the least of their problems. Personally, I would have been complaining that the course featured too many Mitsubishi Shoguns.

Whatever, you could get round in about thirteen minutes, assuming your horse was a good swimmer. Talking of good swimmers, it was only appropriate somehow that Sharron Davies should have been our presenter. There was no gain-saying her description of Badminton as 'the world's toughest three-day event', particularly as it was spoken from somewhere inside one of the world's toughest mackintoshes.

Though happy to let a woman wear the horse-eventer's raincoat, British television has not once allowed a woman to don the sheepskin of football commentary. Reporting for *Correspondent* (BBC2), Helen Rollason wondered why not and pointed out that it was different in Italy. She led us to Donatella Scanatti, a football commentator on Italian television for ten years, and also to Sister Paula, a nun and a Lazio fan (she was shown at a game, not only scrutinizing the play, but also working her way diligently through a large tub of popcorn) who gets work in Italy as a television pundit. Imagine Jimmy Hill in a wimple. Actually, cancel that thought.

In Britain, the call for nuns to have parity with Alan Hansen is seldom heard; what about the call for a woman to do the commentating? *Match of the Day* already has a female summarizer, and it would be a short step from there to match coverage. How would it go down? Rollason took a vox pop on people entering a Chelsea game; and who should pop up to offer his vox but David Mellor.

Mellor took the sensible and broad-minded view that the only qualification was reliable immersion in the game. But then he rather spoiled the effect. 'A woman should only do it because she's a John Motson with looks,' he added. So, to sum up: Mellor says women can come on board, but they will have to know a lot and look right. A stiff challenge. But weren't these the very same mountains Mellor had to climb on his way to becoming the face of the Football Task Force?*

* The Football Task Force was a short-lived, government-encouraged but entirely powerless committee which spent the final few years of the twentieth century bringing about absolutely nothing that anybody can remember.

HONEST KEV KEEGAN: THE HONEYMOON

7 JUNE 1999

'I've got to be honest, as I always will be,' said Kevin Keegan to Gary Newbon on ITV, just before conceding that England could have played better against Sweden. 'Kevin as honest as ever there,' said Bob Wilson after this extraordinary, perceptive and, above all, honest admission.

'Honest as the day is long, isn't he?' said Richard Keys, after Keegan had made much the same post-match speech to Sky Sports' George Gavin. 'Honest, as you would expect of him,' echoed Clive Allen.

Honest Kev, we may surmise, is a bit of a hit with television. This may not be entirely unrelated to the fact that Honest Kev – unlike certain previous holders of the England manager job – doesn't seem to think television should be treated like an itchy rash. The expression of semi-complicity which Glenn Hoddle grudgingly mustered for post-match interviews used to die from his face before he had turned away from the camera. On a really good day, the final question would have to be directed at his retreating back. Contrast Honest Kev, who at least has the patience to stay until the questions have finished, and who signed off from Saturday's tunnel encounter with Gavin by saying not just 'thank you', but 'thank you ever so much'.

Honest Kev had tried to staunch our disappointment at the preceding ninety minutes (during which the tally of English shots on target matched the tally of English players sent off; one of each) by saying: 'The one thing we take out of this game is character.'

Clearly we are at the beginning of something huge here –

nothing less than a reversal of our traditional attitudes. Unless I misunderstand their tone, what Keegan and those in his thrall are asking us to do right now is turn our minds from such frivolous and worldly things as points and qualifications for the finals of tournaments and to seek succour instead in enduring and important abstract human qualities, such as character and honesty. This is impressive. Indeed, the Keegan era seems to be intending to bring about nothing less than a revolution in our moral thinking. It poses the quandary: would you rather have a manager who was out of his depth but never less than honest about it, or a manager who lied through his teeth and won the European Championship? And it urges us to answer: 'Honesty, every time.'

Can this revolution prevail? Nil–nil draws at home to Sweden probably don't help. Richard Keys was anxious to know: 'Is the honeymoon period over?' and both Sky and ITV visited the press box after the game in order to canvass football journalists for their opinions on this. This was a haughty and cunning device whereby critical remarks about Keegan could be packaged as a comment on the print media and its legendary impatience rather than as a comment by television on Honest Kev – a sneaky way of getting juicy issues into the programmes without acknowledging any responsibility for them. Television at these moments is like the embarrassed purchaser of a sex aid: 'It's not for me; it's for a friend.'

Anyway, the consensus in the box seemed to be that Keegan was still on his honeymoon, but that the hotel was terrible, the food inedible and he had forgotten to pack his swimming trunks, so there was every possibility of his taking an early flight to reality next Wednesday if England failed to beat Bulgaria. But he would do so honestly.

HONEST KEV KEEGAN: BACK TO REALITY

14 JUNE 1999

Kevin Keegan: Football Messiah? (Channel 5) wondered whether those features thought to be the England manager's chief assets – his passion, his commitment – might not in the end produce his downfall. Would Keegan be the man to pilot England to long-absent success? Or would his head explode first?

History suggests Keegan has felt the pressure on the big occasion. Rather more worryingly, it suggests he has felt the pressure on the little occasion, too. The most extraordinary thing about his famous dust-up with shy, harmless Billy Bremner was that it happened during – of all things – the Charity Shield. And the match in Hamburg in which Keegan punched someone and earned an eleven-match suspension was, likewise, a friendly.

The programme thrust into plain view some further disquieting contradictions. For instance, at the vertiginous height of his fame as a player, Keegan piously refused to endorse cigarettes. Yet he happily did commercials for 'the great smell of Brut' which, surely, has contributed at least as much as smoking to the pollution of the atmosphere.

Also, the programme reminded us, there was that hard-to-excuse permed phase in Germany, when Keegan went around coiffed, not like a leader of men, but like a Manhattan poodle. Forgivingly, a German journalist informed us: 'This kind of haircut had everybody in Hamburg.' I took it the phrasing arose from the fact the speaker was working in a second language. Then again, it was quite a perm. Perhaps this person knew exactly what he was saying. To adapt the

Beatles: 'I once had a haircut – or should I say, this haircut had me.'

All in all, the programme's drift was that, for someone in public life, there was a potentially dangerous degree of emotional incontinence here. 'This is the only job I've ever wanted,' Keegan told Newcastle United fans before he became the team's manager. So was the England job, though. And dinosaurs would return to roam the earth before Keegan left Fulham, Kev always implied; yet, without so much as a solitary Stegosaurus on the horizon, he was off to Lancaster Gate.

In the aftermath of such about-turns, Keegan has tended to fall back on the classic excuse of the romantic scoundrel: he meant what he said at the time. To analyse this coldly, what Keegan is never less than nakedly honest about is the fact that he can't necessarily be trusted. But, the plea is, at least he's honest about it. It's what you call a win-win situation.

Unfortunately, England's last two games have been a draw-draw situation. As one of the contributors to the programme prophetically said: 'Somewhere down the line, there will be bad results.' Indeed. Less than twenty-four hours down the line, Channel 5 were showing England failing to beat Bulgaria.

Here was a good illustration of what passion and commitment, divorced from tactical cunning, can get you: fifteen minutes of panicked dashing about and mistimed tackles, and then seventy-five minutes of cluelessness and sulking. It was not pretty to watch. And, with Jonathan Pearce doing the commentating, it wasn't pretty to listen to, either. 'Sheringham's header! Oooorgh!'

The function of Pearce is, as far as one can make out, to produce a lot of noise, to be a cheerleader for Team England,

and to show passion and commitment at the expense, if needs be, of characteristics formerly cherished in commentators, such as perspective, sobriety and wit. Very much a commentator for the Keegan era, then.

But given his brief to be bare-chested and war-painted on our behalf, it is strange how often Pearce seems to be trying to pass himself off as a librarian. His commentary seemed designed to suggest a lifetime's immersion in the Bulgarian equivalent of the *Rothmans Football Yearbook*. The arrival, for instance, of a Bulgarian substitute sent Pearce into a 5,000-word dissertation on the player's recent history: 'His two goals last weekend won his club side their first title since 1994.' And so on and on, for hours.

Perhaps we are intended to forge, from this painstakingly displayed background work, a link between Pearce and John Motson, that one-man mission to the Planet Arcane and the acknowledged master of statistical retrieval from deep space. But whereas Motson is clearly enchanted and enthused by his stats, Pearce just sounds as if he is reading this stuff out. The retirement from international football of the tremendous Hristo Stoichkov was certainly worth remarking. It drew this from Pearce: 'The former furniture shop assistant and electrician from Podkova, Bulgaria, departs the scene.' Nobody on earth actually talks like this, so why does Jonathan Pearce?

Over on *Match of the Day*, England got their most thorough kicking of the evening from Alan Hansen. At his most frightening, post-watershed best at these times, Hansen cogently argued that it didn't matter what Keegan did in the way of motivating people if those people couldn't actually pass a football. Fair point. Was it just coincidence that Hansen was dressed in undertaker's black?

CHANNEL 4 SHORT-CHANGED IN CRICKET DEAL

5 JULY 1999

Inspired, almost certainly, by the recently concluded cricket World Cup, England and New Zealand have devoted much energy to perfecting a new, intense and supremely television-friendly version of cricket: the one-day Test.

They didn't quite pull it off, somehow losing focus a little and eventually allowing the match to drift on for two and a half of the allotted five days. But these are early days and by the end of the series, who knows, these two gifted teams could be wrapping up the whole thing by tea on the Thursday. No more tedious Saturday afternoons, then, and no more patchy Mondays. Say what you like, it's a way forward.

It's possible that Channel 4 will be less supportive of this exciting new initiative, having recently written a large cheque for Test cricket on the assumption that it would furnish many hours of broadcasting over the next few years, rather than the odd forty minutes here and there. Already the title of the channel's nightly highlights programme, *Today At The Test*, looks to be in trouble and may have to be adapted in the future to *This Morning At The Test* or, more simply, *Today's Test*.

Still, while it survives, the first thing to say about *Today At The Test* is that, at 7.40 p.m., it's positioned at a time in the evening when people might actually watch it – a fairly simple broadcasting notion, though one the BBC never really seemed to get the hang of. Somehow the Corporation formed the opinion that cricket fans were the same people who watch re-runs of *Prisoner, Cell Block H* and/or study for Open University degrees – people whose needs would happily be met by an 11.50 p.m. start. Which may have been true in a lot of cases, but many will be grateful to Channel 4 for taking a broader view.

The programme was broadcast from an entirely conventional, pitch-side commentary booth – assuaging at a stroke the fears of those who thought the channel's project to youthify cricket would oblige them to present the sport live from the dance floor at the Ministry of Sound, with Pete Tong spinning records in the background.

The format didn't crack any moulds, either. A special guest and a member of the commentary team joined Mark Nicholas in picking over the day's play. Again, people's worst fears have not materialized: thus far the special guest has not been a former weather-girl with her own chat show on Channel 5, nor a deeply unfunny London pub comedian with a regular gig on a quiz about Seventies television. Rather, we've had players who have taken some part in the day's action and thus might reasonably be expected to have something straightforwardly illuminating to say about it. Even if they're Phil Tufnell, or 'Tuffers', as Mark Nicholas prefers to call him.

Tuffers says 'yer know' a lot. In fact, Tuffers says 'yer know' for England. On Thursday, settling down straight away, he managed nine 'yer knows' in his first two answers and thirteen by the completion of the opening session. At tea, Tuffers had moved on to an astonishing twenty-five 'yer knows'. The final session was a less busy and more frustrating one for him, but by close of play, Tuffers was twenty-six 'yer knows' not out – a stalwart performance which will have done his 'yer know' average for the season no harm whatsoever.

The graphics – again, with no ingratiating nod towards the teen market – are clear and pleasing in shades of Andrex. And as for studio gimmickry, the much-remarked 'Snick-ometer' (a sonogram for gauging whether ball has clipped bat or pad on its way through) had a quiet debut. In a programme notable for the moment that Richie Benaud described a lame shot as 'a real windy woof' (an expression which only he could get away with), Nicholas further introduced 'The Danger Zone', a device by which the path of the ball towards the stumps could be analysed by freezing the image and rendering the batsman see-through. This would have been more impressive if the batsmen hadn't been doing such a good job of that themselves.

There are no plans yet that we know of to feature England and New Zealand in an edition of *Clash of the Titans*, a series of documentaries on major sporting face-offs – for example, that particularly bitter 1991 Ryder Cup at Kiawah Island when an American side, pumped full of post-Gulf-War patriotism, decided to leave no butt unkicked in their fight to take back the trophy from the Europeans. Even Dave Stockton, the American captain, had to admit now that the team hats he commissioned in khaki camouflage were a touch de trop. And the 'Wake the Enemy' phone calls placed to the Europeans in their hotel rooms at 5.00 a.m. were perhaps not in the purest spirit of sporting engagement. But what's to be expected from a competition with only honour at stake and no prize money? Clearly, when you remove the incentive of financial gain from sport, all sorts of truly base motives emerge.*

* See also football's Charity Shield, which regularly descends into violence. Sometimes money is the only reliable buffer between sport and total lawlessness.

POOL DEEPER THAN WE KNEW

26 JULY 1999

Sid Waddell is known first and foremost as the Voice of Darts, a role in which his perceptive analyses, his erudite analogies and, above all, his shouting, have secured him the status of a living legend. But let it not be overlooked that Sid's portfolio also includes that other sport of kings – pool.

So Sid was in Cardiff with Sky Sports for pool's World Championships – 'the biggest event in nine-ball history' apparently. Until the next one, anyway. Sky – being Sky – like to show the breaks again in slow motion and with a healthy twist of reverb on the soundtrack, so that the clack of the balls sounds like fifteen guns going off in the Grand Canyon. In such a context, Sid is the only realistic complementary option.

Sometimes a player's name is all he needs. When Sid pronounces, in broad Geordie and a state of guttural excitement, 'Kawabata', it sounds like the battle cry of the Teenage Mutant Ninja Turtles. Sid further reckoned the enthusiasm of Cardiff's pool-watchers was such that, if they had to, 'some of them would get here on biplanes wrapped with gaffer tape'.

You or I might see a low-rent pub game. Sid dives in deeper and returns clutching shining evidence of an epic sport, twice as cerebral as chess and conducted by hyper-conditioned Olympians on a treacherous surface. 'No nap at all. It's like a pat of butter out there,' shouted Sid.

He had some complex thoughts, too, on the variance of pool-playing characteristics according to nationality. 'Some of the Filipinos don't use draw so much,' Sid mused. 'Do they look for angles more than other people?' Questions, questions.

With Sid's fires of excitement burning hot even by his own astonishing standards, Britain's Steve 'Night Rider' Knight took on former world champion Fong-pang Chao for a place in the semis. Fong-pang had a dapper mien. 'Looks like the sort of lad who wouldn't be out of place as a gentleman gigolo on a cruise liner,' said Sid. The Night Rider, meanwhile, looked more like someone who might have helped bolt some of the bigger bits on to Fong-pang's ship. In a moment of high drama, Fong-pang pulled off an outrageous jump shot, making the cue ball leap over a couple of obstructions and pocketing the ball on the other side: an Evel Knievel stunt, albeit on a very much more limited scale.

Not to be outdone, the Night Rider was soon reaching for his own, specially truncated, jump-shot cue. But there then followed several moments of wrestling with a disobedient plastic case, which deadened the suspense rather. 'He obviously doesn't use it very often,' it was observed, 'because he's having trouble getting it out.'

Nevertheless, Waddell decided at one point that the tournament was exciting enough to be described as 'a boy scout jamboree wi' money'. And without hesitating, he added, 'and you know what Baden-Powell used to say: "Do your best or bust." ' I'm not sure that's exactly how the founding father of the scouting movement expressed it, but point taken.

With David Duffield commentating on the Tour de France on *Eurosport*, television last week offered us a rare opportunity to enjoy not one, but two of sports commentary's great extemporizers. When I joined Duffield, somewhere in open country, he was in the middle of a lengthy, and by no means atypical, rumination on the topic of the privatization of French national industries. Bikes were going by but it was clear that, for Duffield, who has whole hours to fill, they were merely an opportunity, a pointer to greater, more resonant things: monologues about restaurants, eclipses, pet-keeping and arable policies. Like Waddell, Duffield is, I think, some kind of genius.

There was no cycling or pool or cricket on BBC1, but there was *Auntie's Sporting Bloomers* presented by Terry Wogan. No other programme title, I find, causes the contents of the stomach to brim in the throat quite so efficiently. Does anyone refer cosily to the BBC as 'Auntie', apart from the BBC themselves?

Here's a series which, granted access to the BBC's entire sports archive, smirkingly shoves aside the footage of things worth seeing again to get to the pictures of people falling over – ice-skaters, skiers, gymnasts. It seems to me that, in order to find this stuff funny, you have to miss the point, massively, about what it is that ice-skaters, skiers and gymnasts do. A gymnast falling over would only be a joke, surely, if the risk of falling over wasn't actually central to gymnastics.

Before a warmly appreciative but strangely invisible audience, Wogan performs his usual, self-saving act of detachment, letting us know, mostly by pantomime use of the eyes and eyebrows, that the dismal thinness of the programme, the challengingly unfunny nature of its script and the bowel-straining poverty of what it offers as entertainment have occurred to him well in advance – probably even before the cheque for his services was credited to his bank account. He adopts that practised, set-upon look of his which says, 'I wish I was elsewhere, doing something different.'

Well, in this case, so do we, so maybe an agreement can be reached.

LEWIS A SNIP FOR BARBER

23 AUGUST 1999

Always avid, the BBC's team for the World Athletics Championships in Seville rises to fascination in an almost parental degree for the doings of 'young British hopefuls'. In heats containing glamorous American multimillionaires, trusty Jamaican gold experts and dour Moroccan record-busters, our commentators will alert us to the presence, in lane seven, of a Fiona or a Delbert, about whom we may have heard little before, but in whose tender hands, apparently, rests the entire future of, say, British 400 metres hurdling.

Then, as the American, the Jamaican and the Moroccan power off into the distance in a cloud of jewellery and high-performance sunglasses, the commentator will update viewers on Fiona's performance, normally using the classic formula 'Fiona with a little bit of work to do at this point'. That's commentator-ese for 'Fiona will be lucky to finish at all at this rate' and it's normally followed, not long afterwards, by its companion statement 'She'll be very disappointed with that.'

With the temperature running so high for the hopefuls, the gauge positively explodes all over the studio for Denise Lewis who, in addition to being a British athlete, is an established achiever. Lewis gave us a weekend's worth of drama in the heptathlon, an event which involves running, jumping and throwing things – not at the same time, though on the same day, which is almost as bad.

She was up against Eunice Barber, a welcome presence at these championships, not least because of the opportunity she provides for puns around the theme of 'the Barber of

Seville'. Barber took an early lead, but Lewis crept back in the shot put and the 200 metres, and, though she finished in second place, everyone in the studio was deeply impressed with her. 'She actually had to go to the well a couple of times,' said Sebastian Coe – an event I must have missed.

The mornings are the best times, in fact. The sun, though full and warm, has yet to start burning holes in the track and in the lycra of the competitors. The stands are largely empty and what noise there is echoes to the distance. The big names from the running events are mostly still asleep in their hotel rooms, or down at the chemist. And in their place, enormous Germans roam the stadium, clutching lumps of metal.

'They don't come any bigger than this in discus circles,' said Stuart Storey, as the screen filled with just a small selection of the muscles belonging to Lars Riedel. He didn't look like the kind of guy who would just laugh it off, were you ever to spill your drink on his discus. Clearly if one is to move in discus circles at all, it's as well to move carefully.

Anyway, so there I was, a bit later, watching the Test match on Channel 4, and this bloke comes in to bowl. And I thought, blimey, it can't be him, can it? And do you know what? It was.

Last year Ed Giddins, along with a mate of his, was flogging Christmas trees from a garage at the end of my road. I often wondered what a Christmas tree salesman did in the months between January and November, which are traditionally slow ones for the trade, and now I know. He plays cricket for England.

In any other circumstances, this switch of fortunes would have the beautiful implausibility of a *Boy's Own* tale. One would marvel at the astonishing alchemy which could turn a tree-seller into an international sportsman in little more than the time it takes to say, 'Lovely shape, that one; a tenner to you.' But, unfortunately, this is cricket we're talking about. In this case, it just makes you wonder about England.*

Channel 4's new cricket mission has been an unqualified success in all but the cricket. If only the cricket had been prepared to meet Channel 4 halfway. Some careful analysis of replays of English bowling revealed that Andy Caddick couldn't find the right length and that Alan Mullally couldn't find the right line. Quite a combination, then. You almost wanted them to turn the technology off. It seemed heartless to use it.

There were signs that the beneficent patience which had characterized the channel's approach early on was beginning to give way to tetchiness at last. 'Well, it just won't do, will it?' said the presenter Mark Nicholas during a particularly rich carnival of incompetence, England's last three first-innings wickets having just fallen in less than ten minutes and with only three runs added to the score. 'It's way below what's required.' Everyone needed a break.

DES DEFECTS; GINOLA CHANGES SHAMPOO

20 SEPTEMBER 1999

Desmond Lynam. You remember him. Sports presenter. Moustache. Bit of a hit with the ladies. That's the one. Well you won't believe this, but the story is he's got a new job. Yes, really. And with ITV, too. Something of a hush-hush

* In slow moments, Giddins and his pal spent a lot of time trying to land a ball in the tree-wrapping machine from the other side of the street. They were pretty good at it. You would never have known they were cricketers.

affair, apparently, apart from the full-page advertisements ITV placed in the broadsheet newspapers (giant portrait of Lynam over the slogan 'The Summer's Biggest Signing') and before that, the blanket national news coverage of his defection, which caused the *Guardian* to put an enormous picture of Des across their front page and place the story about the four hundred people who had just died in a train crash in India somewhere inside.

On Wednesday, following a sensible cooling-off period, Lynam was in a pitch-side kiosk at Stamford Bridge, waiting for Chelsea to play AC Milan. He had made a warm-up appearance the previous night, deep into Bob Wilson's highlights programme. It's Wilson, of course, who most feels the knock-on from Lynam's arrival, which is destined to nudge him away from the live action and across to the recaps – in other words, into that weird, late-night region known in sports broadcasting as the highlight zone. I don't know whether Wilson lost sleep over Lynam's arrival before, but he's certainly losing it now.

Anyway, here, finally, was the first-team debut. Lynam was sitting almost side-on to his desk when the camera first caught him, which is always a sure sign that he's about to wax a little wry. 'Good evening,' he said. 'I had a feeling we'd be meeting again.'

OK, so maybe the coolest thing he could have done would have been to ignore the hullabaloo altogether: just turn up, clock on and carry on working as if nothing had happened. But when your latest career move has drawn the kind of rapt attention which more normally accompanies divorces involving heirs to the throne, you can hardly not nod to the fact.

Lynam nodded to it again when re-acquainting himself with Terry Venables, another defector from the BBC ('They kept us apart too long'). And he nodded to it a third time when we returned from a commercial break after the match. In a moment which may not have been entirely off the cuff, Venables was telling Lynam that he sensed the new boy actually rather liked the breaks. And Des said: 'You get a cup of tea away.' The appeal of ITV has never been made more graphically clear: money to burn, lots of live football and you get a cup of tea away.

Incidentally, the exact manner in which Des would lead into his first commercial break was the subject of feverish betting pre-kick-off, with the solid, if unoriginal, 'Don't go away' closing at 2 to 1 on favourite. 'Hey – don't butt out during the ads,' caught the eye at a thoughtful 7 to 2, the cutely archaic 'We'll return right after these messages,' attracted money at 11 to 1, and 'Tell you what – kettle time,' was the rank outsider at 100 to 1. But Des played it totally straight and the bookies cleaned up ('Here it's Chelsea nil Milan nil, and we shall continue very shortly'). He's back and he's still not predictable.

Shocking news, however, during one of those commercial breaks, for anyone who cares deeply about football: David Ginola is now using an anti-dandruff shampoo. A bolt from the blue, this. There had been, to my knowledge, no press release from Tottenham Hotspur detailing a change in the condition of David's scalp and there was no sign of any flakiness in Channel 5's documentary profile of Ginola. Well – apart from the usual kind of flakiness.

Yet there he was, plain as the scurf on your shoulders. And where once he had shaken his head and spoken to us of his hair-care needs and a bottle of L'Oreal Elvive had popped up, now he shook his head and spoke to us of his hair care needs and a bottle of L'Oréal Elvive Anti-Dandruff Formula appeared.

Yet, strange to report, David was saying exactly the same things about this new shampoo as he used to say about the old one – how he needed to look good, how he had to rely on a shampoo which was muscular enough to wash the strength back in, how he was worth it, etc. Also, while he was saying the same things, he appeared to be standing in exactly the same locations in exactly the same order. You might even say it was the old commercial, with all the references to the old shampoo cut out and some references to the new shampoo bunged in.

But that can't be so, can it? I mean, it would rather diminish our faith in the original endorsement if that endorsement could simply be cut and pasted around subsequent products. And does David have dandruff, or does he not? Until such time as we get some official clarification on this from George Graham at Spurs, we remain in a state of confusion and anxiety.

SWEDES DO IT FOR TURNIPS

11 OCTOBER 1999

Much, as we knew, was riding on the outcome of Sweden v. Poland. Anything less than a Swedish victory and it was cheerio England. No European Championships for the manager Kevin Keegan. Not much for Kev at all, in fact, until the next World Cup qualifying campaign. Just the occasional friendly against the Faroe Islands or Tonga, and the opportunity to make faintly uninspiring remarks afterwards about how well young Joe Cole (or whoever) seems to be adapting to the international stage. Keegan's original idea that he could do the job part-time would have looked strangely prophetic.

But if the Swedes came good, then the entire future of English football was back on again – or potentially, via a pair of play-offs. In the edgy discussions ahead of and during the game on Sky Sports, it was made clear that both 'a lifeline' and 'a back door' were in Sweden's gift. Would the Swedes open the back door and throw the lifeline? Or would they open the lifeline and throw the back door?

In the Sky studio, Stuart Pearce – sporting an England tracksuit top and thus flouting section 17, paragraph iii of the Live Sports Broadcasters' rule book, which expressly forbids the wearing by pundits of replica kit and/or anything else which looks like Boy George might have designed it – expressed his opinion that Sweden were 'a very honest side'. Not for them, he implied, a dodgy deal with the opposition for the sake of a laugh at England. 'They don't travel well, these Poles, do they, Stuart?' asked Richard Keys, and Pearce confirmed that they did not.

Two steady pointers there, then, but the tension refused to dissipate. Keys, our anchor in this sea of nerves, was probably right to call the match 'the most important game that England haven't played for a long, long time', though some might say the finals of any major tournament in the last thirty-three years could also qualify. But it was definitely – what with the rugby on ITV and the shops being open and the match being subscribers only – one of the most important games that England hasn't watched for a long, long time. 'I think it'll be a really dour, rubbish game,' said Ray Wilkins, playing his own small part in the further miniaturization of the viewing figures. But it wasn't about the quality of the football; it was about getting the right result and never mind how. Very much an English occasion, then.

A lot was thought to hinge on whether the Poles would play for the draw which was all they required. Wilkins, revealing himself to be something of a student of the Polish mind-set, thought that this much was certain. 'It's a totally different mentality from what we're used to, Richard,' he said. 'If that was us in there, we'd go out to win the game.'

'And maybe lose it,' said Keys, who seems promptly to have regretted this little moment of satire and saw fit to add a small clarifier when we returned from a break. 'When I said England would lose, I'm not having a go there,' Keys said. Just so long as we're all clear on that.

The panel gave some weight to the feeling that this entire predicament was an embarrassing one for England, and that any side genuinely worth a place in Euro 2000 would not have to ask Sweden to fight their battles for them. Yet Pearce, seeking the inevitable extenuating circumstances, would not hold with the idea that a qualifying group containing Bulgaria could in any way be described as second rate. 'Bulgaria, you weren't sure what they were going to throw up,' he said. That did sound off-putting, one had to concede.

Ray Wilkins attempted to steel us with the argument, heard from Keegan a while ago, that Euro 2000 simply would not be the same without England, a point of view worth discussing with the Dutch and Belgian police forces, who must host the tournament, as well as with the owners of bars and cafés in the vicinity of the selected match venues. And with that we went live to Stockholm.

Sky had men on the ground in Sunderland too, though, where, we were excitedly told, Kevin Keegan would be watching the match on a television in the football club boardroom. Twenty minutes into the game, the screen split dramatically and we watched, agog, as Keegan entered the Stadium of Light through the tradesman's entrance and took his chances in the goods lift in the company of a member of the catering staff. It wasn't made clear whether or not this was the back door referred to earlier in the programme, but Keegan had gone through it anyway. An omen?

Sure enough, the Swedes did the business. 'All right,' said Keegan afterwards, 'we've gone in the back door. But who's to say we won't come out the front door?' Indeed. But who's to say they won't get confused in the kitchen, take a wrong turning in the sitting room and come out the French windows? Until we have the confirmed floor-plan for Euro 2000, it's surely too early to speculate.

UNSTEADY EDDIE MISSES OUT

1 NOVEMBER 1999

It was Eddie Irvine v. Mika Hakkinen for the Formula One world drivers' championship at Suzuka and, as so often, it came down to lap times. 'Irvine's fate is in the lap of the gods,' ITV's Martin Brundle said. Sadly, the gods were lapping at an average of half a second slower than Hakkinen's McLaren, so that was that for Eddie.

Nice try, though. Since his teammate Michael Schumacher returned from injury, Irvine has been able to employ what is effectively the English national football team's recipe for sporting success – namely, getting someone else to do the heavy work. Just as England could have qualified a lot faster for Euro 2000 if they had persuaded Sweden to play all their matches for them, so Irvine can now ruefully reflect that if only Schumacher had been around throughout the season to do his driving, he would probably be world champion by now.

What with this critical, head-to-head situation about to go off, and the week's shenanigans concerning some controversial extra millimetres on Ferrari's barge boards (finally deemed to be within the statutory tolerances), there was much to talk about on Murray and Martin's F1 Special (ITV). On the FIA ruling, Murray took the cosy line that what the authorities say goes, Martin arguing that a rule's a rule. 'You can't be a little bit pregnant,' said Brundle finding, as ever, the apposite metaphor.

Astonishingly, their judgements were thrown into chaos just hours later when a post-programme spot-check revealed that the pair's matching ITV rally jackets exceeded the statutory tolerances on stuffing for presentational outer garments by as much as 44 per cent. They looked as if they might turn into an air balloon at any second and lift off.

But there were a million stories out there in the paddock that never sleeps, and damn it if in the run up to the big race ITV wasn't going to bring us several hundred thousand of them. Reporter James Allen was dispatched to a rubber plantation in the jungle in Malaysia to assemble a piece on the origins of tyre material. I'm not making this up. 'It takes a lot of trees to make a set of Formula One tyres,' said Allen enthusiastically, against a backdrop of quietly perspiring fronds.

Also, the Suzuka grand prix was to be Damon Hill's last race before retirement and, to mark the passing of a true British great, Murray Walker took Hill for 'a gentle evening stroll down the pit lane' (I don't think we were intended to make any satirical connection with Hill's not entirely full-blooded performances for Jordan throughout the season).

'You going to do the things that ordinary people do – talking to the family, playing with the kids?' asked Murray. It wasn't, perhaps, the smartest question to put to one of sport's most famously committed family men. 'I do that anyway,' said Hill, looking slightly misunderstood. We'll miss him.

It was 4 a.m., British time, when the race coverage began. This is a television zone traditionally occupied by peculiar, decades-old football documentaries and commercials for telephone 'dating' lines. In ITV's London studio, Jim Rosenthal had Tony Jardine to chat to, live and one-to-one. It was by no means the couple's first date, so maybe it was the tension of the occasion, or maybe the extreme smallness of the hour, or maybe just the strength of the coffee in the green room, but the pair of them seemed to be in the grip of a strange hysteria.

Rosenthal asked Jardine if we could be confident that Schumacher wouldn't simply take Hakkinen out at the nearest convenient corner in order to hand the championship to his teammate. This was a perfectly reasonable prognosis, based on a fairly sound reading of the historical evidence, yet for some reason it reduced Rosenthal and Jardine to helpless laughter, lasting many seconds.

Jardine then told a joke. 'What's the difference between the British American Racing team and a cocktail stick?' Rosenthal said he had no idea. 'A cocktail stick has got two points,' said Jardine, only just able to get the line out as his own laughter sucked the wind out of him. Well, it's been a long season, I guess.

In Japan, Murray Walker was equally demob happy, at one point producing his impression of Mika Hakkinen. 'Mika has been saying it will be the first one to crack,' said Murray, deliberately giving the second half of the sentence a Finnish finish, as it were, so that it came out, 'It woll be thur furst wun to cruck'. Actually, the impression wasn't that bad, but coming less than twelve hours after the broadcast of the grand finale of the lookalike and soundalike contest *Stars in their Eyes*, it could only fall a little flat. Rather like Eddie Irvine's championship hopes. 'They all deserved to win,' insisted Walker, attempting consolation at the end. 'They all tried terribly hard.' Our old headmaster used to use that line. We weren't convinced by it then, either.

McENROE ON THE HERITAGE TRAIL

6 DECEMBER 1999

'All great events and personalities in world history reappear . . . the second time as farce.' Thus Karl Marx, shortly after going to watch John McEnroe in the ATP Seniors Tour of Champions at the Royal Albert Hall.

'Just like old times,' said the BBC's John Barrett on Saturday afternoon. Well, sort of. At one end of the court stood McEnroe, vengefully querying the eyesight of the umpire and picking at the shoulder of his shirt, as he always did, as if even that held a grudge against him. And at the other end stood Jeremy Bates, losing.

And at stake? Well, that was a difficult question. Suspended from the Albert Hall's rafters was a shiny new car, and if this tournament's grizzled winner wouldn't actually be driving away in it, he would almost certainly be leaving with a cheque large enough to buy it, and a couple more like it.

But beyond basic acquisitiveness and vehicle sales, what else was powering this strangely stiff contest, this peculiar imitation of top class tennis (a brilliantly accurate imitation in flashes, but an imitation none the less)? The pride of old soldiers, perhaps. Yet when McEnroe spoke in a post-match interview of his hope that the crowd had 'got their money's worth', his seemed to be a pride which was very mindful of the possibility of a fall.

Everyone there would have been judging him explicitly against what he once was and is no more. McEnroe knew days when a crowd could have high expectations of him and he could exceed them. So what would it be like for him now to be always in pursuit of the crowd's expectations? Maddening, possibly. Or maybe not. Maybe a relief.

In any case the crowd for this sport-style experience lapped him up. There is no crowd in sport readier to be pleased than a tennis crowd. Tennis crowds find the arrival on court of a stray pigeon funny. Tennis crowds even think Henri Leconte is funny. When McEnroe gave us his heritage version of a strop (a needless, but just possibly contractually obliged, curse-free showdown with the umpire over an over-ruled line-call), the crowd gave him their heritage version of a slow handclap.

And John Barrett and Mark Cox lapped him up, as well. 'Rumbling like a volcano,' said Barrett, with relish. 'He really is a formidable competitor and clearly enjoys competing,' explained Cox. 'Loves playing in front of a crowd.' The BBC lavished serious time and proper camera angles on the tournament, choosing it in preference to the Davis Cup final (a real, contemporary contest, with real consequences) on the grounds that there was 'no national involvement' in France v. Australia, whereas a tournament featuring semi-retired Americans who set the world alight twenty years ago – well, there the nation would happily involve itself. The choice says nothing untoward about the BBC, who were right. But it does make you wonder a little about tennis.

And on the subject of heritage experiences, Channel 5 showed *Miss World 1999*. 'Hi, I'm Miss American Virgin

Islands, and my ambition is to become a forensic scientist.' They didn't used to say that in John McEnroe's day.

Among our judges for the evening: the very lovely Eddie Irvine, whose hobbies include car-racing; and the gorgeous Lennox Lewis, whose ambition is to travel the world and fight people. Lennox was completing a remarkable week, which started out with an appearance on Ian Wright's chat show, continued with an interview in the *Grandstand* studio and then saw him swaying along to Cliff Richard's Millennium Prayer as part of the star-studded finale to the Royal Variety Performance. There may still be some dispute in the air about the nature and number of the championship titles that he unified by defeating Evander Holyfield, but there is no arguing with Lennox's claim right now to be the undisputed heavyweight champion of the *Radio Times*.

At Miss World, during the meet-the-judges section (evening wear, no bikinis), Melanie Sykes asked him what he was looking for. 'Personality, poise, how she carries herself,' said Lennox, a politician to the very ends of his braids.

Contrast Irvine. Sykes put it to him that staring at women in bikinis would have to be more exciting than 'driving around the same race track again and again'. And, keen as ever to be an ambassador for his sport, Irvine said: 'It's a helluva lot more exciting.'

THE LONGEST DAY

27 DECEMBER 1999

Christmas day. Never an easy time to be a satellite sports channel. I'd hazard a guess that a larger slice of the British population was tuned to the quiz show *Who Wants to Be A Christmas Millionaire* on ITV than was watching the finals of the European Latin Dancing Championships from Helsinki on Sky Sports 3, which went out at the same time. And it's just possible that more people spent Christmas Day dressed in a sheep outfit, suspended from a telegraph pole and yodelling than watched the many hours of karting and sumo wrestling with which Eurosport chose to mark the festive season.

Elsewhere were blockbusting movies; Sky Sports 2 had a pro-celebrity golf competition from Lake Tahoe. Wayne Gretzky, the ice hockey player, got his ball stuck up a tree. Maybe he should stick to ice hockey. Charles Barkley, the basketball player, had the worst swing that has ever been shown on television. Maybe he should stick to ice hockey, too. 'Oh, you've got to be kidding,' the commentator said, at least once. If only.

Back on Sky Sports 3, Sabine Kramski from Germany was doing the samba. Actually, now we were talking. One of Sky's team of Latin Dance experts had previously sniffed at the Russian entry. 'We're actually looking for a little more pelvic action in the samba,' she said. Not a criticism you could level at Kramski, who had pelvic action to spare. Only a unique resilience to bruising, and a paramedical team standing by, could guarantee the safety of her dancing partner, Michael. More in need of a breastplate than anyone since 1066, Michael was, alas, wearing a shirt slashed to the navel. Like Barkley's swing, it was painful to behold, but Michael smiled bravely to the end. It was Christmas, after all.

On Sky Sports 1, Brazil were playing Italy in the 1970 World Cup. Good game, but it didn't throw up any surprises. Damn those Christmas schedules with their repeats. The worst was still to come: Sky Sports 2 padded almost the whole of Boxing Day with that tired old comedy, Test Match Cricket: South Africa v. England Live. Meanwhile, back at the golf, John Elway, the American footballer, had so badly overhit his approach shot to the ninth that a helicopter was being scrambled to look for signs of it in the Nevada desert.

As one flicked between the channels, it was as if a law had been passed, demanding that people spend Christmas doing only things that they had little experience of or were in some way incompetent at. There was Gretzky playing golf; and there was the athlete Kris Akabusi playing tennis. That was on Cliff Richard's Pro-Celebrity Tennis, which is something of an annual institution on Sky Sports 3, though one was disappointed this year to see it broadcast so late on Christmas Day evening. (Last year, fittingly somehow, it went directly up against the Queen's speech.) But in all other respects, this film of Cliff's yearly tennis bash in Birmingham did not let us down.

'Hi, guys,' said Akabusi. 'You're watching Cliff Richard's Pro-Celebrity Tennis. Aw-raaaght!' That was one of the less tonally appropriate sentences spoken on a sports channel this year. Cliff's shindig is about as cool as an event could be which, uniquely, combines a tennis tournament, a Cliff Richard gig and a Christian rally. But the television coverage is certainly 'aw-raaaght' for Cliff's publicity department. Sky's Kelly Dalglish and Nick Rothwell took turns seeking testimonials to Cliff's greatness from members of the crowd, who love him to the marrow of his being, or thereabouts. 'He's a good tennis player,' said one, 'a good person. And he's got a good bum.'

As the police and local authorities know only too well, if ever Cliff didn't make it as far as the final, this crowd would be burning cars in Birmingham city centre deep into the night. Luckily, again this year, he made it right through, where he was seen off by a formidable combination of Hank Marvin and Ilie Nastase. (Nastase has grown no smaller in retirement. If these days he looks a shadow of his former self, then it's one of those huge shadows seen on the walls in frightening movies.)

Nineteen ninety-nine, of course, has ended in unwanted and aggressive controversy for Cliff, with the undignified ruck surrounding his Millennium Prayer single, in which the Lord's Prayer is set to the tune of 'Auld Lang Syne' – thought by some to be shockingly manipulative and in poor taste, as well as extremely difficult to cut a rug to. It was nice to see those arguments laid aside here in Cliff's closing rendition, performed on court. Wouldn't you have loved to have been a fly on the wall at the choreography sessions during which Cliff worked out exactly how he would dance while reciting the Lord's Prayer? Imagine the tussle which must have gone on there between showbusiness and the demands of humility made upon Cliff by his faith.

'I've even started playing golf,' Kris had just warned us. Save that for next year, maybe.

2000

EUBANK ATTEMPTS ORAL THEKTH ON SKY

31 JANUARY 2000

Everyone had been expecting an early knock-down, but no one had thought it would come as quickly as this. Less than seven minutes into Sky's coverage of the Julius Francis v. Mike Tyson fight, our studio compere Paul Dempsey invited Chris Eubank to share with us his thoughts on the raw phenomenon which is Iron Mike. After all, as Dempsey pointed out, Eubank had been 'intimate' with Tyson. 'If I can use the phrase,' he added.

As is his wont on these occasions, Eubank philosophically tilted his face to one side, as if the sheer weight of his thoughts caused his head to require the additional support of a shoulder. The Tyson he knew, he eventually said – in the measured, explanatory tone which, of the present generation of broadcasters, only he and Melvyn Bragg have truly mastered – was 'intelligent, conthiderate'. The 'preth,' said Eubank, had painted 'a very bad picture of him.'

OK so far. But at this point, Chris's train of thought, gathering speed, took him up a slightly surprising branch line; the one which goes past Tyson's rape charge. Tyson, Eubank pointed out, has always maintained he was innocent. 'She agreed to oral thekth,' said Chris.

Kapow! We cut back to Dempsey, whose face seemed to have gone entirely white. You cannot agree to oral thekth on Sky Sports. Certainly not before 9.30 in the evening. And probably not even after that. 'Chris, thanks,' Dempsey said, a little more urgently than he might normally.

'That's what he said,' continued Chris, not immediately willing to let this one lie.

Who knows what was going on in Dempsey's earpiece at this moment. Nothing in his training as Sky Sports' boxing front man had prepared him for oral thekth. But whether on his own initiative, or because his producers were screaming at him, Dempsey confronted the crisis, dug deep into himself and pulled out something superbly, unimpeachably pompous. He looked straight into our living rooms and said: 'We dissociate Sky and Sky Box Office from those comments. That was a personal opinion.'

A personal opinion! On a sports punditry panel! Whatever next? It was like that classic moment from the film *Dr Strangelove* when a fight breaks out between the generals and Peter Sellers shouts: 'You can't fight in here – this is the war room!'

Anyway, the next time we went back to the studio, Eubank was gone. Purged. Erased. Stalin himself could not have managed the matter more smoothly. It was like he had never been there. All that remained of him was the arm of an empty chair beside Barry McGuigan.

Then again, perhaps Sky always intended to remove Eubank at that point and bring in a replacement about forty-five minutes later. ('It's Marvin Hagler,' said Dempsey. 'Marvellous Marvin Hagler,' the modest retiree corrected him.) And we did catch up with Chris in the arena later during the fights on the undercard when Sky adopted the risky tactic of getting him to comment briefly during the sixty seconds between rounds. (Risky because the average Eubank sentence is really only just warming up after sixty seconds.)

But he never got back in the studio, so I think we have to account it a first-round knock-out.

The Eubank/Dempsey contretemps was more entertaining than anything that later happened in the ring. As usual with boxing, Sky's team didn't so much assess the event as weigh its pre-publicity. Which meant this fight came in weighing tons. Unable openly to make jokes about Julius Francis (to do so would have been to mock the subscription-paying audience), Sky's people resorted to smuggling them in instead. 'I suppose the cynics would say he was having a look at the canvas,' said Dempsey as Francis inspected the ring. 'I suppose the cynics would say he might need them in there with him,' said the commentator Ian Darke, as some soldiers led Francis into the arena.

'If he believes he's got a chance, then he's got a slight chance,' said Nicky Piper, who obviously wasn't one of the cynics. His interviewer pressed him: 'But do you think he's got a chance?' 'Not really, no,' Piper said.

'OK, it was a mismatch . . .' Ian Darke conceded afterwards. Well, maybe it was OK with him, but he was getting paid. His audience, on the other hand, had shelled out £11.95 and were missing *Match of the Day.*

Afterwards, American television got to Tyson first. The interview was remarkable for the following piece of fastidiousness on the part of the interviewer, Jim Grey: 'Mike, go ahead and wipe your nose. You've got some stuff coming out of there.'

Then it was Darke's turn. As boxers will, Tyson opened by offering nuff respect and a big shout-out to the Home Secretary. 'I'd like to thank Mr Jack Straw for inviting me into his country and taking the slack for me,' said Tyson. Which was well put. It would be interesting to know what

Straw makes of his new status among the American bruthas. He is Britain's first Homey Secretary.

Tyson had one more thing to add. 'Thank you to the Kray family for sending me flowers . . . I appreciate you, Reginald Kray.'

We couldn't see Dempsey at this point, but I reckon he was out cold on the floor.

FIVE GO TO ITALY

7 FEBRUARY 2000

According to J. P. R. Williams, the former Welsh full-back, now aged fifty, modern rugby is 'an absolute disaster and a shambles'. The notion of a full-time, professional rugby player is 'absolutely ridiculous'. The game is 'poor to watch', the players are 'overpaid', and the entertainment value, at both club and international level, is 'dreadful'.

Apart from that, though, the game is in great shape and television didn't see why it shouldn't raise a hearty glass to the opening of the Six Nations tournament. In J. P. R.'s day, of course, the Six Nations was merely the Five Nations. More recently, it threatened briefly to become the Four Nations when England sold the Twickenham rights to BSkyB. But it pumped itself up to Six Nations when Italy decided to join in. It may well go down to One Nation, however, if Austria carries out its plan to invade everybody.

As Steve Rider observed on *Grandstand* (BBC1), the arrival of the Italians, necessitating a few trips to Rome, has added 'a very attractive new long-weekend venue to the schedule'. Not that this alone would have swayed the organizers. That said, plans to incorporate in future years

Bali, Palm Springs and a team representing the Sandy Beach Hotel in Barbados are thought to be well into the negotiation stages.

'The Scottish fans are the first to enjoy the delights of the Eternal City,' Rider went on, and we then went into a brief film, which was eternal in its own way, and featured shots of mopeds, girls with long hair and, inevitably, a kilted gentleman playing his bagpipes at the Trevi Fountain. I could be wrong, but I'd swear I saw one of those stone lions flinch.

It was a good job the city was providing the visitors with some fun, because Italy were about to treat Scotland to the delights of an eternal rugby match, crushing them in a manner which one felt was rather presumptuous for new-comers, even rather rude. As I understand it, when you've been newly introduced to a club, you wait a decent interval before trashing the secretary at snooker.

Still, whatever the outcome, the match was, as Nigel Starmer-Smith in the commentary box pointed out, 'a moment of history for all of us'. Not just some of us, note; all of us. 'How sensible it is to see a full crowd,' Nigel added.

In keeping with the solemnity of the occasion, Princess Anne was on the pitch, surrounded by her own personal seven hills, in the form of some exceptionally well-formed minders. As a consequence, the first ruck of the tournament happened five minutes before kick-off, as the cameras tried to get unobstructed pictures of the Princess Royal shaking hands with the two teams. A television first, that. Another moment of history for all of us.

Reporting on the atmosphere in the Welsh camp, ahead of their tricky fixture against an unusually large French side, Jonathan Davies visited the Welsh captain, David Young – the survivor, like Davies, of a temporary but lucrative brush with the code of rugby league. (League players, Young pointed out, tend to regard union players with the kind of queasy contempt which Molesworth reserved for Fotherington-Thomas. Or as Young put it, using the appropriate rugby terms, 'The first thing they want to do is put one on the end of your snitch.')

Predictably, discussion turned fairly rapidly to some of the issues raised so thoughtfully during the week by J. P. R. Williams. Davies recalled the game's amateur days and asked, 'What's the difference between them and the professional era, then?' To which Young replied, 'Money.' Fair point.

Other differences are to be found in the rule book. Along with Italy, a new set of regulations has been introduced for this Six Nations, and the BBC – dutifully fulfilling their role as a public service broadcaster – gave us the low-down in simple terms. Briefly, it's OK to throw people up in the air at line-outs, provided they are members of your own team; but players seen throwing anyone else around unnecessarily will be yellow-carded and despatched to the sin-bin for ten minutes to cool down (or, as seems just as likely, to work up a proper head of bitterness and resentment).

I don't wish to sound like someone who has had their snitch put out, but any legislation which diminishes the likelihood of fighting during a rugby match is legislation aimed directly at the honourable pleasures of the television viewer, and is thus to be resisted.

Over on Sky Sports, England trounced Ireland in a blizzard of statistics. Lines of attack, handling errors, missed tackles – you name it, Sky Sports put a number to it. Contrast the following conversation between Starmer-Smith and Gavin Hastings during Italy v. Scotland on BBC 1. Hastings was pretty sure a penalty kick, ruled dud, had actually passed between the posts. Starmer-Smith considered this possibility, during a solitary, inconclusive replay, before declaring,

'You'd have to really slow it down.' On Sky, they'd have slowed it down, divided it up, computerized it and set it to music before you could say 'J. P. R. Williams'.

BBC PULLS PLUG OUT FOR BOAT RACE

27 MARCH 2000

'The two big motivating things are fear and hate,' said the rower Johnny Searle, referring – of course – to the Boat Race (BBC1). Or 'Fear and Loathing in Putney' as we probably ought to know it. And what a trip! Across choppy water into a headwind that could have turned back the Armada, and through every shade of British spring weather, from beaming sunshine to horizontal sleet. The BBC tipped their cameras to the skies at one point and it was like Turner's *Rain Steam and Speed* up there, albeit with Fulham Football Ground where the train should have been. (Somehow Turner never got round to painting Craven Cottage. His loss.)

This was no day to be presenting live television from a boat. So bad luck, Steve Rider. Five minutes into the broadcast he was as grey as the sky and, on account of the cold, he had probably lost most of the feeling in his extremities. The Olympic oarsman Matthew Pinsent joined Rider for a while and even he looked uncomfortable, hunched against the wind in the bow of the BBC's rental (£5 per hour, plus a £10 deposit for the oars). To my mind, if you're on a boat with someone as experienced as Pinsent and he starts to look unhappy, there's really only one sensible way to go: overboard. But Rider clung on. And still that slightly spooky smile of his held. It always does.

'A new millennium and a magnificent new trophy,' said Rider, before showing us what he carefully referred to as 'the Aberdeen Asset Management Trophy'. A new millennium, indeed, but still no change to the BBC's famous policy on advertising: they'll do as much of it as they're told to. It was a splendid trophy, though, a bold new silver construction apparently modelled on the air traffic control tower at Los Angeles International airport. Only slightly bigger and with a plinth.

You'd need muscles and height to hoist such a thing aloft, and luckily for Oxford they were fielding the tallest crew that had represented the university in the history of the race. Average height: 6 ft 4.625 in. I know this for a fact because Barry Davies told me. The programming seemed richer than ever this year with Boat Race stats. For instance, did you know that, in the course of the race, each oarsman would take 600 strokes? And that they would have put in roughly an hour of training for each of those strokes? And did you know that they would each burn off 6,400 calories? And that 6,400 calories is the equivalent of 213 of Marks & Spencer's prawn and mayonnaise sandwiches? And that if you laid 213 of Marks & Spencer's prawn and mayonnaise sandwiches end to end, they would reach from one side of Barnes Bridge to the other? Well, you do now. (I added a few stats of my own at the end there. This stat thing is infectious.)

The BBC were with Oxford during some of those 600 hours of training and on Saturday they showed us the film they brought back. Suckers for punishment, these university rowers, who like nothing better than a 5 a.m. alarm call. Why? They're students, for heaven's sake; surely they've got all day? Here's how committed Oxford were: they went all the way to Spain for a training camp – and they made sure they ended up in a bit that was cold.

Still, it wasn't all work. The crew were definitely watching *The Simpsons* at one point, though it was probably an early-morning episode. And Tobias Ayer, one of the rowers, took time out to show us a trick he specializes in, which involves balancing a dirty sock on his nose. Thanks for that, Tobias. We were just beginning to think you guys never had any fun.

With the hard work behind them, and the hardest work to come, the crews made their way from their boathouses to their boats, the cameras tracking them intently. They came out one by one, like American footballers at Super Bowl. Indeed, in past years, exactly like Super Bowl, this procession to the boats was quite often a parade of steak-fed Texans and blokes with enormous jaws who had been reared on the rapids of Colorado and could bench-press a steer 790 times. But 2000 is an Olympic year and the big boys are working on their acts elsewhere. So the Brits got a look in.

Some people knock the Boat Race, saying it's a peculiar piece of elitist pageantry, a curio rather than a sporting event, and that the attention paid to it by television is incommensurate with its status within the world of rowing. But this seems unfair from many angles. At the very least, it's to devalue the amazing consistency of these Oxford and Cambridge crews. The Boat Race comes round every year and they always qualify for it. That remarkable achievement alone, surely, justifies the presence of the cameras.

I, for one, wouldn't have wanted to miss the scenes of Oxford jubilation afterwards, which involved a lot of bouncing, but on dry land this time. 'A total Oxford celebration,' Davies called it. 'This wonderful new Aberdeen Asset Management Trophy . . .' said Rider, still, to his credit, plugging away.

FIRST GRAND NATIONAL AD

10 APRIL 2000

Off to the Grand National, that annual parade of the finest in equine athleticism, where the spiffiest specimens the horse world can muster rub muscular shoulders with each other. Where was your money? As the BBC's lengthy and vividly attentive build-up unfolded, I was divided between Celtic Giant ('he's got a fibrillating heart,' Peter Scudamore took the trouble to mention) and Listen Timmy ('the metal tube is to keep his air passages open').

But who was I to brush aside entirely the competing claims of Dark Stranger ('disappointing over three miles last year')? Not to mention Kendal Cavalier ('very slow and not that good,' according to his own trainer. We used to have a Vauxhall Cavalier that was a bit like that.) And what about The Gopher? ('Seriously wanting at this level' in the words of one of the form guides.) Worth a tenner each way, surely?

'Every horse that lines up on the tape on the day has a chance,' the jockey Mick Fitzgerald told Sue Barker as they sheltered from the rain in the BBC's lively interview enclosure. 'It's part of the fairy tale that is Aintree,' he went on. And there was a sudden blinding flash, and Mick Fitzgerald turned into a pumpkin.

Where was one to turn for succour and advice? In this most bafflingly open of fields, who would come through with the compass and the map? Scudamore did his best. Saturday's going seemed to suit him. It provided him with the opportunity to point out 'one of three jockeys I know of in professional jumping who wear contact lenses'. Now, that's what I call an inside track.

Talking of inside tracks, one of the loose horses took one at about the halfway stage of Saturday's race. His rider was long since dumped and was perhaps even then picking carefully through the fronds of a destroyed fence in search of his contact lenses. The horse raced on proudly, kicking up high along the front of the grandstand, the roar of the crowd in its ears, the actual race veering off to the south.

What was in its head at that point? It's not a popular view, and you certainly wouldn't want to voice it around Jenny Pitman, but they're not very clever, horses. A trainer once told me that if a horse got into the sea without a rider, it would carry on swimming in the direction it was going. It would not occur to it to turn around and head for dry land, the way it does to the average family spaniel. Think on that, next time you're putting your money down.*

Back at the course, Scudamore's powers of analysis were turned on the images of the jockeys as they waited in the weighing room. 'I should think every dentist in the country watching will think, I'll phone that man and help him out after the race,' said Scudamore. Later Scudamore would take his place among a selection of former jockeys, each recalling for our jollification their failure ever to win a National, and tell Barker: 'You never won Wimbledon. At least we can blame the horse.' Truly, the afternoon belonged to him.

They were calling it 'the 2000 Martell National' but in truth, of course, it was the First National AD – or After Des.

* Richie Benaud, the cricket commentator, maintains that it is wisest never to bet on anything that can talk. Surely this is round the wrong way: never bet on anything that is dumb, particularly if it's as dumb as a horse.

It was always on these big, live occasions that the BBC were going to miss Lynam. Hours of outside broadcasting, on one occasion under threat of a terrorist explosion, stretched his professionalism in ways that getting Alan Hansen to talk about slow motion replays from, say, Coventry v. Bradford on *Match Of The Day* never could.

But Lynam has moved on, and we must, too. Barker jovially accepted the mantle – or rather the mock-sheepskin coat – backed up by Clare Balding. Roving in the loose boxes (they can't touch you for it), Balding had a memorably unfruitful encounter with jockey Richard Guest, who was hard at work saddling his horse and didn't seem to want to be interrupted.

Speaking through a nervous laugh, Balding said: 'You've got a very small saddle there as well, which I suppose isn't great for the big fences, is it?'

It possibly wasn't what Guest wanted to hear, minutes before tackling the most mountainous obstacles in British racing. 'I've had them a lot smaller,' he said, still not quite looking as if he were ready to burst into song.

'And you're excited about it?'

'Over the moon, yeah,' said Guest, without a glimmer.

'Are you really?' Balding went on, 'because you just sound a bit quiet and I suppose you've got jobs to do, that's why.'

'Busy, yeah,' said Guest.

I don't suppose these few moments of television are likely to feature on Balding's personal showreel, but there was something rather heartening about them. Sports events are so complicit with television these days, so eager to please. But here, at the National, clearly not everybody was about to play the game. It didn't hurt to be reminded that these television people, with their cameras and their wires and their intrusive demands on people at busy times, are to some extent in the way.

'You could have had him at 40 to 1 yesterday,' someone said after Papillon's victory. Now they tell us.

MANSELL PAYS AND DISPLAYS

24 APRIL 2000

The ban on cars in the Silverstone area on Saturday did not extend to Formula One models, fortunately, so the qualifying session was able to go ahead.* And the ban didn't apply to Jim Rosenthal's car either, so we were able to watch it all unfolding at home.

I'd hazard a guess that when Rosenthal signed up to front ITV's grand prix coverage, he wasn't imagining that the gum boot would figure very significantly in his presentational wardrobe. I reckon he was thinking more along the lines of cotton short-sleeve shirts, some casual slacks – perhaps the occasional cheeky Hawaiian number for those balmy evenings in Barcelona and Monaco.

But then the British Grand Prix got moved forward to Easter and all of a sudden Rosenthal was looking for grip in the wet. When we first saw him, he was up to his knees in some of Northamptonshire's stickiest loam, apparently attempting a one-man re-enactment of that famous old television time-filler, The Potter's Wheel. Behind him was the

* Extraordinary downpours had left Silverstone's fields unsuitable for weekending visitors in cars. Mud is all very well at the Glastonbury Festival, but Formula One tends to be a little less pagan in spirit.

top third of somebody's car. The rest of it, we were to understand, was directly below it under the mud.

'They're not car parks really, are they? They're fields,' was Rosenthal's point when he returned to the dry in the studio. The former world No 1, Nigel Mansell, was on hand and revealed himself immediately to be a forceful and energetic person to have around when the conversation turns to the provision, or otherwise, of hard-standing parking facilities.

Mansell, in his heyday, had a reputation for being a little understated, or even monotonous – quite unfairly, it now turns out. The problem was that, back then, people only wanted to talk to him about winning grands prix and driving for Ferrari and being incredibly rich and famous, when clearly he just needed a subject he could really get his teeth into – such as car parking – and he would have been away.

He positively warmed to the theme. He twinkled, he smiled, he lit up the studio. His eyebrows – apparently enjoying a whole new lease of life in retirement – worked overtime. 'Happy birthday, Eric. Hello, Hazel,' he said, offering a little message for the folks back home. This would have been unthinkable as little as ten years ago.

Mansell also turned the considerable weight of his experience to the topic of young Jenson Button – inevitably one of the weekend's big issues. Button had spun off during practice – or, as Mansell put it, 'he had a bit of a whoopsie on the circuit'. I stand to be corrected, but Mansell is, I think, the first person to use the expression 'whoopsie' on a national television broadcast since Michael Crawford in his famous role as the accident-prone Frank Spencer. So congratulations to him on that.

Anyway, Mansell's larger point about Button was that he would be all right 'if he stays on the black bit of the circuit'. I don't think anyone could really disagree with that – nor with Mansell's splendid summing-up of the qualifying session: 'It was all a question of timing.' Qualifying sessions so frequently are, but the point cannot be made often enough.

COULTHARD AND BEST WORK OFF THE HANGOVER

8 MAY 2000

Out in Barcelona, ITV kept an anxious eye on David Coulthard, who was stepping into a Formula One car less than a week after stepping out of a crashed Learjet. How was he physically? How was he mentally? How would he fare at 'one of the most physical circuits on the grand prix calendar', according to Martin Brundle. 'He's bruised down the right-hand side; there's a lot of right-hand bends here . . .' warned Tony Jardine.

Actually, he did just fine, thanks. He finished second. 'Let us remember the tremendous pressure that David Coulthard has been under this week . . . My heart goes out to him,' said Murray Walker, admiringly. But that's racing drivers for you. We'll never fully understand from the outside, but behind the wheel of a car travelling at 200 m.p.h. is where these people find their serenity. Damon Hill used to say that leading a grand prix was like being the only person on earth. If something traumatic had happened to you recently, if you had something you wanted to get away from, and you were a grand prix driver, probably the best place for you would be inside your car, going as fast as you knew how.

Also fearlessly back in the hot seat after a near-death experience, George Best returned to work on *Soccer Saturday*, that marathon and highly valuable show in which Sky Sports ask a few ex-pros to park themselves in front of a monitor and keep an eye on the afternoon's football for us.* Contractual niceties prevent us from seeing the action the pros are seeing, which makes the programme very much a verbal experience, and even, in its more energetic moments, a gestural one. Indeed the more one watches *Soccer Saturday*, the more one realizes that it is, essentially, a highly refined and thoroughly modern version of the old parlour game, charades, with Rodney Marsh saying, in effect, 'It's a football match; five syllables; two goals so far; no sendings off.'

Anyway, Best was put in charge of Arsenal v. Chelsea, and though he seemed a little more sallow and quite a lot more gaunt than the last time we saw him in action, he made a decent fist of it, with one or two inevitable, just-back-from-injury wobbles. At one point, he was squinting at the monitor and trying to make up his mind whether it was Thierry Henry who was down injured, or somebody else. In came the voice of Marsh, urging Best to get his act together and make up his mind. 'Give me a break,' Best said. 'It's my first day back. Make yourself useful. Go and get me a drink.'

Laughter, as *The Reader's Digest* is fond of telling us, is the best medicine. Especially extremely dark laughter.

*After decades of pioneering alcohol abuse, Best's liver finally rebelled and he was admitted to hospital in early 2000. He emerged vowing teetotalism and perhaps the creation of a new family.

JIMMY HILL: THE WAY FORWARD

JULY 2000

Desperate times call for desperate measures and, sure enough, as Euro 2000 climbed to its peak while English football sat at home staring dejectedly at its own boots*, Jimmy Hill delivered to the nation a 30-minute address on the state of the game. Or, at least, to that portion of the nation which can get Sky Digital.

Non-subscribers may be largely unaware of the direction taken by Hill's career since the World Cup in France in 1998 when the BBC told him that, though they hated to lose him, they thought he ought to go. Foolishly, the corporation seems to have been assuming that Hill would retire. Jimmy Hill is no more likely to retire than Perry Como is to sing The Prodigy's 'Smack My Bitch Up'.

Sky swooped in to offer Hill his own chat show, plangently titling it *The Last Word With Jimmy Hill*. This they have posted on their digital service which is, shall we say, at the fledgling stage in terms of viewer pick-up. But let's not underestimate the potential audience. I personally know two viewers who have seen the show (myself and our cat, who walked through the room while it was on) and logic requires that there simply have to be others.

Incidentally, whoever chose 'Jimmy, Jimmy' by The

* England were eliminated in the group stages after three performances of gruelling mediocrity. Euro 2000 was widely agreed to have been one of the most exciting and colourful international football tournaments in living memory – a total party, bursting with Portuguese flair, Dutch craftsmanship and French brilliance. England, in effect, merely had a walk-on role as a bloke carrying a tray of stale sausage rolls.

Undertones as the programme's theme music was either deaf to the lyrics or in possession of a darkly subversive sense of humour. At any rate, in the title sequence, Hill smiles boldly out at us while Feargal Sharkey sings, 'Poor little Jimmy/ Wouldn't let go.' Is this a dignified way to preface the thoughts of one of the game's senior statesmen at a time of national crisis? I only ask.

In this England special edition (no cosy fire, à la Bill Clinton – just an appropriately sober, bare stage), the camera closed in tight on Hill's head as he solemnly announced: 'We are in danger of becoming a Third World football nation.' Not wanting anyone to think he was merely 'hitching a ride on a typically knocking journalistic bandwagon', Hill pointed out he had, at least, had the decency to start knocking England before the tournament opened.

This was during an extremely vivacious performance as the studio analyst for Sky's coverage of England's pre-tournament friendly against Malta, during which Hill had the courage to say that he couldn't really see the point of interviewing Alan Shearer if all he was going to give you was the usual old flannel. That was a great moment, because though everyone had thought this for years, nobody had actually said it on television, and certainly not directly after an interview with Alan Shearer. Hill also said, after Malta, that England couldn't possibly win Euro 2000 and that it was 'misleading propaganda' to suggest they could. Among his reasons for believing this were such small details as the fact that England had finished nine points behind Sweden in their qualifying group, possessed nobody with a left foot and, just for starters at Euro 2000, would be facing a team (Portugal) containing two of the best players in the world.

Referring to England's qualifying record, Sky's Richard Keys had, back then, countered Hill as follows: 'Does that matter? That was then, but this is now.' Keys may well have been playing devil's advocate, as his role demands, but as an expression of the history-shorn fantasizing that seems to accompany the English national team wherever they go, this would be hard to beat.

Hill's address included, tangentially but inevitably, a shot of a Belgian police lorry squirting water against the stomachs of topless English supporters in Charleroi*. Hill called upon the Government to 'make it unpleasant to be a hooligan', but, disappointingly, he didn't go into any details about the kind of unpleasantness he was looking for.

Finally, though, he got round to a series of germane bullet points. For me, point two ('Learn from abroad') and point three ('Improve coaching quality') were both contradicted by point four ('Control foreign imports'). The English professional game needs more foreign players, surely, not fewer. They do, after all, represent the standard everyone is meant to be aspiring to and they have already made a considerable difference. In the past, a young central defender coming through the ranks at, say, Chelsea, would only have to think to himself that he needed to be as good as Michael Duberry to be in with a shout of a first-team place. These days he realizes that he needs to be as good as Marcel Desailly. Standards can only rise in those circumstances.

But point one was unimprovable: 'Accept our limitations'.

* Ahead of England's match against Germany, fans misbehaved with café furniture in Brussels and Charleroi. achieving mass coverage in the British press. In the same week, however, there was a riot following a basketball match in Los Angeles, during which a crowd of 20,000 had to be contained within the arena while police tried to staunch the looting, car-tipping and gunfire going on in the streets. At one point a tree was torn up, stuffed through a police car window and set on fire. An awful truth dawned about the chair-tossers in Belgium; even England's thugs aren't very good.

English football has had no problem bigger than its refusal to admit that it has a problem. And here was Jimmy Hill, leading the way to confession and solution. A troubled nation could switch off at the end and feel comforted that at least someone out there had it all under control. Someone who will not be silenced.

ACKNOWLEDGEMENTS

Most of these pieces first appeared in the *Daily Telegraph*. A handful at the beginning of the book first appeared in the *Independent on Sunday*. I am grateful to David Welch, the sports editor of the *Daily Telegraph*, and to the staff of the paper's sports desk and library. I am also grateful to Simon Kelner at the *Independent*.

I would like to thank Diana Eden, Georgia Garrett, Nick Hornby, Anthony Lane, Paddy McAloon (who gave me the title), Peter Straus and Richard Milner at Picador and, most of all, Sabine Durrant.